Chasing Lost Times

A Father and Son
Reconciled Through Running

GEOFFREY BEATTIE AND BEN BEATTIE

MAINSTREAM
PUBLISHING

EDINBURGH AND LONDON

First published in Great Britain in 2012 by
MAINSTREAM PUBLISHING COMPANY
(EDINBURGH) LTD
7 Albany Street
Edinburgh EH1 3UG

ISBN 9781780575209

A catalogue record for this book is available
from the British Library

Printed in Great Britain by
CPI Group (UK) Ltd, Croydon, CR0 4YY

1 3 5 7 9 10 8 6 4 2

CHASING LOST TIMES

Geoff Beattie is a professor at the University of Manchester and a celebrity psychologist. His PhD is from the University of Cambridge, but he grew up in North Belfast. He is the author of nineteen books, including one novel. His work has either won or been shortlisted for a number of major prizes, both national and international. He has presented a number of television series on BBC1, Channel 4 and other stations; he was resident psychologist on ten series of *Big Brother*. He also presented two series on the psychology behind sport, called *Head to Head*, for Radio 5 Live. He started running seriously at the age of 13, the year his father died, and has trained every day since without any break or let-up. He sees this as profoundly psychological.

Ben Beattie was born in Sheffield, and this might explain why he loves running up hills. His father encouraged him to run when he was seven or eight, but the encouragement felt more like pressure at the time. After a significant gap, Ben returned to running four years ago, and his times and placings have improved dramatically. His PB for the half marathon is currently 72 minutes, a few minutes off elite status. He was third in the Kassel Half Marathon in 2011; his father was some way behind.

Acknowledgements

I would like to thank my agent Robert Kirby from United Agents, who saw the merits in a father and son exploring their compulsion to run more or less from the start; Bill Campbell from Mainstream (whom I have always been keen to work with) luckily concurred with this judgement. A small section about my father first appeared in *Protestant Boy*, and I thank Granta for their permission to reproduce it in a slightly different form here. A section on Mauritius first appeared in *Why Aren't We Saving the Planet? A Psychologist's Perspective*, and I thank Routledge for their permission to reproduce that here. Carol's description of her accident first appeared in *Get the Edge*: *How Simple Changes Will Transform Your Life*, and I thank Headline for their permission to reuse that description. Sale Harriers is a wonderful running club, and I thank them for their support and their cameraderie (particularly Fechin). They make Manchester's rainy winters (and summers) almost bearable.

– Geoff Beattie

I would like to thank the members of Steel City Striders and Hallamshire Harriers for helping me to become competitive again. I'd also like to thank the members of the Team Planet-X, plus the support staff, for making the 24 hours of the Thunder Run more pleasant than it really should have been. Most importantly I am thankful to Joanne for putting up with me, to my mum for being my biggest fan and to my dad for introducing me to the joy of running in the first place, even though I didn't appreciate it at the time.

– Ben Beattie

Contents

1

Slipping In and Out
of Consciousness

September 2011

I was sitting on a raised platform in the brand-new Westfield shopping centre in Stratford, east London, in the shadow of the new Olympic stadium, with nearly a year still to go before the Olympics. The shopping centre had been open for just one week and was full of excited shoppers, all trying to navigate the confusing malls. Like all such carefully constructed shopping malls, they were purposely designed to confuse and disorient the shopper so that their visual system would work overtime, in terms of processing all of the visual cues in the immediate environment, including all of the advertisements and the brand messages urging them to *buy, buy, buy*. It all seemed to be working because groups and couples hurried by, laden with their new purchases, which were bursting out of brown, apparently eco-friendly bags, the latest marketing gimmick. There seemed to be an awful lot of collisions, that's all I noticed from my raised platform, as if their visual systems were getting a little over-stimulated and a little over-confused. It all smelt new; it all smelt a little like fear.

It was a day full of energy and excitement and a sort of generalised anxiety, and I sat on the platform, red eyed, supporting my head with my hands and blinking uncontrollably with extreme fatigue. I was fighting to stay awake. A charming and friendly couple were led onto the raised platform by one of the promotions girls (Rachel – 'singer, dancer, actress', 'cruises a speciality, really, you have to start somewhere') for me to be filmed talking to them about closeness in British society for a big PR campaign funded by an international skincare company. I was the face of the campaign, an extremely tired face today. The husband had recognised me from *Big Brother*, I could see it in the slightly furtive glances he sent my way, and he evidently had seen me analysing the cast of *The Only Way Is Essex* a few days previously on *Ghosthunting with . . . The Only Way Is Essex* on ITV.

'There were a lot of stones flying about the place,' he said enigmatically, but I knew what he meant; he had obviously watched the 'poltergeist' activity down in deepest Essex. He wanted to be analysed by this famous psychologist.

'I love your work,' he added. We sat down on a white sofa in front of the cameras. I didn't want to disappoint him but I couldn't keep my eyes open. The cameras were rolling. I could feel the blinks getting more frequent and longer. I panicked because I felt that my eyes were closing; I was falling asleep right in front of him.

I slapped myself – I had to – and I could see the man's wife looking at me curiously. We all shared the same small white sofa in front of the cameras; my facial slap was unmissable in the circumstances. She could actually feel it because we were sitting so close, even though I tried to do it on her blind side.

'Sorry about that,' I said, as if it was some sort of nervous tic. I could see the woman looking at her husband; I could tell that she was looking for reassurance – after all, she was right next to me, our buttocks were touching. So much for the apparent lack of closeness in society today.

'It's an experiment,' the husband said back to her, in a reassuring sort of way. 'He's testing how we react to odd little events. I've seen him doing this on *Big Brother*. He's always playing little tricks on the housemates. He analyses their . . . what do you call them? . . . micro-expressions to decode their body language. He's just analysed yours. What do you make of her so far? Have you got her sussed out yet? I bet he knows everything about you, love, just on the basis of how you reacted there. He can read you like a book. It took me years to work you out, and he's done it in an instant. What a top guy.'

I just nodded, and as my head moved downwards, so too did my eyelids. The blink occasioned by the head movement became a real eye closure; my eyes seemed to stick. My eyes were now shut. I reacted against this – I had to – and heaved my eyes open suddenly, almost explosively. I was fighting this great desire to sleep. I had been there before. The last time, it was in the middle of the action itself: I felt fatigued, I had been going for hours, and my eyes started closing, for longer and longer. It just felt like I was resting my eyes . . . everyone seemed a long way off . . . tunnel vision, I'd never experienced that before . . . and then I felt myself going down, drifting into sleep, that's how it felt, and then I heard the wail of the ambulance, and then I was asleep for a bit, and woke up as they wheeled me into the hospital, and I remember ice, and lying in a bath of ice, shivering and wondering whether this was part of the dream. But today I was still awake. The lovely couple merely thought that I was testing them again, endlessly testing them.

The PR lady in front of us was looking a little confused.

'Is this what psychologists do before they start an interview, to get their interviewees to react more?' she asked me in a break. 'Are you warming up their motor neurones? This is all very clever stuff.' She beamed at the couple. 'This is a real treat from Britain's top psychologist. He's here for one day only at Britain's newest shopping mall. You are very fortunate people.'

They gave me thoughtful answers to each of my questions, and I tried, as always, to use direct eye contact to encourage them, but keeping my eyes wide and interested was draining all of the remaining energy out of me. My head suddenly fell forward onto the very large bosom of my interviewee, so that I actually headbutted her breasts. I apologised profusely. She

11

was getting quite concerned about how I apparently liked to test people. I apologised again. I was so embarrassed by this latest lapse that it energised me for about a minute or more. I became temporarily quite articulate again. The couple could see the difference. They could clearly sense that there was something wrong with me but they just didn't know what it was.

Rachel, the promotions girl, could also sense that there was something wrong and asked me if I would like some Coke, and then added, 'The drink, I mean.' I think that this was telling; I thought that she had her suspicions. I could feel myself lurching across the stage, as she sent someone off to fetch some Coke, the drink that is. But I clearly needed something urgently. Another younger couple had joined me on the sofa. The girl, very pretty with bright-red dyed hair, giggled a lot but really tried to answer every question with a lot of thought. I usually feel that I can build a bond with strangers more or less instantly, but not when I am this tired, not when I feel like this. Her boyfriend had got strangely sweaty palms, perhaps caused by my odd demeanour. I felt like explaining; I wanted to say, 'OK, I have had a big weekend, you're absolutely right, a bit crazier than I thought, in fact a mad fortnight, more than the human body was designed to bear. I'm running on empty, surviving on Red Bull and energy bars, trying to get some energy from somewhere. But my body is closing down, it's telling me that it's had enough, that the party's over, it's time to go to bed, to relax, to chill.'

I spent a weekend *Ghosthunting* with the Happy Mondays a couple of years ago, with Shaun Ryder and Bez on full throttle. I've seen how people can get carried away with the action and how they need props to keep them going; and when the props are removed, then comes the fall. Shaun didn't seem to need much food that weekend; all I remember him eating was one Brussels sprout for dinner, off my plate, and as he ate it like an apple, his pointy ears moved up and down. When it came to the interviews, I remember him wanting to use the nice, clean, flat surface of my television to keep the party going. They had come prepared for their night of ghosthunting.

That night Yvette Fielding organised a Ouija board session on a coffin, but the glass kept sticking as it moved across the surface. She thought it was dirt from the old chapel falling onto the coffin, but it was something the boys had put there in the break to get themselves up and ready for the night's further activities.

'I'm buzzin',' Bez kept saying. Just buzzin' from the gear that had been on the coffin lid. The next night they were not quite so lively, and I remember that mood, and that I had tried to keep them up in each of the interviews in front of the cameras as they sagged in front of me. But it was me who was sagging now. I was falling asleep in public in a shopping centre on a Monday morning in front of curious shoppers who vaguely recognised me and wanted to come and sit on my sofa.

When the filming finished, I said my hasty goodbyes and stumbled off towards the Underground, colliding with the crowds coming in the opposite direction, and sat on the seat with my eyes closed. If it hadn't been for my new £400 Holland Esquire jacket, I am sure that I could have been mistaken for someone who was destitute trying to catch forty winks in the middle of the day. I had a bag with me, with some gear in it, and I was desperately trying to find some place to use it. I felt like an addict, not a word I like – it's more a psychological dependence for me, after all – but I suppose my body does crave it, so addiction might be the right word. I needed to get somewhere urgently.

I had spent the day before with my son Ben, pushing ourselves through this in our own ways and we'd both survived. The problem was he was rested, I wasn't. I had been out there in California and then Chicago pushing the boat out every single day. I had arrived back in the UK on the Friday, and hadn't slept because of jet lag on the Friday and Saturday. On the Saturday I had tried to drive over to Sheffield from

Manchester to pick Ben up, but the Snake Pass was closed at the summit because of an accident so I had to drive all the way back and then catch a train to Newcastle. I had some urgent work to do when I got there, some revisions for an article for *Nature*, so the day before was hardly restful. And Ben and I shared a room, and I lay there in the dark listening to Ben talking to himself in his sleep at regular intervals, the tone loud and disturbed.

He had quite sensibly taken the day off after his big weekend; I was back at work and trying to work normally.

Ben and I have had a complex relationship, as many fathers and sons do. Freud might not have been right about the Oedipus complex, with competition for the wife/mother, but there does seem to be some implicit and often fraught comparison always at work there, in my experience at least. There was a time when a weekend with his father would have been the worst thing in the world imaginable for Ben, but somehow we got through it because something drew us both in and pulled us together. That thing that has left me stumbling through London with a large brown leather bag in my hand, looking for some kind of fix – perhaps there is no other word for it.

Ben had rung me up to see how I was. We have different personalities, different ways of doing things. I tend to be quite chatty, and quite open, while Ben can often be a man of very few words, sometimes single words. But I was delighted that he had rung; there had been a time when it simply wouldn't have occurred to him to see how I was after a day like that. We'd laughed at how wasted we both felt. We had parted at the station in Newcastle the day before, on a dreary and grey Sunday afternoon, both moving with difficulty. This thing that we both love had caused that.

I eventually found what I was looking for: it was a gym, and I changed with eyes that were now half closed, then climbed up some stairs and ran out along Essex Road in Islington and up onto Upper Street, but despite the exhaustion I was happy to be back in that familiar pattern once again. The three half marathons in the fortnight were over. I had pushed myself with the world's hardest half marathon, the Pier to Peak Half Marathon in Santa Barbara in California, a climb of 4,000 feet, more or less equivalent to running up Ben Nevis, without any subsequent descent (and I live in Manchester so I never see hills, which made the whole thing more challenging), then the Chicago Half Marathon, then the Great North Run – on top of the jet lag and the work and the runs every day in-between because I never stop, and all of the usual emotional issues that surround going away for over three weeks, with my children back in England. I am sure that Ben was secretly proud of his dad, but he would never have thought to say it.

I thought that Ben had done amazingly in the Great North Run. It had all been leading to this so far, a time of 1.13.02, 45th out of something like 55,000 runners, but he still wasn't happy; my time was very disappointing, embarrassing even: 1.45.06. But it was my own fault. I had managed to persuade myself that three half marathons in fourteen days would leave me supremely fit; instead it just left me supremely tired. I had been hoping for 1.36, the time I had done in Cardiff a few months previously (which Ben likes to point out was a hundred yards or so short). Ben still felt that he hadn't tried hard enough, he hadn't pushed himself enough. What sort of Oedipal urge was behind it all?

I have always been a runner, endlessly pursuing some unreachable goal, and Ben has had to deal with this all of his life. He has had to adapt to it, in his own way. I suspect it's like dealing with someone with a strong, unwavering set of religious beliefs that reside within, no matter what external events occur to shake those beliefs to their foundation. Saying that I am a runner is, of course, a somewhat bold statement to make. It almost feels like a declaration or a claim, a public announcement that I belong to this great group called 'runner'. It is a particularly bold claim because I am not, and I never have been, a runner like Alberto Salazar or Brendan Foster or even

Ron Hill, a runner that you will have ever heard of for running because of speed, accomplishment or sheer bloody effort. I'm always worried that someone will say, 'You call yourself a runner?' But I am a runner nonetheless, inside, and I would say that first and foremost I am a runner, probably more than I am a 'psychologist', or a 'family man' or a so-called 'celebrity academic'. It feels to me not so much like a bold claim as an admission of some sort. I have been a runner for 40-odd years, long before I became any of those other things. I train every day, regardless of time zone, weather or illness. Of course, I have trained with stress fractures to my ankle (I suspect that many runners have done this), but I have also trained with what was later to be diagnosed as septic arthritis ballooning my broken ankle so that I couldn't walk, let alone run; but I could still hobble and that was enough. I needed to get onto the running machine and hobble for a couple of miles so that this odd pattern of absolute consistency would not be broken. The next day I was in Accident and Emergency because of the ankle, probably not as a direct consequence of this extra run, so I was secretly pleased that I had got the extra run in. I have raced with a shoulder dislocated the week before in a bad fall in a 5K race, with other runners now asking me why my shoulder looked so frozen and my gait appeared so odd.

Running is something that acts as a bridge to the Belfast of the '60s, which was my home, and the narrow wet mill streets of the north of the city. That's where it all started. There is something very familiar about running, the anticipation, the movement and rhythm that takes a while to build before it becomes smooth, but perhaps most of all the feeling afterwards: it's not so much a great glowing 'runners' high' but something harder to describe. To me running feels like some sort of self-correction process; work or indeed any aspect of life can leave you feeling slightly off-balance, off-track, but the run soon fixes that. It pulls me back to the real me. I have needed running to get back on track many times in my life.

I sometimes think that running is one of the few things that really does connect me to my past, as my father, mother and brother are all dead. Since I also grew up in the Belfast of the Troubles, many of my friends and neighbours have also passed on, most prematurely and abruptly, a number murdered in the conflict, leaving within me a general feeling of disconnectedness except when it comes to this one activity that provides me with some connection. I feel like I'm reaching out to connect with something on my runs, this one desperate gesture, like the gesture in Michelangelo's *Creation of Adam* on the ceiling of the Sistine Chapel. It's an intentional gesture, iconic and meaningful, a great desire to touch the past, to hold on to it, to feel belonging.

Running is something that my own family have had to live with, perhaps to endure over the years; it has provided the structure and sometimes the narrative of much of my everyday life. Meals were always organised around my running, and sometimes whole days, holidays certainly. I thought that my children would end up hating this activity, but it turned out to be more complicated than that, much more psychological. Ben is now, of course, a very good runner, the only one of my children so far to fully embrace this sport (although another son, Sam, is becoming more regular in his running and has for some time been incredibly disciplined with his gym training; he also has great potential). But Ben is more obsessed than I ever was, if such a thing is indeed possible. It has taken over his life as well. He says that he feels good about this, but we will see how this might change in the future when all of its many consequences will become apparent as the years progress.

Ben and I seem to have a good relationship now through running, certainly not perfect, but this was not always the case. For many years I felt that Ben might have hated me. This, I appreciate, is a very strong word for a father to use, and I do not mean it in a metaphorical or abstract sense but in a quite literal way. He seemed to hate me because of what he saw as my shortcomings as a father and as a man. He never told me so because that is not in his nature, but he showed me, through his lack of interest in my life, his avoidance of me whenever and wherever possible, his rejection of everything that I stood for: academia, discipline in training, my understandable obsession with success and money (understandable perhaps given my poor background from those mill streets of Belfast) and running. This, in many ways, is a familiar story – the eldest son rejecting the hopes and aspirations and values of his father – but here it felt stronger than this, much stronger.

But then sometimes life surprises you, and now Ben is a runner and he says that as a consequence he understands me better. I sometimes think that Ben and I have been on some kind of journey, to find each other and possibly ourselves, through probably the only thing that really connects us. That is why we decided to write the book and to do it from two perspectives, that of a father and that of a son talking independently. Sometimes we will write about the same experiences that we have been through together, sometimes our experiences will differ, as I travel the world of the celebrity academic and Ben pounds the streets of Sheffield endlessly, tirelessly and single-mindedly. There is a very old saying that history is only ever recorded by one person, the victor, but in the pages that follow I want to ensure that this never happens and that our history will be recorded and contested by both of us. And anyway, perhaps with running there is no real victor, just quiet voices in the end pounding away and enduring what they have to. I am a professor of psychology and I believe that the articulation of difficult and painful thoughts and memories is an important and indeed necessary part of healthy living. But those psychologists who have researched this issue of emotional disclosure might never have examined a case like this. I already feel that this journey will be a story about pride and shame, despair and maybe elation, joy and sadness, longing for the past and relief that the past was somehow survived, in more or less equal measures. This will necessarily be a story of loss and gain, a story of the man being father to the son and perhaps sometimes the reverse, a story of the excavation of concealed hate and love, and a story of suffering and longing and desire and fulfilment – maybe a story of ordinary life itself, and maybe not. Maybe a story of life lived through running will look and feel different from all other lives. I wouldn't know, I've only lived one life and running has been at its core. Will it be a story of genuine reconciliation? Who knows? Ultimately it depends on the pain that we're both prepared to endure on and off the road.

Ben and I sat at Newcastle station and I tried to communicate to him how much I loved him and how proud I was of him. I tried to kiss him on the cheek, this 28-year-old man with stubble (it's just my way, I can't help it, it makes me feel better), but he pushed me away.

'People will think you're gay, you know. Kiss me here and they'll think you're definitely gay.'

But I grabbed him by the neck, pulled him close and kissed him anyway, and walked off to my platform with leaden legs and this strange gait that most runners would instantly recognise, that comes from blistered feet and tight, iron-solid muscles. I think he smiled though when I kissed him, a father prepared to signal his closeness through his body language, despite all the warnings and all the embarrassment.

But I glanced back, and he was reading some running book, which was sitting precariously on his lap, and he never looked back at me once, not once, as far as I could tell. And I was alone again.

2

The Middle of Nowhere

The house in which Ben grew up overlooked the moors outside Sheffield. It was a vast, bleak landscape – there was nothing really visible through the patio doors that opened onto the back garden except a great, rising hill covered in heather, green then purple in the changing seasons; and then the whole vista would turn white with the deep snow that would come with winter in the Peak District.

I had wanted this house ever since I first saw it, sitting there on the Snake Pass as you travel from Manchester to Sheffield across the great spine of England that is the Pennines. Hollow Meadows had been built as a workhouse at some point in the nineteenth century and later became a school for truants and then a TB hospital and later still an asylum, sometime in the 1950s, a severe building in many ways with a serious purpose: to keep the poor or the bad or the sick well away from the city of Sheffield. It would have been a long walk to get back to town from here, but many apparently still tried. I ran into Sheffield many times from Hollow Meadows. But the view when you sat in that old building was redolent of more ancient histories, untouched by any modernity or fad, and humbling in some mysterious way. It was a wild view, and very few walkers tramped up along the paths visible from our house on this particular bit of the moors. It was bleak and windy up on those hills, regardless of the season. It tested the body when you were up there, running into the wind, leaning into it, like holding a door shut against some determined intruder. I moved there with my wife Carol and three children when they were still very young, and we lived right in the centre of this old complex that had now been turned into nine houses. Our house was in the middle of the enclosed courtyard and had the original staircase from the workhouse. Despite its sorrowful past that must have been intertwined with a lot of individual suffering, it always felt like a warm and welcoming place, with stars overhead at night in clear skies without the city's smoke or fumes. I had never seen stars like that before.

I loved the quiet, rugged moors just outside the window, and my runs of eight or nine miles through them with dusk approaching on cold midwinter days, alone, mud splattered, fingers icy, but with my heart pounding, looking out on a primitive landscape that seemed to take on my noisy pulse, as if I had projected it somewhere else. The moors felt alive and fiercely robust, in fine health, fit and well for millennia, and there was I in the middle of it all, just the visitor, just temporary, just passing through. I was allowed fleetingly to view its great rugged beauty through my running, which helped me understand its permanence through my movement and impermanence. I love mountain ranges far away and the idea of running through them (which is an interesting ambition for someone who does not like running up hills); I love snow without footprints, unsullied and pure, and trails that wind to infinity that hint of adventure and maybe even some sort of spiritual enlightenment at the base of the clouds, even just 'yes, I see'. I love the feeling of history and permanence and place that you can get when you run.

But I have an image in my head of nature more potent than most, and that is an image from Nanda Devi in the Himalayas, a picture taken way above the snowline. White peaks touching the sky above the 'Goddess of Joy'. And there in the foreground a suntanned face with white goggle marks around the eyes and a fresh growth of beard, a Westerner smiling for the camera, like a tourist above the world, pale skin touched by the sun, reddened in parts, an unmistakable joy in his face,

21

that smile of his, the eyes crinkled into life, the sign of a human being testing himself in the wilderness, in tune with life, in tune with nature, in tune with himself. This image is my brother Bill. He was a good runner but not competitive; he had too many other competitions with himself. And I have another image of him as well, an image of him wrapped in something green and filthy, the kind of thing that climbers would have to hand, that they might dump at the end of the day's climbing, or at the end of an ill-planned expedition, and I can see the rough contours of his body through the grimy, green tarpaulin, his face and body covered, just lumps and bumps visible on the stretched plastic, as he was laid to rest a day after the photograph, under some filthy stones with his name scratched on a rock like a warning to fellow travellers in this remote and dangerous region, like Coleridge's Mongol king. 'Beware, beware,' that's what that pile of stones said about someone who never had any illusions, those bright, flashing eyes closed for ever. And that is my emotional legacy. A legacy of loss, a legacy of recognising that everything human is temporary and transient, and a realisation that everything you hold dear will pass, no matter how much you want it to stay forever. There is always the danger that I am emotionally blunted by life and the small unpredictable events that have shaped me, and perhaps I am emotionally disempowered by this whole cumulative experience. Perhaps running gives you some control over your life in ways that other things do not. Bill loved Sheffield with its rock climbing and its crags and edges just outside the city, and sometimes I think that's why I moved there in the first place.

I have another radiant image of my brother in the mountains, but it is a curious image because he is not physically present in the scene; rather, it is an image of an object glistening by a river, like a totem, something that represented him. One summer he invited Carol and me to Chamonix for a summer of climbing in the Alps, but when we got there eventually, after many mishaps, he had already gone. He was too easily bored to wait for us; it had taken us days to hitch-hike there. He had gone somewhere else to climb; his fellow climbers said that they knew that, they just didn't know where he had gone to – somewhere else in the Alps, he hadn't bothered to tell them. Presumably he assumed that I had changed my mind, playing it safe again. We had no tent and no money and I spent the first day wandering aimlessly around the town and the surrounding fields for somewhere dry to sleep with a 17 year old, who was terrified of any spider that scuttled, any daddy-long-legs that flapped, or anything with or without legs that could crawl up her body at night. It was never going to be easy to find sanctuary there. But I tried and eventually I found a beautiful bubbling Alpine stream that jostled its way under an ancient moss-covered bridge. The view of the still snow-covered Alps in the background was spectacular, the water was pure, and the bridge afforded shelter from the wind and any rain. I was ecstatic.

Carol had big, doleful grey eyes that looked out from under a black fringe. She sat on the dry grass in her flimsy summer dress and started to sob gently into her hands. She said that she never wanted to go anywhere with me, ever again. She made me promise to start sweeping the riverbank for spiders (like the bomb squad from my native Belfast, I had to secure the area inch by inch). Every time I found a spider, like a magician I made it disappear, without her ever noticing. She was sobbing so much, with the tears blinding her eyes; she was easily fooled by my sleight of hand, as the small black spider balls were flipped to the floor. I worked my way from where we sat to right under the bridge and then I saw it. It was sitting there on its own as if it had been arranged deliberately and carefully, like some iconic work of art in an exhibition, full of symbolic significance, layers of meaning. It was a tin of Heinz baked beans, the metal still shiny, with a ragged top, hastily and hungrily opened without a proper tin-opener. This was the sign that I had been looking for. Others had slept there, British climbers (you just knew that they

23

would be climbers); it would be a safe place to stay. Some might try to criticise climbers, who are allowed to get so close to the mesmerising beauty of nature, for soiling the environment in this way. But I had no such feeling of revulsion. I needed a sign and that was it.

We slept there that night and Carol felt secure because others had been there before. The next morning there was no sign of the tin can; the stream had probably pulled it into its journey. Months later when my brother and I finally met I discovered, by accident, that it was he who had enjoyed the beans on his first night in Chamonix, where rather than pitch a tent he had decided to rough it for one night. We were frequently drawn to each other in this kind of mysterious way, so his loss was always hard. He loved the mountains but like many climbers he left debris behind; he knew that the mountains could take care of themselves, that nature always triumphs. The debris of human life is always swallowed up. I like the way that running helps me view the many facets of nature, some good and some bad. It helps me put things in perspective and see things from a safe distance.

In Hollow Meadows we had a boxer dog called Louis who was my treat to the children and myself when we first moved into the house. We brought Louis back in a cardboard box from a breeder in Doncaster when Carol was at work, and the first thing that he did was pee all over the kitchen in excitement. Carol had not been consulted about us getting a dog, but her anger subsided quickly and the children loved him from the start. We all did, Carol especially. Louis would stand by the patio doors and his head would twitch one way and then the other as he watched the sheep on the hill in front of the house. I took him for runs even when he was a pup and we would run together up that sharp hill in front of the house. When he was bigger he would pull on his choking lead, first to the left and then to the right as he tried to break away to get after the sheep. You couldn't let him off the lead much of the time because his enthusiasm for chasing sheep with their sharp, evasive and, it has to be said, arrogant turns would lead him up over other hills and well into the distance sometimes in minutes, with me threatening and swearing at the top of my voice, scaring any walkers within earshot. Louis was one of the most muscular boxer dogs that I have ever seen but his legs were very short. We only noticed this much later when we saw him standing with other dogs of the same breed. He was so short that he looked like a different breed. My kids always said that it was my fault because all that running had stunted his growth.

I had done many long runs in this particular section of the Peak District, up to Stanage Edge from the Snake, where Bill used to climb, then along Long Causeway to Stanedge Pole, and down over the flagstones to Redmires Reservoirs, long before I decided to buy the house in Hollow Meadows. I think that it was on one of those runs that I noticed the house in the first place, or rather I noticed the abandoned mental hospital, now derelict, and I became excited when the renovation started. It was the perfect location for a psychologist who sometimes doesn't like people that much but rather likes to be on his own, in the middle of nowhere with a wild half-crazed dog and mad-eyed terrified sheep.

I always saw Hollow Meadows as a place for children. There was a stream in the hollow down at the back of the field opposite the house, and then a rickety bridge and large boulders to step over to take you up and onto the moors. These boulders always made the start of any run difficult but the dog didn't seem to have much trouble; he just ran up the gully between them. For me it was a place for children to play and have adventures, and the opposite of my own grim mill street in the Belfast of the '60s. But the images that spring to mind now are sometimes more negative than I would like. My daughter Zoe and her friends, maybe 12 or 13, trapped in the corner of a field by a herd of young bullocks, curious and awkward, bulky, stupid creatures, brazen, pushing forward slowly towards a small huddled group of hysterical children.

Or Ben panting and crying and saying that Louis had got off the lead and stampeded the herd of white cows up the back field, by biting their tails to make them run. When I got there the cows were still panicking and mooing loudly, and the dog was nearly exhausted with all the fun and excitement, his jaws covered in foamy saliva. The farmer was standing there with a shotgun in his hand, but I told him quietly and confidently that if he shot my dog he'd be fucking well next, and I said this in my strongest and thickest working-class Belfast accent. Growing up in Murder Triangle in North Belfast with many close friends who had become infamous through the Troubles ('your pals have made it to the front pages these days,' my mother would remind me; 'one of them has killed more people than Billy the Kid') can have advantages when you need to threaten somebody like this. I knew what a real threat sounded like; I had grown up listening to enough of them on my street, and had seen enough of them actually carried through, to know what genuine threats sounded like. They were never that loud or in your face. My threat sounded menacing enough even though it had no substance whatsoever. The farmer put his gun away, swearing under his breath, and saying that the next time he would ring the police and they would shoot the fucking dog instead of him. 'That's what they're paid for,' he said. This sounded to me like such an odd comment that it has stuck in my mind. Dog shooters, that's what the police were. But I know what he meant. I could see my son looking at me, shyly and proudly, maybe even very proudly.

I liked to tell my children about my background in Belfast, and my gang from the 'turn-of-the road', and what became of them in the Troubles. It was, of course, as much a story about me as it was of them. I worked my way out of there, without any excuses – and believe me, I would have had many excuses to draw upon if that had been my choice. Several of my close friends were murdered, most of them in the bars and clubs at the 'turn-of-the-road' itself. After all, we never liked to wander too far from home. A number of them were convicted of murder; some were convicted of multiple murders. My friend Robert had his throat cut in a back alley. Bill was shot dead in our local pool hall. Somebody walked in and said, 'All right, mate?' and then opened fire with a sub-machine gun, and then shot him six times with a revolver to be on the safe side, if that's the right phrase. The manager of the shop next door described the noise as 'like a hammer hitting corrugated tin'. Bill was shot dead by a man who didn't even bother to cover his face but murder charges against the three IRA defendants were dropped after the key witness whose car had been hijacked and used in the shooting refused to testify. My friend Dennis was shot dead in a drinking club in Silverstream.

The coroner at Dennis's inquest said, 'We have heard a lot about Chicago-style killings in Belfast, but this was more like a Wild West saloon-style killing as portrayed in the pictures. Here we had two outlaws coming in and starting to fire in all directions.'

Shots were fired outside Dennis's home just before his funeral was due to start; many of the women in the house became completely hysterical.

I knew a lot of these outlaws and some were now in the Maze Prison or Maghaberry serving multiple life sentences, and I would visit them when I was home, just back from California, or wherever, with a tan that would light up a room, and tell them about my academic exploits and my running. Jim, serving eight life sentences, did a half marathon in the grounds of the Maze one year. He and I had asked Carol out the same night, as we walked home from a disco in the church hall. A fight had broken out and somebody got hit with a hammer, and the disco was abandoned, so we were both trying to make the best of a bad job with a last-ditch effort at a date. Jim and I go back a long way. But that day on the visit to him in prison, all I was interested in was his time for the half marathon. I had been in the gang with the rest of them. There is nothing too surprising about that, it would have been odd if I hadn't been, and I have tiny, almost invisible scars from a knife wound on the fingers of my left hand as a small reminder of the wee bits of bother we used to get into with other gangs. I can just about make out the scars. But I had passed the eleven-plus and gone to a very good school, and at nights I would work at a little yellow card table in our front room and then go down to the corner, to the 'turn-of-the-road', to see what was happening, to see what the lads were up to. They were all proud of my academic achievements and sometimes when we met lads from other gangs they would ask me to tell them how many O levels I had (12), or the grades of my science A levels (all As), in the days when this was extremely uncommon. And these other guys would shake their heads in disbelief.

'Fucking hell, Beats,' they would say, 'how the fuck did you manage that? Did you take something? Did you get your hands on some fucking brain-power stuff?'

The gang was always breaking into local shops and the local chemist's (where, embarrassingly, Carol's mother worked). They didn't know what they were getting some of the time; it could well have been brain-power stuff. I had to decode the labels and explain what it was. Perhaps I had squirrelled the brain-power stuff away for myself. All they knew was that the lad at the corner with the short dark hair and the leather jacket, which Robert had nicked for him, had this weird string of qualifications, and he could read and speak Latin and Russian; and even more weirdly, he went running every day with bare legs in the winter, and his run would take him back through Ligoniel Village, or 'Comanche Territory' as we knew it, and the Comanches would throw bricks at him just before he got to St Mark's Church and started heading for the invisible 'Peace Line' on the road.

Back in the field above Hollow Meadows Carol was crying helplessly, threatening to get rid of the dog if it did that one more time. I smacked Louis on the side of his great heavy head and swore at him, and the foamy spit shot off into the wet grass. I dragged him home, which was easier than normal because he was so tired, and threw him into the warm kitchen before getting him a bowl of water. He lay on his side heaving with exhaustion, lapping the water with his tongue out of the side of his mouth.

I had managed to buy the house in Hollow Meadows on a lecturer's salary (the manager of Sheffield Wednesday lived in one of the other houses) by having a second job. I wrote for *The Guardian* regularly about life in the North, including sometimes the darker and seedier side of life in the North during Thatcher's recession with the steelworks and the mines closing. I wrote stories about big macho men skulking round Shoppers' Paradise supermarket in Crookes for the family shopping in the afternoons so that they wouldn't bump into their mates from the steel furnaces simply because they couldn't face the humiliation of it all. And women popping into the building society four or five times a week to pay in 25p or 15p 'to even up their account' so that they could get out of the house and have a bit of a chat with the cashier.

And sometimes there were good-news stories, or things that looked on the surface like they could be good-news stories, like the steelworker Brian who couldn't wait for his firm to close because he was a keen marathon runner and he was looking for more time to train. Brian was one of the lucky ones kept on right to the end in his particular factory with enough time for officials from the Department of Employment and the redundancy counsellors to come to them to prepare them for life on the dole. Brian said that he only became worried when the woman from the Department of Employment told them that all of the rules and regulations about unemployment benefit were so complicated that nobody really knew what anybody was entitled to anyway. Brian went to a lecture on finding a job where it was suggested that steelworkers might like to think about dog-walking, pet-sitting and fish-feeding for neighbours on holiday as new job opportunities. Then the big day came, with a full day to fill, and he persuaded his wife, who was very unfit, to come out for a run with him, only to find that he couldn't keep up with her. He had never had asthma in his life but suddenly there he was puffing and panting and gasping for breath on a street in Sheffield. He tried going out with his old running club but the same thing happened; the rest of the runners couldn't understand it. It got so bad that he couldn't even walk home from the jobcentre without continually stopping. He had read somewhere that nerves could bring on asthmatic symptoms but he refused to believe that that was what was happening to him. He thought perhaps it was his house-cleaning, which he did while his wife went out to work, or the fact that there was a lot of dust in the factory in the last few weeks before it finally closed. But either way his running career was over. Some of these articles were repackaged as books: *Survivors of Steel City*: *A Portrait of Sheffield*, *England After Dark*, *On the Ropes*: *Boxing As a Way of Life*.

My daily routine was odd for a university lecturer with a young family. Out talking to redundant steelworkers and miners, in the crowd at bare-knuckle fights raided by the police, out scouting round the town with a burglar in his car looking for 'opportunities', hanging around nightclubs and casinos, in the know after hours with the local CID and the hangers-on and the ten-bob millionaires, as they call them in Sheffield, and the models and the girls from the massage parlour on their nights off. I rarely went to bed before 2.30 a.m., and never got up early. Going to bed that late became another of my compulsive routines, even on my wedding anniversary, which is 31 December. Carol would be crying, as I got ready to go out on my own. My mother showed her displeasure.

'If I'd a fucking gun, I'd shoot you myself,' she said.

I would also come home late for dinner most nights, to Carol's annoyance.

'Where have you been?' she would say, suspicious and angry, and often rightly on both counts.

I look back at these books of mine with black and white

photos, which I took myself, of slim, toned girls that I knew well, dancers or models or promotion girls, 'good-time girls' my mother called them, with great early '80s hairdos, blonde and layered, dressed in leather thongs doing high kicks in the front room, in front of their bored mother on the settee reading the classified ads, and think about all of the distractions around every corner to a guy like me with a gold VIP card to the clubs and casinos. I got much closer to one or two them, almost inevitably.

When I got home in the early evening, the children would be delighted to see me, even if I was late, and then after 20 or 30 minutes of excited play ('You just get them wound up and then leave it all to me to get them settled again,' Carol would say) I would start putting on my running stuff. Our favourite game was called 'Wolf at disco', and it was thought up by me. It consisted of me standing outside the bedroom door as the children bounced up and down on our double bed, and I would shout 'Wolf at . . . disco!' and the kids would have to stop bouncing and lie down on the bed as quickly as possible and stay quite still, without any movement. The last one still moving was out. They loved this game, although its name, which they liked to chant, has got interesting connotations given that I spent so much time out in clubs. Sometimes the anxiety in their faces was palpable when I told them that I had to go out again, to get myself out that door and onto the moors, every day without fail, while the dog leapt and jumped across the floor in anticipation.

This compulsive running, without deviation or excuse, is something that I have done every day since I was 13. At school for a while I was running not just every day but usually twice on a Tuesday and a Thursday, nine times a week in all. Belfast Royal Academy was a good school with a great academic record, and I shared classes with boys and girls who were not from my part of Belfast. But in my seven years at the Academy I didn't once invite a single Academy boy or girl to my home and the outside toilet without a light and the backroom without much wallpaper because the walls were too damp for the wallpaper to stick to. One friend did, however, come uninvited on one occasion, but he just wanted help with his homework and he didn't stay long. One of my mates set fire to his school blazer by popping a lit cigarette into his pocket before he left. His father returned about half an hour later with the scorched jacket and stood in the middle of my front room, tense and irate ('steaming', my friend said), as my mother categorically denied that it had happened in her house, and told him that he was wrong to make such accusations. She had genuinely seen nothing and assumed that his accusations were the result of prejudice on his part and little more. I hadn't seen the butt of the cigarette being flicked into the pocket but I had seen the smirk of one of my mates soon after and I knew that this meant something. I just wasn't sure what it meant at the time until we were left on our own. This particular mate of mine was also murdered during the Troubles.

And to be honest I never really felt part of that great school. Rather than mingle with my classmates at lunchtimes I went for a run and had a late school dinner on my own. It didn't seem that lonely or that unusual, except perhaps in its frequency and except perhaps looking back. I did this every single day, which with the passage of time seems very significant indeed. One of my mother's best friends was the dinner lady so she would serve me late and give me two apple crumbles. I thought that the teachers always implicitly regarded me as quite different from the rest (but, of course, this could have been my imagination). In a chemistry class one day, and it was the 'A' class for A-level chemistry and therefore full of serious students, I remember once laughing too loudly at a letter that our teacher, an old wizened spinster with bad teeth, was reading from an ex-pupil that had gone to Cambridge. The letter was meant to be an inspiration to us all. Maybe we could make it to Cambridge one day, if we tried hard enough. There was some word in this letter that I found hysterical; I can't remember what it was now. I think it may even have been 'scholar'. It was an unfamiliar word, or unfamiliar in that particular context, that just sounded ludicrously pompous to me. It sounded funny at the time, don't ask me why now. I laughed out loud. It was a sudden, uncontrolled splutter of laughter, a common sort of sound; it was only me who saw the joke and the sound seemed to echo in the wood-clad laboratory. Maybe I had expected others to laugh at this word, prompted by my anticipatory guffaw; I had liked to think of myself as a bit of a funny man in class, never taking anything too seriously, or that's how I liked to portray myself, always able to get others to join in – but not this time. The teacher paused almost mid-word and hesitated, as if fighting for control, then exploded in a rage at me. She was so angry that spit was coming out of her mouth, from between her bad teeth, as she shouted; she slammed the letter onto the lab bench and stormed off. In my view, she got far too angry given the nature of the offence. I could see something in her eyes, as she glanced back, just the once, which said something about boys like me from that part of town, from the 'turn-of-the-road', from that Loyalist ghetto that bred such violence and such resistance. 'No matter how you try with them,' that was what her eyes were saying, 'no matter how hard you try, and, Lord, I have been trying.' She asked to speak to me outside, after she had calmed down, just in case I didn't understand the implicit messages, and she said slowly and calmly, 'Beattie, you come from the gutter, and that's where you're going to end up, mark my words. I'm never wrong about these things.' These words have been burned into my memory for decades. I stared back at her with resentment and a fury that I really felt inside, but did not dare express. I could have hit her, that's what I felt like doing, and that's what many from my street would have done, or cried, but luckily I didn't do either. I just nodded my head with aggressive, sharp little movements in time with every word she said, and stared back at her and kept control. I was good at keeping control. I was very disciplined; that was important to me. I never made excuses about not going for my run, I never made excuses about not doing my homework despite all my messing about in class itself. And I ended up getting a first-class honours degree, and doing my doctorate at Cambridge, at Trinity College, no less – no widening access, state-school quota, backwater college for me.

I felt guilty about coming home late and then going off for my run, of course I felt guilty, so I would ask Ben, the eldest boy, to come with me. He told me recently that I didn't just ask him once; I would ask him again and again and again until he agreed. His mother would often intervene.

'It's raining, he doesn't want to go. Can't you get the message?'

But I was persistent. Ben reminds me that I would often bribe him as well, to get this fair-haired boy with bare legs in the middle of winter out the door with his dad, dressed in his father's running clothes, far too big for him, and over the rickety bridge and up through the scratchy heather into the wilderness. And Ben always knew that I wouldn't compromise on the run. I couldn't run slowly just because he was with me; he had to keep up with me and the dog because otherwise it wouldn't have been a proper run. I could see the anguish in his face sometimes, and I had to learn to avoid looking at him in order to get started. I had to have this run every day and it had to be sufficiently hard. That was the way things were, Ben knew that. He, of course, had no real choice here. It was either run with me in this way or let me abandon him once again, and if he didn't come with me it would be like him agreeing to be left behind. There would have been a subtle shift of responsibility for any separation that would have let me off the hook to some extent.

One night, in July or August, we got to the top of the hill and I could see that he just couldn't keep up with me. He was bent double, gulping for breath. He told me that he had a stitch. He rarely got stitches; I wasn't sure whether it was an excuse or not. But I could see that he was very uncomfortable. It was about nine o'clock, getting dark already, so I told him to stay there on the moors in the middle of nowhere, on his own, until I got back. I wouldn't be long, I said, a few minutes at most; I had to have my run. He knew that it wouldn't be a few minutes and that I was lying. I couldn't have taken him back home and then gone out running; it would have been far too dark even with all those stars up there. I had tried it many times but had stopped a while ago after I had got tangled up very badly in some barbed wire that had been left in the middle of a field; the barbed wire had ripped my shorts and made my balls bleed.

The dog and I started to run off, and Ben smiled weakly, and funnily enough I can remember the dog looking slightly puzzled and running beside me for a few paces and then back to Ben, as if trying to round up the pack and keep us all together. But Louis eventually came with me, so we both left him. We ran down a little path by the river and then turned right at the end onto a road that arched back up towards the summit where we turned onto the moors again and down through some steep waterlogged fields. It was a full circle that took about half an hour. I wasn't concerned about Ben so much that night because I knew there would be nobody about, but I was concerned that my run had been broken up and was now disjointed, hardly a run at all. The dog might have liked these sorts of runs with lots of stops and starts but I didn't.

The loop took about 30 minutes or maybe a little more that night, and the dog and I eventually came down the hill speedily. I glanced down at the spot where I had left Ben, expecting him to be looking up, impressed with our speed. But he wasn't there; there was just no sign of him. I could feel the panic spread through my body. I had no idea where he might be. Had he tried to follow me? Or had he set off home? Or had he gone to meet me, maybe on a parallel path, in the direction that he thought I might be returning from? My panicky guess was that he wouldn't have gone home; that would have been too much like an admission of weakness on his part. My gut instinct was that he had set off in the direction that the dog and I had run off in because he might think that he could somehow catch us. So the dog and I set off on the course again, calling out for him, the fear audible in my voice, even to me.

Eventually I saw him in the distance, trembling and crying, his arms dangling by his sides, not so much running along as shuffling. I hugged him and he cried, with these great heavy sighs that were stopping his breath. A small, frightened child standing quite literally in the middle of nowhere. He was very apologetic.

'I had to try and find you,' he said. 'A sheep frightened me, I couldn't stay there.'

I felt ashamed to my stomach, but I still wanted the two of us to run home, down past the grazing sheep, down through that dip in the hill with the gurgling mud that fills it and down through the coarse heather, back down to his mother. On the way back home he was still trembling but I told him not to tell his mother about me losing him. She might have stopped him ever coming with me again. His mother looked pleased to see us both and she asked him if he had enjoyed the run that night and he burst out crying.

'I don't know what the matter is with him tonight,' I said. 'It's not that hard up there; it's good for him, for goodness' sake.'

'He's only a child,' she said. 'It might not be hard for you because you do it every day but he's only a young boy.'

Ben got dressed for bed very quietly.

But I have another image in my head of my son Ben, a sharp and clear image, which is also perhaps connected with why I started him on running in the first place. Ben always loved sport. He is eight or maybe nine, in this photograph from my memory, with impossibly blond hair and beautiful fine features – I would say angelic looking, if it were not such a cliché. He is standing on the far side of a football pitch, which is covered with a slight dusting of frost. He is hopping up and down blowing on his hands, probably not because it is doing much good but because he sees other boys doing it, and after all, that's what footballers do, they hop up and down like this and then they blow on their hands. He is on his own, about 4 yards from a man in a maroon tracksuit. The man has a moustache, a tache they say in Sheffield, and a slightly vacant expression, hard to read. I'm staring at this man looking for signals. There aren't any. He is just watching the game. Small boys are running up and down the field with the ball at their feet, there are some attempts at passes, lots of shots, most many yards wide, few goals. There is another group of about three boys to the man's right, all hopping on the spot, blowing on their hands. And for some reason they are more openly excited than Ben about the whole thing, more optimistic I would say. The man with the tache, the manager, sometimes turns their way and points to the action on the pitch. They stop hopping for a second and watch the game but soon continue their jumping movements. The man with the tache doesn't turn towards Ben, but Ben keeps looking towards the man with a look of quiet, desperate expectation. It breaks my heart. Carol is standing beside me, in a thick padded jacket.

'Why doesn't he put him on? Those boys played last week and the week before. He's got his favourites.' She is angry and she doesn't try to hide it in any way. She is watching the game but swivelling her head my way, just in case I fail to understand the depth of her emotions. Ben does not look our way: he may be too embarrassed; perhaps he is too engrossed in the action on the pitch. Either way, it is just Carol and me and the man with the tache in this little triangle, stretching across a football pitch, with desire and anxiety and wish fulfilment and anger all mixed up in this volatile little bundle.

'What happens if he doesn't get on again this week?' she says. 'He'll be devastated. Phil Vicars plays every week and he says that Ben is as good as any of them who are on the team.'

I hug her for a second, and I can feel her shuddering with

sadness through that thick, padded coat. It's unbearable and after a few seconds I say goodbye and walk back to my car on my own. I couldn't watch any more and I couldn't catch Ben's eye. That night, I asked him to come for a run with me. For some reason I assumed that he would say no, but he didn't, and that was the very first run. We ran for about a mile without stopping and I noticed that he has a long even stride. I promised to buy him some good running shoes.

'It's more fun than football, isn't it?' I asked as we sat in our front room sipping lemonade.

'Not really,' he said, 'but it wasn't as bad as what I thought it would be. And anyway, it will make me fitter for football. If I'm fitter, I'll probably get on next Sunday.'

I sometimes think that's how it all started; it was, after all, the first step, the first mile. I was just trying to keep him at it on long, wet nights out near the moors for his own sake, but also for mine. But Ben confessed to me that he hated running at that time, probably as much as he hated me some of the time. He had his own reasons for that, which only became clear recently. It was to do with a particular marathon, a particular point in time. I would do the Sheffield Marathon each year, and Carol and the children would wait at the finish for me to give me their support. The marathon was usually held in June and occasionally in July, and there were, on a number of occasions, fatalities because of the heat. It was a tough, hilly marathon and always very hot. The winning time was never fast. The first year I did it without any specific marathon training and with only two long runs in 3 hours 29 minutes, and was quite pleased with the result. I had been in a nightclub until 4 a.m. the night before, drinking vodka and orange because my hazy thinking told me that the orange juice might help with the run.

In the second year I trained much harder with longer runs and I would have broken 3 hours if I hadn't started sprinting for the finish on Penistone Road when I saw the 25-mile marker. I woke up later in the Northern General Hospital on a drip, dehydrated and confused. The first thing that I asked when I regained consciousness was whether I had finished; the second thing I asked was whether I had broken 3 hours. The doctor said that he thought that I hadn't finished at all because I was picked up on the route itself. I had got to 25 miles in 2 hours 45 minutes, I do remember that (a marshal counted the runners passing and told me that I was in 29th position at the time), so I could have walked the last mile and still broken 3 hours but the heat had made me confused on the run itself. This was the first time in my life that I had ever fainted.

Carol had no idea what had happened to me that day, and waited for hours at the finish with no sign of me. We had two children by then: Zoe was three and Ben was just one. Carol couldn't drive so they had all come with me in my car that morning. Carol was there at the finish for nearly nine hours before I finally turned up, having been discharged from the hospital. I had, by the way, been out until 3 a.m. in a club the night before that marathon; you can see that I was more focused for this particular race.

But despite any mishaps, this was an annual family event. On the day itself, which was always bright and sunny, Ben would run with me in the early morning to warm up, and they would all be there at the finish.

Another year I just did the half marathon but was going for a good time and pushed myself too hard again. I staggered down the last few yards of the course and passed out at the finish. I was taken to the hospital and packed in ice to try to lower my body temperature. Carol said afterwards that they were very concerned that I might have a heart attack because my core temperature was so high. I had remembered reading somewhere that the world marathon champion, Alberto Salazar, had been packed in ice and been given the last rites after a 7-mile race in Falmouth, Massachusetts, in 1978 (his body temperature hit 108 degrees), so I knew that it was serious when I came to and heard all that ice clanking around me and felt the wet. I remember regaining consciousness slowly and seeing my children standing above me, all crying, as they stood around my dribbling, incoherent body. Ben recently told me that it felt at the time that we were there for maybe eight hours with me on a drip, but it couldn't have been that long. He had to go and get my medal for me and the officials said to him, 'How do we know that your dad actually finished the course?' He had to describe me and my finish to them to jog their memories. But I was teaching my children a valuable lesson: running could do this to you.

Ben told me recently another story which, in many ways, is much, much more painful than this. One year, he said, he had made me a sign out of a piece of white paper sticky-taped to a stick that read 'RUN DAD, RUN'. The marathon usually fell on Father's Day so this was going to be a big occasion for a happy father. He was going to wave it at me, as I finished the marathon. He reminds me that I always said that I wanted him to run the last half mile with me; the two heroes together, the father and son. And he was going to carry the stick with him all the way to the finish. But this particular year, Carol and the kids weren't invited to the finish. I had my reasons; maybe it was someone with layered hair like from those black and white photos, the sort of hair that would look ridiculous now; maybe it was the fear that someone like that would turn up at the finish because everybody from the nightclubs knew that I did this race every year. I couldn't risk it, I hate embarrassments, and sure enough, that day I came home much later than expected. Ben tells me that he was in his bedroom at the time but he could still hear Carol shouting, 'Where have you been? Who have you been with?' The anger directed at me went on intermittently for hours and my responses sounded feeble as they percolated through the thin walls of the house that we lived in then, feeble even to a child that age, more feeble than expected from a man who had just run 26 miles; more feeble in a different way. Carol had lost her arm in an accident when we first moved to Sheffield, a few months after my brother

40

Bill's death, and when she gets angry with me her injured left arm makes little staccato movements in time with the right, as if the phantom limb in exasperation and desperation wants to strike me. It is uncomfortable and distressing to watch, and if you do see it then it becomes immediately clear where any emotional sympathy should reside. The children caught glimpses of this distressing scene and reacted as they should. Ben told me recently that it was on this day that he realised that his father was not what he thought he was and that, on reflection, he might just hate my very guts. And he also tells me that later that night he pulled the sign out from under his blankets and ripped it to pieces as his younger brother, Sam, slept in the bunk bed beneath him. Ben cried himself to sleep that night, but quietly, not wanting to upset his mother any further. I was out, of course, even though it was a Sunday night.

He was six years old at the time and he says that this was one of the defining memories of his childhood, the night that he stopped trusting me and maybe, just maybe, started hating me. Through running I had managed to expose all of my frailties, both physical and moral, as a runner and as a father. He says that it was as painful as that, and in those subsequent years when I asked him to run with me, from the new house up near the moors, he wanted to tell me to get lost, to go fuck myself as I had said to his mother, but he couldn't, so, on occasion, when the cajoling got too severe, he would go with me on a run in the middle of winter, in just shorts and a tracksuit top that was far too big for him, or in the heat of summer stripped to the waist just like me, and I would abandon him even then. Even then.

3

LOSS

I let Ben read these opening chapters of the book. He was fine until he got to this point about the clubs and the girls, and his father's 'other life', and then I could feel his anger boiling over.

'You always like to come across as a bit of a cad, as a bit of a Jack the Lad. I'm not sure that this quite captures it,' he said. 'Why don't you tell it as it is? Why don't you face up to what you did?' Even today he's still angry at me. Here he explains what he thought of me at the time, as well as some of his motivations to run:

> It is difficult to remember a particular feeling in retrospect. The power of an emotion is such that it consumes you at the time. Looking back now, I cannot ever imagine hating my dad but there was a time when I must have come close. I didn't want to see him or speak to him. I didn't even like to hear his name mentioned. I would fantasise about a time when I would be stronger and I could hurt him, he made me so angry. My resentment didn't centre on myself or even my brother and sister but on the treatment of my mum. In my mind, she could and can do no wrong and didn't deserve such rotten treatment and disrespect. So I would imagine a time when I would be able to beat him – literally. In hindsight, maybe becoming a better runner than him was my way to

prove my manhood and at the same time take something away from him. I could never take away his academic qualifications or his money but I could take away his achievements in running; achievements that he was incredibly proud of. After beating my dad in a head-to-head race, the next obvious target to focus on was my dad's personal bests. This drove me forward.

And Ben was right; I wasn't such a cad as I liked to make out sometimes, life not as untroubled, as carefree. It was a lot more painful than that, almost too painful to talk about sometimes. I married Carol when we were both students at Cambridge. She was my first girlfriend, from the same narrow streets of North Belfast as me. She followed me across the water to university and then later she moved north with me to Sheffield and our first jobs. It should have been a time of great promise. My brother had just got married in Scotland that year and bought his first house, and my mother was happier than she had been in years.

'It's all coming together for this family, at last. You've got a wee job, your brother is settling down,' she liked to say.

Then a few months later, my brother went to climb in the Himalayas. It was to be his last expedition; he was adamant about this. 'I don't even know why I'm going, to be honest,' he said when I saw him last. 'I'm not into it in quite the way I was.'

He didn't come back from that adventure; he died there on Nanda Devi, and there he lies, beneath a pile of loose stones with his name scratched on one of them with hard flint. My last memory of my brother is his friends and me carrying him aloft to his car at his wedding. In retrospect, it was like shouldering a coffin to the grave. It didn't feel like that at the time, but it looks a little like that in my imagination with the benefit of hindsight.

The months after his death were an odd, unsettled time for me. For five months my main emotion was a diffuse and unfocused sort of anger. I had lost my father when I was young and it had taken me five years to cry openly about that loss. My uncle used to say that after my father died 'I just pulled down the shutters'. Then one night in Hyde Park in London, of all places, I drank a bottle of cheap red wine and cried in front of Carol. We had hitch-hiked there to go to a free concert. I didn't mean to do this, to disclose emotionally in this way; it wasn't planned, it just happened. The floodgates opened. I'd never realised that crying could make you feel better, but it did. I'd always assumed that it just made you more vulnerable.

When Bill died I wasn't sure what to do, I just felt angry. Carol's family was very much intact, mine wasn't. Carol tried to comfort me but I told her that she would never understand what I was going through; she would never understand what it was like to cope with loss like this.

Now it was February in Sheffield, and the snow lay thick on the ground, muffling all the sounds of everyday life. We lived together in an old rat-infested coach house with no heat. We went to bed early to warm up. This is Carol's account of the next day:

> I woke up feeling a bit anxious. I was working as a trainee prison psychologist in a borstal in Leicester and commuting every day from my home in Sheffield. I used to leave at half past six and get the bus to the station, then the train, then cycle from Leicester station to the borstal, and the same again at the end of the day, two and a half hours each way. That day I had to go to Leicester Prison to interview a prisoner on remand for murder – it was going to be my first big test. I left the house with plenty of time to catch the bus to the station, leaving a note saying 'wish me luck' to Geoffrey, who I knew wouldn't be getting up for another few hours. There was lots of snow on the ground, it had been there for weeks, and the bus was

very late coming down the road so by the time I got to the station, it was getting very close to five to eight. The bus stop was right outside the station entrance and in those days, there was nothing between the main foyer and platform 1. I could see the train standing at the platform and I thought that I could just make it. I had my season ticket in my hand, although there wasn't anyone checking tickets, and I was also carrying a briefcase and my handbag. I ran towards the train and grabbed hold of the handle of one of the doors, just as the train began to move slowly along the platform. I was running alongside it now, not quite able to get the door open enough to jump in, hampered by the things I was carrying and the leather boots I had on. The train was moving faster now and I don't know whether I jumped towards the step of the train and lost my footing or whether I was just pulled down by the gathering speed of the train, but somehow I found myself standing upright between the platform and the moving train – there was a big enough gap between the two. Then my coat must have caught on the undercarriage of the train and I got pulled under the wheels. I remember calling out for my mum, although I don't think I've ever told her this.

I can't remember exactly what happened next but the train began to stop, and I must have managed to scramble to my feet again because when people came running along the platform and shouted to me, I was standing up. One of the people told me she was a nurse and had been on the train when it was suddenly stopped. She kept saying, 'Don't worry; I expect it's only broken,' when I told her that the train had run over my arm. An ambulance came and took me through the rush-hour traffic with a police escort to the Hallamshire Hospital. When we got there people asked me over and over again who my next of kin was. We couldn't afford a phone in those days and I knew they'd have trouble waking my husband up by banging on the door.

My coat and all my other clothes had to be cut to get them off – I'm not sure what happened to my boots. I didn't see my arm but I couldn't feel anything at all and when the orthopaedic registrar said that it couldn't be saved, I wasn't surprised.

I remember waking up some time later and realising my mum and dad were sitting by the bed, and being very puzzled as to how they'd got there. The next morning when I woke up in a ward, the radio was on and I heard a report about myself – although I guess I could have imagined this whole thing, as I had a morphine drip.

Although it didn't occur to me at the time, one thing which I have come to regret is that I didn't see my arm or know what happened to it. I do miss it and think about it still. It was part of me.

All the time I was in hospital I was fairly positive – the doctors I saw were all very enthusiastic about developments in prosthetics and because I was young and healthy and I had no other injuries, they thought the prognosis was good. I quickly became institutionalised in the hospital – the days took on a comfortable routine, I didn't have to worry about anything much and there was nothing too taxing or difficult to do. The weather outside was still freezing and snowy, but high up in the Hallamshire I was safe from it. I found a way to wash my hair and open the individual packs of butter and jam on the breakfast tray, and I thought that I'd pretty much cracked it. Geoffrey and I even managed to sneak off for some intimacy in the hospital, quite exciting in a strange sort of way. I think that it was important for him to show me that the accident hadn't changed anything. It was his way, I suppose.

After a month I was allowed to go home. I was looking forward to it, but wasn't prepared for the desolation I felt going back into the place I'd left without thinking a month before. Things that had once been familiar had now become objects to be wrestled with and I realised how hard things were going to be. When Geoffrey went to work and left me alone in the cold, untidy flat I cried in a way that scared me – howling and sobbing. It was the first time that it dawned on me what had changed.

I think we went to the rehabilitation centre in a fairly positive frame of mind – almost looking forward to seeing all the marvellous things the doctors had told us about. When we got there the waiting room was full of old men – no young people or women in sight. There was also a line of artificial legs lined up in a corner and other ghastly pink prosthetic body parts sitting around waiting for fittings. To me, at my age, who'd hardly had a day's illness in my life, it was like a vision of a hell that I was about to be dragged into. The consultation didn't do much to help as it focused heavily on the different attachments (including a hook) that could be screwed into an artificial arm, which could restore the functions of holding things, sewing and knitting – none of which I cared much about. I was more interested in form than function – I wanted something to fill my empty sleeve and restore some sort of symmetry. So we moved on to 'cosmetic' artificial limbs. I would be measured up and two artificial arms would be made for me – so that I had a spare in case anything happened to one of them. The arm was heavy, awkward to wear – it was secured by leather straps that went over the shoulder and across the back – and not very convincing close up. The colour was unnatural and unlike my skin colour. There was a mechanism inside the arm which allowed it to be moved into a bent position and locked there – but it was very difficult sometimes to unbend it – I certainly never mastered it in the short time I wore the thing before throwing it in the cupboard to gather dust.

It was a few weeks after I'd got out of hospital; I still had dressings on my arm. We'd been invited out somewhere – it was the first time I'd gone out in the evening since the accident – and we were driving there in the car. We took a wrong turn or something and in no time we were having a full-blown argument. Nasty things were said, as they usually are in pointless arguments, but I was shocked – I had felt until then that I was now surely immune from that kind of thing. I had been in some kind of cocoon of being looked after, feeling that no one would ever be unkind or mean to me again. But I was wrong. The world and other people weren't going to make allowances for me. They hadn't changed – I had. From now on I was going to be at a significant disadvantage.

This all happened over 30 years ago. For me as well as Carol, it is also a vivid, flashbulb memory. I saw Carol the morning of her accident in the hospital before they amputated her arm. I can see the position of her now, the angle of the bed, and the shine of her long, dark hair on the white pillow. I had overslept. Someone at the hospital must have tried to reach me at work because my professor's secretary had come to my house and knocked on the door three or four times to wake me up. She told me that Carol had had an accident, but she thought that it wasn't too serious.

'I think that she's fallen off the platform, that's all,' she said. 'Platforms aren't too high,' she said. 'It's not such a big fall. She'll be all right.'

I can remember to this day that I misinterpreted what she was saying: I thought she meant that Carol had fallen over in her platform soles. My mental image at that precise moment all those years ago was of Carol tottering over on platform shoes, big platforms with four-inch black heels with red stars on them, shoes from our student years imported into this almost dream sequence. I can recall this misinterpretation of a word after all those years and the fleeting mental image that briefly lit up my mind.

My professor was at the hospital and waited with me in the waiting room. As the doctor came in to talk to me I recall jumping up and hitting my head on something and wanting my injury to be serious, but it wasn't. The doctor described what had happened at the station and explained how they would have to amputate the arm.

'Is there any alternative?' I asked, as if he had not considered any. He shook his head without looking at me, and led me in to see Carol. She was conscious when I got there. She didn't smile at me, and I mention this because it's as if I might have expected a smile from her. Then she immediately apologised because she said that she knew what I had been going through with my brother's death.

'I'm sorry,' she said, and she did smile a weak, half-hearted sort of smile. I can hear her saying those words now, and I must say that at that moment, and even now, I felt deep shame that makes me feel a little sick.

I held her limp, lifeless hand in what I suppose was my pathetic attempt to show that this hand, which was to be removed, was still part of her and of us. I was wearing a white puffa jacket that my mother had bought for me that Christmas and it got smeared up and down the sleeve with her blood. When they wheeled Carol off to theatre I had to ring my mother and tell her what had happened. Her neighbours went to the chemist's to get her some tablets and she arrived later that day, on Valium and alcohol, after the arm had been amputated, and stared at my sleeve, as if I might not have noticed the blood that was streaked right down it.

Carol never complained about what had happened to her, but she sometimes got depressed.

'It's only natural,' my mother said.

But she never complained, and she never attempted to justify any failure to do whatever a busy and active life would require. She went on to raise three children and drive and cook and sew all with one arm, and open bottles gripped between her knees, and hold dresses with her teeth as she pushed the sewing needle through, and cut meat for the family held on chopping boards with nails sticking out of them (made by her father), and play competitive badminton with me, serving and hitting the shuttlecock with her one good hand, until one day when some opponent protested that this was surely against all the rules of this most English of games. Somewhere it must be written in the rules, he said, that you couldn't just drop the shuttlecock and hit it with the very same hand. 'It must give you an unfair advantage.' I had thought that he was joking and I'm sure that I must have laughed, but he was quite serious about it. He had this sanctimonious expression on his face as if he had caught us cheating.

'But that's the English for you,' my Ulster Protestant mother said when I told her. 'They're a strange bloody people when it gets down to it.'

Carol only ever complained that she could not greet her children with her arms outstretched in the way that you should, and could not clap her hands when she saw them in concerts or getting prizes or running races, except by slapping her right palm down on her right thigh in a muffled sort of ritual that drew attention to itself with its oddness.

But the pain in her arm never left her. She says:

> I'm surprised. In fact, I think it's getting worse rather than fading. There's a low level of discomfort, rather than pain, which feels like tingling nerve

endings, which is pretty constant, but then this can develop into other, more definitely painful things. For example, quite often at night, if I wake up or can't get to sleep, I just can't find a comfortable way to lie and my arm becomes really hot and the pain is quite intense; or if I'm very tired or maybe coming down with a cold or something, my arm starts to get these spasms of pain darting through it. Also, generally, it doesn't react well to extreme cold or heat. I've been trying to think about the pain, because I've never really thought the sensation was like a 'phantom limb' – I don't feel like I have a whole arm there. Sometimes I have a feeling like my fist is closed very tight and I can feel my finger nails digging into the palm of my hand, and my thumb squeezed underneath my fingers, and I feel that it would be good to be able to open my hand out and spread my fingers.

When it is really painful, the only way I can describe it is as being like the thing has just happened – the train has just crushed it – it is burning hot and feels like there are bits of mangled bone and nerves and sinews all jammed together – it is a feeling of compression and pressure. I don't remember whether this is actually what it felt like at the time. When I have the spasm pain it is difficult not to flinch with every spasm. These types of pain are distracting and can be a bit draining at times. I specially hate it when it happens at night as there is nothing to take your mind off it and I sometimes I think it will drive me mad. I don't take painkillers, as I don't like taking medication.

I have always felt that this pain has been something of a barrier between us. It's private to her; it takes her away from those around her, engulfing her and leaving others feeling

51

useless, unable to do anything to help, with no sensible suggestions to make. And over all those years, I know that I didn't help at all; and, of course, I myself had nobody to turn to. This isn't some 'poor me' bleat, because I never said this at the time, I never complained – what had I to complain about? Carol was my best friend as well as my wife; we were inseparable. But how could I talk to her about what I was going through, given what she had to deal with?

I had never been with anybody else but after her accident I had an affair. It wasn't difficult; the girl made all of the approaches and she knew that I was married. We were both in our early to mid-20s. In retrospect, I think that the sex for me was a mechanism to get close enough to someone to open up to them. This must be one of the best excuses ever, laughable to some, but quite true; at least, that's how it felt. Today, I can't remember the sex, or any excitement or any real desire, but I can remember lying in a bed with dank, cheap, blue sheets, with little bits of silver jewellery on the sideboard, and talking about Bill and Carol and my mother, and fragments of my life in Belfast, and feeling much better for it. Very guilty but better inside. I'm not, after all, the kind of person who could go to a counsellor or a psychologist; they'd probably know me for a start. And I can remember The Human League playing in the background, something about a crow and a baby having an affair. 'A new band from Sheffield,' she explained. 'I know the singer.'

The whole thing was also, of course, unforgivable and Carol never really did forgive me when she found out, which she did almost immediately, 'for being so pathetic and letting both myself and her down'. She said that at one level we were finished, but I felt that she needed me and I certainly needed her. We thought that a family would bring us closer together; soon afterwards our wonderful daughter Zoe was born and Carol's life changed dramatically again, but this time for the better. I felt that I could never leave her; I loved her too much, and I respected her more than anybody else in the world. I still do, but there are many other layers of emotion in there as well now, not surprisingly. But, of course, you establish patterns in your behaviour through your actions. Behaviour can become habitual and things that at one time demanded reflection and worry, stop requiring this. I needed people to talk to intimately and I had found a way. We soon had three beautiful and happy children who idolised their mother. But I had found a personal and selfish mechanism to cope with life.

Years later, Carol found out about another much longer and much more serious affair, and this time she and I agreed that I should apply for jobs elsewhere. I was offered a professorship at the University of Strathclyde in Glasgow, still in my 30s. The kids and I went to view houses on the banks of the Clyde, and I wrote for *The Independent* about how the great shipbuilders of the Clyde were now reduced to building model boats to sail in the local park (still incessantly working even during the interview process itself). But my new girlfriend, Jennifer, got pregnant and, as a consequence, I stayed in Sheffield. Jennifer and I had a lovely daughter, Clara (and three years later a son, Billy, who is the image of me), but I stayed with Carol and buying Hollow Meadows, my dream home in many ways, was a sign of my commitment to her.

Carol asked me not to talk to our children about my other family; it was simply not to be mentioned. And for years afterwards I lived this odd and anxious double life, still with Carol, but trying to bring up two new children elsewhere, even after accepting a Chair at Manchester. When Jennifer subsequently moved on with her life (because it was obvious that I was never going to leave Carol) with a new, much younger man, I would find myself waiting endlessly for Clara and Billy on the street outside her house because the new boyfriend didn't want me in the house, presumably because of his own insecurities. Then the children and I would go for a walk in some park in Sheffield in the rain, with the kids bored and moody, because there was nothing else to do at the kinds of times I got there. We had, after all, no home to go to. But I knew that I had nobody to blame but myself for any of it. And any emotional suffering, and believe me there was plenty, had to be borne by me alone, silently and without discussion, and I knew and understood that perfectly. It was clear to me that I could never, ever ask for any sympathy, and I haven't. My mother put it simply: 'Slap it up you. What did you expect?'

Ben was probably right. I'm not much of a cad as it turns out, or much of anything else for that matter. But oddly, running kept me going and I kept at it, throughout.

4

In and Out of Love

Ben

I don't remember exactly when I fell out of love with running. I continued to run occasionally. I had put on weight and was far more concerned with pursuing other interests. It seems simplistic now but I think the fact that I stopped running was a way to get back at my father; to hurt him like he'd hurt me.

When I was about 17 I finally received confirmation of something that I always suspected to be true. I was at a party with my closest friends. There were about ten of us, both girls and boys. I got the feeling that everyone knew something that I didn't; that they were talking about something and I wasn't included. I like to think that I am an observant sort of person, and it was clear to me from the whispered conversations and the furtive glances that there was something going on. Years later, I was accused by two of the people at the party of being 'fucking paranoid'. This may be true but perhaps it is entirely justified, given what has happened in my life so far. Finally, I could take no more of being a pariah and I cornered one of my female friends. I demanded that she tell me what was going on.

My memory of this moment is undimmed; she said to me, 'I'm doing work experience at Lydgate Infant School and the teacher I'm helping out asked me how old I was and which school I went to. When I told her, she said to me, "You may know the son of the father of my children."'

I may have paraphrased the first part of this, but I have

always vividly remembered the clumsiness of the second part. That awkward sentence has stuck with me forever, and that was my old school. My father seemed to have no shame. Some of his latenesses had started to make sense. He had two kids with somebody else, so he had another family, and he wasn't even good at time management when he had just one. He was always too busy, always running around, trying to fit everything in.

This wasn't a huge shock to me, to be absolutely honest. I wasn't a naïve boy and I was aware that the relationship between my mother and my father was not perfect. What was shocking was to have it confirmed to me like this, and to be confronted by it. My overriding emotion was one of embarrassment, however; embarrassment and anger that all my friends knew and weren't going to tell me.

The two activities that characterised my father, that made him the person he is today, were running and study. He was, and is, a celebrated academic and an obsessive runner. He had always encouraged us all to follow him down this path: improving body and mind. It was at this point in my life that I gave up on both. The decision wasn't a conscious one in either case. Now it seems like an act of pure rebellion but at the time it seemed more born out of laziness or indifference.

Whether consciously or not, I managed to craft myself a life that seemed as far away as possible from that chosen by my father. My faltering education finally ground to a halt and I ended up as an assistant manager of a city-centre bar. I was drinking most days and smoking heavily. We had always been told as children that we must never smoke and never ride motorbikes. It was always those two things. They were seen as the most dangerous and the most stupid things imaginable. For the record, I've still never ridden a motorbike.

I had reached the very pinnacle of rebellion. I decided that I would forge a career as a bar manager. My friends ask me now, 'What were you thinking?' like it was a deliberate choice that I made. But I had simply backed myself into a corner. I couldn't see a way out so I had to adapt, to adjust my expectations. It was never my dream but I didn't know what else I could do.

The funny thing is that although this seems like the actions of a young man trying to gain maximum separation from his father, what I was actually doing was following a path that was set out by my dad years before. Of course, at times in his life he had smoked the occasional cigarette and the 'characters' that I now associated with in the Sheffield nightlife scene – the bouncers, the bar staff, the drinkers – were the very same ones that my dad had studied and written about in the late '80s and early '90s. Most of them remembered him with considerable fondness.

I did still run at this point, if you can call it running. I achieved a PW (personal worst) at the Sheffield Half Marathon in 2002 when I collapsed at 11 miles and was put into an ambulance. Somehow, through tears of shame, I managed to convince the ambulance crew to allow me to finish on the proviso that I visited first aid at the stadium. I finished in just outside 2 hours. I look back at photos from that race and I look older then than I do now.

After a few years working in the bars of Sheffield and living in shared houses, I was offered the chance to move to Macclesfield to help open a new 1,200-capacity bar. In hindsight I was already desperately unhappy but thought that somehow getting away from Sheffield would help. As the demands of working incredibly long hours with lots of stress and very little reward grew, I became more and more unhappy, eventually spiralling into what I can only describe now as despair.

The one positive of this experience, however, was the slow rebuilding of the relationship with my father. As Macclesfield was only a short train ride from his home in Manchester, I would occasionally visit him and we would go for a meal together in town. I think that during those meals, I finally began to understand him a bit more as a person. I was always in awe of his achievements but very wary of him. We were never close enough that I could say with any real certainty what his motivation was, why he acted in the way he did. I never understood why he had done the terrible things that he had. During those meals I began to understand a bit more. He wasn't a bad person. He had made mistakes; he had backed himself into corners as well. He was trying to do what was right. We spoke like adults when we ate in Manchester. He explained a lot to me that I hadn't understood. For years I was angry with him for what he had done, but it was only then that I started to find out why he had done it.

My Macclesfield adventure ended like most of my experiences: in shame. One day I woke up in the bedsit above the bar that I shared with my partner at the time. I couldn't move. I was being held down by an invisible force. I had been having regular panic attacks and now I felt crippled by an endless one. Somebody called NHS Direct but I knew there was only one solution. My sister was called to drive over and pick me up as my mum and dad were on holiday. We drove back to Sheffield in total silence as I came to terms with the fact that I was quitting in shame once again.

I was dreading seeing my father when he got back. All I remember thinking was that this would not have happened to him. He wouldn't have let himself down like this.

5

Some Lost Times

I have always found it difficult to recall happy memories from my own childhood, although I have little trouble recalling many of the very sad ones. Perhaps I come from a particularly sad family in which the balance between happy and sad experiences was not quite right. My father and brother both died suddenly and without any proper goodbyes, and maybe that was a major part of the problem with what remained of my family and the grief that clung to my mother.

My brother died in the Himalayas when he was barely 30; my father was 51 when he died, 12½ years before my brother. He had gone into the Royal Victoria Hospital in Belfast for routine observations; at least, that's what he told the family. He didn't even tell us that he was going into hospital until the day before; he didn't want to worry us. My mother, my brother and I visited him the night before his operation. In my last conversation with him, on the Sunday night in the Royal, I told him that one of my guinea pigs had died. I just blurted it out, as a bit of a joke, a distraction, maybe something to say to break the emotional tension that I could feel in the ward that night. He looked really saddened; he sat up in bed in his blue-striped pyjamas, and his glasses moved on his face, falling forward. I couldn't bear it.

'No, I'm only kidding you, Da,' I said laughing. 'I'm only joking, Da. It's only a wee joke.'

It was part of my strange repertoire at the time to help people: I would tell someone made-up bad news and then explain to them that it was only a joke, so that I could be responsible for bringing good news their way. The good news was, of course, only good news because of the made-up bad news that had preceded it. After all, telling your father that a guinea pig is still alive, and still sitting there in the corner of the hutch, still not doing very much but still squeaking a little, is hardly great news, in and of itself. But my father smiled with such relief when I told him; he was so pleased that I wouldn't be upset by any loss. He knew how attached I was to my fat, indolent guinea pigs in their large, brightly coloured hutch out in our wet, grey backyard.

The next day he never regained consciousness. He lay in a coma for a week and he died the following Sunday. Every day on the way home from school during that fateful week, as the bus made its sharp left at the 'turn-of-the-road', I would glance nervously at my house to see if the blinds were down, my stomach in my mouth. Those words about an albino guinea pig, with a squealing, spoiled demeanour, were the last I ever said to him. Those were the last words with my father for a lifetime. I was doing exams that week, and I did extremely well in every one of them and never once made an excuse, although I am confident that it would have been very easy: 'I'm sorry, I can't come to school this week, my father is in a coma in the Royal Victoria Hospital. I am sure that you will understand.' My mother expected no less of me.

My mother liked to talk about my father whenever I was home visiting her. She still lived at the 'turn-of-the-road', but eventually in a new Housing Executive house. Her stories about my father were always introduced in exactly the same way. 'Do you remember . . . ?' she would ask when starting to talk about him, and I would nod in a non-committal sort of way, because the truth was that I didn't really remember many important details about my father any longer, but I was too embarrassed and ashamed to say so. I think that it was a sort of defensive forgetting, a form of repression to ease the pain. But I had heard the stories many times and my father had been reborn in the telling, and I could do nothing about that.

I have images of him as well, somewhat disconnected images that don't really add up to a whole, complete person. I remember the way he smiled (but then again I have photographs to remind me), and the way his glasses sat on the end of his nose when he was reading. I remember how he stretched his arms out to put his coat on and how he tugged his cap down on his forehead. I can, of course, recall vividly the night of his death (too vividly really for my own comfort), and my Aunt Agnes being annoyed that nobody had come to pick us up to take us to the hospital to see him, although I wouldn't have been allowed to see him anyway, as he lay there without sense or feeling (however, my mother always said that he knew that she was there beside him, because he used to play with her wedding ring; she clung on to this desperate idea for many years). I can see the expression on my aunt's face from that night (even now), and the face of my Uncle Terence, 'the Big Fella' everybody called him, who stopped us going into the hospital. I remember the rain that night, the puddles in the car park of the Royal. I can picture those grey puddles now, I just have to close my eyes and look. I remember my father resting in his coffin in the front room for the days in which 'he was home', and how ridiculously well he looked, on that white shiny satin, with (I was told) some powder on his face, in the glow of the pink lampshade that seemed to light him up.

'Those colours bring out the best in your da,' my Aunt Agnes said to me when they brought him home. 'It's just like he's had a good walk in the fresh air up to the wee shop and down the Ligoniel Road. He loved that walk. He's a handsome man, your father, he always has been.'

My mother always said that he looked so good as a corpse because he had died in good health. 'He just had an operation and didn't come out of it,' she explained. It made quite a lot of sense then; it still does.

I remember how my father walked and the smell of his overalls. But his voice has faded in my memory. I watched a TV programme once in which a hypnotist said that human memory is a bit like a video recording of life, with all the events stored on some kind of biological spool, waiting to be played over and over again, if you just knew the right way in, if you just had the key to unlock it. But I have always thought that this wasn't quite true because no matter how hard I tried, I just ended up with fragments of images and events.

I remember one afternoon up the Hightown Road, with me kicking the rugby ball about, him lying there reading his paper, his glasses over the end of his nose, the smell of the air. I can remember booting the ball up into the air and chasing it over the ground covered in prickly yellow gorse and loose sharp brick. I remember feeling that sharp brick through the soles of my thin trainers and then stumbling on a shard of broken glass, which somehow managed to pierce the side of my ankle. My father had to carry me back to the car. I don't remember how his voice sounded or what we talked about that day. I just remember him struggling under my weight, and wheezing with the effort – he had a bad chest sometimes. I remember that his glasses dropped off on the way back, and that he had to put me down on the wet grass while he picked them up. His glasses fell off a lot; the frames were loose.

I remember smells from him. I can recall the smell of engine oil, engine oil that's been on the road and seeped into old overalls. His nickname was 'Half-shaft' because he worked as a motor mechanic for Belfast Corporation at the Falls Road depot. He worked with bus engines and smelt of the oil that they put into buses, even on his days off. I can always remember the smell of those old overalls, weeks between washes; we didn't have a washing machine in those days and the smell was everywhere. I still love that smell.

But I have another image from that time, as well. An image that has never faded or been diminished by time, slightly disconnected, it stands out on its own, but it is an image that has haunted me for a lifetime. On the night of my father's funeral, after we had laid him to rest in Roselawn Cemetery with the wind lifting the dirty green carpet used to cover the wet clay grave, we were in my aunt's house for the sandwiches and tea because our own house wasn't big enough for the friends and family. Everyone was there, drinking quietly, the gentle and sporadic sobbing made worse by the memory of the coffin juddering down into its final position; everyone except my beautiful cousin Myrna, that is, who inexplicably had gone to work that day. Nobody had explained why. Life at the time seemed to be full of things that were never properly explained, at least to a 13-year-old boy. My cousin walked in right in the middle of our quiet, Protestant sort of wake. She seemed to cling to the doorframe, not entering, just standing there staring at us all, and I can picture her now, an image etched on my mind forever, an emaciated grey ghost, already dead in the eyes and the mouth.

I had heard, overheard to be more accurate, that she had got some kind of eating disorder, anorexia nervosa, 'slimmer's disease', my mother called it, but I hadn't seen her for months, as the slimmer's disease took hold. She avoided seeing relatives. But there she stood in the silence and the sadness, and everyone looked at her and nobody said a thing, as if she looked normal and healthy and was just late for the funeral. I think she walked slowly past us all into the kitchen to stand alone, the place where food is prepared and eaten, but not for her.

She died a couple of weeks later of pneumonia and was buried in the row opposite my father, which is handy from the point of view of people bringing flowers to either grave. Her mother, my Aunt May, a sweet, lovely woman with a giggly, girly voice, always said that what triggered the anorexia was a chance remark from a doctor at work during a routine medical examination, a remark that she was a little overweight. From that day on, my aunt always said, she never ate properly again. It sounds almost ridiculous that such a life-threatening disorder could be triggered in this way, but many years later I supervised a postgraduate student who analysed anorexia nervosa in the families of sufferers and it was extraordinary the number of interviewees who pointed to a similar 'chance remark' as the cause of the whole thing. Anorexia is a complex psychological disorder with cultural, personality and biological factors all linked in its development, but human beings like to identify a single cause that they can pick out and say, 'If only that hadn't happened . . .' This single cause is usually something fairly random (so that any normal family could potentially be affected) and external to the family itself (so that no blame could ever be attached to the family). The PE teacher who commented that Tracy was too fat to be any good at games, the boyfriend who said that Jane's bum was too big for her skinny jeans, the doctor who quipped that his patient could do with losing a little weight. It was always things like that. It reminded me of what Friedrich Nietzsche wrote in *Twilight of the Idols*:

> *To trace something unknown back to something known is alleviating, soothing, gratifying, and gives us moreover a feeling of power. Danger, disquiet, anxiety attend the unknown, and the first instinct is to eliminate these distressing states. First principle: any explanation is better than none.*

My family, and many other families, had found an explanation, one which stressed the power of the word, of the chance remark (and I suppose, by implication, the dangerous power of the carelessly chosen word of those in authority). Nobody ever disputed my aunt's account and it became the true version of what had become of my beautiful cousin. I sometimes think that in that awful year of my life my prejudices towards my own weight – and I think that I have many – and other people's weight, were probably laid down forever. I believe that I run every day partly to keep myself looking lean, and this is both a rare blessing and an absolute curse for someone as busy as me, running along the Pacific Coast Highway in the dark, having arrived at LAX at night, lest I miss a single day of training. Knowing this, you can imagine some of the scenarios that have formed the basis for my life.

When I say 'prejudices', by the way, I really do mean prejudices. I have had my unconscious implicit attitudes measured using an instrument called the Implicit Association Test (or IAT). This, I suppose, is one of the perks of being a psychologist. Attitudes basically are our underlying predispositions to act, but many psychologists argue that these predispositions, such as they are, are not all open to conscious reflection. Some lie buried in our unconscious and these are called 'implicit' attitudes. The IAT tries to measure them not by asking for self-reports but by seeing how quickly people can associate images from the various relevant categories (for example, fat/thin in the case of weight, black/ white in the case of race, low carbon footprint/high carbon footprint in the case of environmental attitudes) with words signifying 'good' and 'bad'. The IAT measures associations in the human brain. Having had my implicit attitude measured in a whole series of domains the one, and only one, strong prejudice that I seem to have is an anti-fat bias.

Of course, this story about Myrna may tell you why weight is an important issue for me but why have I ended up with an anti-fat prejudice, why not an anti-thin prejudice? After all, it was not the fact that Myrna was a few pounds overweight (maybe more, maybe less) that killed her. Well, perhaps it was the implicit message in the story: the implicit message being that if you are overweight then you can be killed by a chance remark; the unconscious message being that being fat makes you too sensitive to others' insensitivity; the unconscious theme being that being fat means that others can control your life and even your death. My compulsive running may just reflect my unconscious desires to escape from my father's destiny, but it may also reflect this deep-seated desire to put myself out of harm's way from chance remarks (and thereby make myself less vulnerable in life). It may be core to my psychological make-up and mean that I have an implicit and unconscious bias against fat people, who have not made the effort to shield themselves in this way. Of course, the fact that my implicit attitude actually does connect to some core behaviour in my everyday life, namely my determination to run, is very encouraging from the point of view of my academic work since I am researching this in a number of domains including the environment and race. It is also, of course, more than a little depressing for me.

I have one other brief image of Myrna; however, a positive image this time. In it, several of us, as children, are sitting and playing in a sloping field with a slight dip in the middle. It's funny that I can recall the dip so vividly, but we were all sitting in or around it, playing some sort of game. This was a meadow full of flowers, a carpet of bright, shimmering, yellow buttercups, hardly without a gap, and I have a vague recollection of the way Myrna sat and laughed that day; it was a very girly laugh just like her mother's. I think I remember the sound. But this is really just a fragment of an image with no real narrative, with no beginning or end. I don't know how we got to the meadow or what we were doing there other than playing a game, but I don't remember what game it was, or whether Bill was there or not. I don't remember whether I plucked some of the flowers to take home to my mother, which I often did, but maybe not in the case of buttercups, or whether I left them all there undisturbed. I don't remember where the meadow was. This is, it would seem, a very limited and transient image, not sharp and clear, not like the other image of Myrna in the doorway, which has stuck firmly in my mind; that grey look and the deadness in her eyes on the day of my father's funeral, permanently etched on my imagination. This darker memory, unfortunately, is crystal clear and shows no evidence of ever fading.

These are some of the things that I remember from my

childhood but on many occasions I wish that it was very different. I wish that I could be more in control of my memories, so that I could balance them out a bit more. I wish that I could recall the good and the bad with equal clarity and with equal precision and force. But sometimes no matter how hard I try, it is only the bad memories that spring somewhat uncontrollably to mind and torment me with their presence and their detail. According to a number of psychologists, however, there are steps that you can take to facilitate the retrieval of autobiographical memories, including the good ones, and some of these steps may seem a little surprising. One technique to aid more detailed and more accurate recall of childhood memories is to try to recall a memory while displaying the same bodily behaviours that would have accompanied the laying down of the original memory. It sounds very odd, but many psychologists claim that it can work.

Sometimes when I run memories do come back, not smoothly but in a stuttering sort of way; images of my childhood and my family. But it can be a hard and painful way to remember the truth, especially about my father because he wasn't there to watch the running develop into a lifelong obsession. He's just not there.

6

What My Father Taught Me

So I am a runner with a daily ritual, a purifying, cleansing ritual. But this is not a daily ritual like brushing your teeth or showering, because you have to explain it to others, you have to say, 'I am just going for my run,' or, 'Can we eat later because I have to have my run?', or 'Don't put the children to bed yet because I will see them after I have had my run.' Brushing your teeth was never like this. And once you articulate your position, and your identity, you lay yourself open to challenges. 'Have you done a marathon?', 'What time did you do?', 'I'm doing a fun run; I'm a runner too, just like you', 'What are you training for?', 'Have you ever actually won anything?' It's an oddly self-conscious way of purifying yourself and your body when you lay yourself open to comments, challenges and random asides like this. And of course, it has to be built in to the routines of everyday life.

I have my school partly to thank for my life's journey in running. In my first year they held a house cross-country championship, which was compulsory. I had a date in my diary for the race. I had started playing rugby at this great posh school and it was a sport that I wanted to excel at, to please my parents and my Uncle Terence as much as anything.

'Geoffrey is a rough little bugger. He'd be good at rugby,' Terence would say.

I didn't really know much about cross-country running, so I persuaded two of my mates from my street to run with me out in the clay fields just past Harmony Hill. We slipped out of our house, as if it was something shameful that we were about to do, with our shorts and our plimsolls in our bags, and changed in the wet, cold rain. We hid our bags under a hedge and stood there looking at each other.

'I think we had better start running now,' I said, and we started off across the field, puffing and panting, looking for a way out of that field and into the next. It gave us a chance to catch our breath. We had run maybe for 40 seconds or a minute.

'This is too much like hard work,' said my friend Colin. We came to a tarmac path; we could either climb up the road towards the summit of Divis and the television mast, or run down the road. The consensus, that is to say, the vote of the other two, was to run down the road, our feet clattering along it in the cold, autumnal rain. We ran for maybe a mile, maybe a little less and then we decided to turn back, up that little climb that had been so easy on the way down. Colin walked first and then Jackie. I tried to keep running, although it felt like running on the spot. I couldn't stop puffing, desperately gasping for air; it almost felt like drowning. I looked around, and even though they were walking, they were only a few yards behind.

'Lift those legs!' shouted Colin. 'One, two, one, two; keep them up for fuck's sake!' We eventually got back to the hedge where we had hidden our clothes, and we pulled out the wet bags. The thorns cut our legs, which were caked in mud. We hadn't brought any towels so we slipped our jeans over our muddy legs and dandered home, stiff and tired.

At the race itself, there were about 60 or 70 boys, all lined up. Some looked like runners, many did not. Most wore rugby shirts with their house colours, blue, green, yellow or red. Mine was blue for Cairns House. We set off in the grounds of Belfast Castle, down a lane and then left across a path and into a field. There seemed to be a number of boys in front of me, who went off quickly, but there were many more behind, so I was probably about 12th or 13th. I knew that I hadn't really trained for the race; I just wanted to see what it felt like, to see how sick I might feel afterwards.

Perhaps my interest might have been restricted to this annual compulsory event but in my second year in school I dislocated my elbow in a judo class and had to give up rugby, so I thought, why not run? The cross-country master taught us Latin, and it was common knowledge that he had only one lung and a huge enthusiasm for the sport. On Wednesday afternoons we would run 'over the top', across the castle grounds, climbing towards Napoleon's Nose on the top of Cavehill. It took me many years to realise that Napoleon was on his back on this hill, and that the nose was in profile, because from the 'turn-of-the-road', where I lived, Napoleon's Nose just looked like a large rock (and I thought that he was standing upright and the nose was pointing out) and didn't really look much like a nose at all, let alone Napoleon's own nose. It was only from the richer parts of town, like the Antrim Road, that you could understand why the rock had been named in the way it had.

It was on these runs, running with a large group with many stops to wait for the slower runners, that something developed. On days in December in the snow up on Napoleon's Nose, you would find us in vests and shorts, passing walkers in duffel coats and thick padded jackets. We would run past them, our fingers blue, with this great heroic swoosh. Perhaps it was all subliminal; our unconscious stimulated. 'Over the top', that's what we called it, with echoes of the trenches in the First World War and the 36th Ulster Division at the Somme. 'The greatest loss and slaughter sustained in a single day in the whole history of the British army', in Churchill's words. As boys we all knew about the Somme.

'Not a single man turned back,' my mother always said. 'My father told me that. He was in the army so he knew what he was on about. Not a single one, remember that.'

We had no heroic battles to fight, no way to prove ourselves. Although perhaps it was to come with the Troubles for some, I just had this.

Races on a Saturday morning were all over Northern Ireland. We were ferried about on a school bus, and would find when we got there white-legged, skinny boys with thick country accents that were almost incomprehensible. We would be out in the freezing cold, trying to follow a cross-country course only marked out by sodden, yellow flags. One day in December, in the middle of nowhere, I saw a flag on one bank of a swollen river and a flag on the other bank. There were no other runners about so I jumped in and nearly froze to death; I had failed to notice that there was another flag maybe 50 yards to my left and some stepping stones on that part of the river. I turned blue and shook violently. My feet and hands were very painful to touch. The Latin master let me shower first and then it was back home to the terraced streets of North Belfast and Jackie and Colin standing there, now smoking 20 a day, asking why I was bothering.

'What are you trying to prove? It'll kill you, that shit,' they would say. It was not a glamorous beginning and not necessarily easy to explain, but that was the start, my start.

On some nights I would see the runners from Duncairn Nomads or North Belfast Harriers in all shapes and sizes, in odd outfits, long before designer running gear, pounding the roads, never the pavements, up our way. There was always something oddly brave and heroic about the whole thing, like sticking your neck out to be ridiculed, like standing out from the crowd. I would run up the Horseshoe Road and down through Ligoniel, and as I passed St Mark's Church, crossing one of those invisible territorial markers that demarcate sectarian Belfast, moving from one ghetto to another, sometimes a half brick would fly past me as I signalled clearly and unambiguously, perhaps even arrogantly, that I belonged to one tribe and not the other in the Belfast of the Troubles. Funnily enough, Belfast is the only city in the world where I have ever had bricks thrown at me for running. A friend had an egg thrown at her in Salford – it smashed on her chest just below her chin – and another friend had someone spit right in her face as she ran past a group of girls in Salford, but I have never seen anyone stoned. It's not the running as such that causes the response, but fear, fear of the unknown, that's how I like to think about it, fear of things that you don't understand or things that you might never understand. Some guy who doesn't know the rules, who didn't seem to realise that there was a war on, here in Belfast. Armoured cars, soldiers with guns, burnt-out buses, scorched roads, and this dickhead out for a bloody run as if he didn't give a shit about anything, the arrogant fucker. Doesn't he know that we shoot people for less? I think that it was fear. And there was just so much fear back then in Belfast.

What I realised from the start was that this activity could more or less take over your life. The formal routine back then was a long run with the cross-country club on a Wednesday up in the grounds of Belfast Castle on the Antrim Road; five or six laps around the waterworks, which was about a mile right round, on a Thursday afternoon; and often a cross-country race on a Saturday morning. In summers on a Wednesday afternoon there would be a bus trip out to a sports field in the country and the sweeping curves of the 400-yard grass track. But this was just the basics, and the real structure developed from there. It spanned the entire week. At school, rather than go to the chess club or drama class, or simply hang around with the other boys at lunchtime, I chose to go for a run – self-consciously, I have to say, because I hated people seeing me. I would go out through the school gates and around the waterworks every lunchtime except Wednesdays. And this meant, of course, intentionally or unintentionally, that I didn't mix with the other pupils at Belfast Royal Academy in the way that I perhaps should have done. It almost makes me laugh looking back, both as a psychologist and as a human being, at how disciplined I was in this.

When I became a little better known and the BBC did a television documentary about my early life in Belfast, one former pupil and friend commented on my running and the fact that I ran at lunchtimes rather than mixing with the other pupils. He said, 'It was as if you chose not to fit in.'

But that's not how it felt at the time. Perhaps it was a fear of rejection, perhaps it was the symbolic running away, running out of the school gates and up through the waterworks towards where I lived, towards the working-class 'ghettos' of the city. I had managed to get into this school and this school took me away from everything that I knew. And after school I would trudge, lonely and alone, back to Legmore Street. Or perhaps it was simpler than that; perhaps I just liked the solitary nature of running, the fact that you don't have to depend on anyone because, after all, when it comes down to it, there's nobody you can depend upon.

Sometimes I was very self-conscious. I could sense people sneering as I ran past them. They would often make comments, sometimes they would throw things; but I learned to cope with that eventually, especially the comments, which I had found most difficult. By then I had started running from my house. I would stare out of the front window of my house down at the hardware shop at the bottom of Barginnis Street, and the dull wet streets round about, and I would go out for my run then in my little vest and shorts.

'You'll catch your death of cold!' my mother would shout after me. 'That's not good for you, you know. Your father had rheumatic fever when he was a boy and that gave him a bad heart and killed him in the end. Do you want to be next?'

Ever since I could remember, I was told that my father had a bad ticker because, it was said, he had had rheumatic fever as a boy. Maybe the running was indeed some sort of talisman to protect me from his fate, or maybe the opposite: maybe I unconsciously wanted to get soaked right through in the wind and rain in Belfast, to get rheumatic fever to join him, because I do know that I missed him more than anything. This is the problem when a psychologist tries to analyse the causes of his own behaviour: there are too many possible explanations and the sample, by definition, is a little too small. All I do know is that I loved my father more than anyone or anything in this world. My mother always said that she had never seen a son and father so attached, and in every black and white photograph of my childhood I appear to be sitting on my father's knee, rather than my mother's. Many families have their divisions and mine seemed to be divided right down the middle: me and my dad, my brother and my mother.

My father worked on the buses up the Falls Road, and he would take me to scrapyards every Saturday afternoon, just the two of us, to look at the old rusty bangers that he might be able to do up. We would get the bus and then walk to these great fortresses of old cars and scrap metal, protected with rusty gates and barbed wire, and shifty men coming out to greet us suspiciously, covered in oil and grime. This was where we got our first car for £14 at Bates' scrapyard beyond the top of the Ligoniel Road, just past the bus terminus. I can remember my father to this day spitting on his hands to seal the deal, the Bates' wild Alsatian dogs snarling and growling in the background, and my father's smile of quiet satisfaction. He knew more about cars than they did, and he knew the engine was sound; he had got it to turn over eventually. He paid in cash, counting the pound notes out; it was probably all the money he had in the world. He had saved for years for our first car behind my mother's back because he never talked about how much it cost. She used to ask me how much he had paid for it but I never told her. He was one of the good men around our neighbourhood, in my mother's words; he would hand over his pay packet on a Friday night when he got home from work, and my mother would take what she needed for the family, then give him a few pounds back to go down to the bar with the men. He wasn't a big drinker so he saved the money, but he always paid his way and he bought that car with the money he had saved. We drove back down to the street that Saturday afternoon. All the kids came out because it was the first car in the street, and they lined up to look at it, and one by one I invited them to sit in the back with me.

Our lives changed because of it. We used to drive to Bangor on a Sunday in one or other of these old cars, and out towards Donaghadee. My mother would look into the big houses near Holywood.

'Look at that one, Billy,' she would say. 'Go a bit slower. Imagine living there. Look at the chandeliers all lit up in the middle of the day. They don't care about their electricity bills. Maybe one day our Geoffrey will buy one of those. He'll get one for himself, and maybe he'll buy us a wee bungalow as well next to it.'

And my father would drive slowly enough for my mother to study the interiors of these grand houses that looked as if they were on show. This was how the other half lived – ostentatiously, their lights on in the middle of the day. We lived in one of those little mill houses up in Ligoniel, two-up two-down, with an outside toilet and damp walls in the back room, and usually an engine stripped on the floor in that room, sitting there on newspapers, soaked in oil, just in front of the sink where you had to wash. But, of course, I loved that house, when we were all there together. I can remember that tired feeling on a Sunday evening and the sun setting on the way home, with the car from the scrapyard pulling us back to Ligoniel. Later, my father got a new job at the tech and he started taking me to school in the car because he started much later. We would pick up two of my school friends on the way there. He went out of his way on this journey; generous to a fault.

I don't remember my father ever being ill or angry. He was a good-natured man, good-tempered – 'soft' was a word I heard used about him. I remember all the cars, all bought from different scrapyards, and their registration numbers – NKF 148, DZ 1135, SAO 277 – even now, which is perhaps a little odd. And without too much trouble, I can still smell those cars in my imagination, their old, battered leather seats and their dusty ashtrays that pulled out, with the corners solid with dirt. It was a certain old smell that didn't really belong to me or my family, because all the cars were second-, third- or fourth-hand, maybe even more, but it was a comforting smell nonetheless because they all smelt the same. My father always had to work on them, as they sat on the street outside; he was always tinkering with them; there was always some knock or rattle to be fixed. Our neighbours would tap on the door on cold winter nights to say that their car wouldn't turn over or had a banging noise underneath, and he would go out in his overalls in the wind and the rain and slide himself below the car to take a look, lying there on some wet newspaper for hours until the car was fixed. He would come back looking pleased with himself.

'I got it going,' he would say.

'Did they give you anything for the wee job?' my mother would ask.

'They tried, but I wouldn't take anything off them; it wasn't a big job.'

'But Billy, you've been gone for hours.'

'Your father would have been a rich man if he had charged for all the work that he did,' my Uncle Terence used to say about him after he died. As it was, he wasn't a rich man, and we had very little. My brother Bill inherited his last car but crashed it within a couple of weeks and my father's final legacy had gone.

'I never knew anybody, man or woman, who had anything bad to say about your dad,' my mother always liked to tell me. 'The night he died I saw grown men sobbing in the street. You don't get that very often around here in North Belfast. Imagine men crying openly in front of other men. Big Minnie said that it was a first around here; she had never seen anything like it before. She found it a bit disturbing, to be honest – the men weren't even drunk and they were still crying.'

My father had no real interest in sport; maybe he would put a bet on the horses on a Saturday afternoon but he had no real interest in football and certainly not in athletics. According to my mother, he had been a very good roller skater when he was younger because his father had a travelling skating rink, but I never saw him skating. She said that he took her to the beach once and ran down to the waves as if he was just about to dive into the water, but then he just stopped abruptly and paddled his feet and ran out again; he couldn't swim.

'He used to tell me that he went to the swimming baths every Saturday but that was just for a wash, I later found out,' my mother told me.

My father would take me on walks up the Horseshoe Road, up to the 'wee shop' with the Fanta bottle sign, and then down into Ligoniel. It was our regular Sunday afternoon exercise. It was just a leisurely stroll, but it became one of my regular runs in the years after his death. Up to the 'wee shop' and down through Ligoniel, noticing every little twist and turn in the road and the little spring of water on the right-hand side of the road, just to try to remember him better, smiling and strolling on a warm Sunday afternoon before life changed, just to try to stimulate my memory.

But even this memory became tainted. That little bit of path from the 'wee shop' down to Ligoniel became infamous in the Troubles and stained with emotion, with the cold-blooded murder of three young Scottish soldiers. One of them was seventeen; two were brothers. The three of them were just stood in a line and shot in the head by the IRA. The story that everyone in the neighbourhood heard was that they had been drinking in the town centre and were lured up to the White Brae by some girls, the classic honeytrap. There were beer glasses at the scene of the murder; the young lads thought that 'they were on to a good thing', in my mother's words.

A boy of 12 found the bodies. He said, 'We were just standing there frightened and not knowing what to do. Two men came along and one of them touched the head of a man who was lying over another. His head fell back and the man said, "They are stone dead."'

An editorial in the *Belfast Telegraph* at the time read: 'After all the horrors of recent weeks and months, Ulster people have almost lost the capacity for feeling shock. But the ruthless murder of three defenceless young soldiers has cut to the quick. These were cold-blooded executions.'

The route that I took with my father every Sunday became an odd little run of sharp, contrasting emotions, hardly just reminiscent of happy personal memories, but it was the only route that reminded me of him so I stuck to it, though I did shudder slightly every time I got to that spot where the young lads were lined up with their beer glasses and shot in the head. But I still managed to smile a little when I passed the bubbling brook on the way up, and thought of my father cupping his hands to get us both a drink on those warm afternoons of my childhood.

My father would build me guiders out of old bits of metal and wood and sets of pram wheels, and then I would set off on that ritualistic journey of 12 or 16 repetitions to the top of the park gates and then back down, over and over again, until the bats started to circulate by the lower gate. I would come home with my shirt damp with sweat. My brother Bill liked to hike and rock climb, and walk up the Mourne Mountains with his friends, but I was happy in these little lonely rituals of mine. I would play soldiers on our floor for hours, and then pull the guider to the top park gates and ride down, over and over again.

'It will make you fit,' my father would say. 'All that exercise will give you muscles.'

When he died I felt that my world as I knew it had simply gone. I could hardly cry at first. My uncle said many years later that I simply pulled down the shutters and never talked about my father any more. My mother lay in bed at nights calling out his name, with these long pauses as if she was expecting him to call back, and I lay weeping into my pillow, because I could not let her see me doing this. Her life was now bad enough; I couldn't make it worse.

I recently read *On Men: Masculinity in Crisis* by the

psychiatrist Anthony Clare. In this book he reflects on the psychological effects of the early loss of a parent. He writes:

> *It is not surprising that the death of a parent may be less disastrous for a child than loss through divorce . . . The death of a parent is usually recognised as a severe blow and results in an outpouring of emotion in support of the child from the other family members and in a process of grieving in which the dead parent is remembered with sympathy, pride and affection. The widowed parent shares in the child's loss; together they can maintain an idealised picture of the dead parent and can, even through death, build a sense of connectedness.*

But I felt that his loss could not be shared and that grief just had to be borne. I don't recall hugging my mother or my mother hugging me in a sympathetic way, except in great, heaving paroxysms of grief, which tended to be in public, and just made me feel worse. I just felt responsibility, maybe too much for my age.

'You're the man of the family, now,' my uncle would say. 'Bill is away a lot of the time. You are all that your mother has got.'

'He would have been a vegetable if he had survived that operation,' my mother used to say, trying to cheer me up, maybe trying to build some sort of connectedness. 'The blood clot went to his brain. You wouldn't have wanted a vegetable as a father.'

I could never comment on this, it seemed so stupid. I wanted him to be there with me in any state; and I ended up keeping the image in my head.

My rituals became much lonelier after he died, lonelier and more meditative. I suppose that I was a 13 year old trying to make sense of a strange, unpredictable world. I became strangely fixated on nature and living rough and escaping and being chased by unknown people. I loved films in which the heroes were chased endlessly, like *The 39 Steps*. I became obsessed with spending time in huts and hideaways in the glens around the mills nearby, diving into the dam with its dead dogs on summer afternoons; and with lifting the bookcase with the encyclopaedias up and down, 50 or 60 times with lots of repetitions, until the encyclopaedias would fall out onto the floor and my mother would shout up the stairs, asking what the bloody hell I was doing, banging about up there. I started running more seriously about this time, recording my distances and times. Perhaps it was all just the beginnings of mental discipline or a way of dealing with fear and uncertainty, or a form of obsessive compulsive disorder. Perhaps I found safety in my routines.

So here I am, a professor of psychology looking back at the start of my running career, trying to understand my basic motivations. Did I not want what had happened to my father to happen to me? Was that what this was all about? Or did I realise that I was going to have to be very disciplined to get through life? Did I realise that there was to be no public display of grief, no shouting out his name in the middle of the night, and that I needed an iron will and the discipline of running? Or was there a completely different motivation? Was I running out into the driving wind and rain of Belfast to get nature to do its worst? This may not necessarily be that far-fetched an idea. My brother Bill challenged nature in the hills and mountains of Afghanistan and Nepal, and joined my father when he was barely 30 on the 'Goddess of Joy', Nanda Devi, in the Himalayas. He was alone, climbing for the summit, and died needlessly and senselessly, and in a way that meant that the little house in Legmore Street would be for the remainder of its days a small, dark and sorrowful damp hole. Or was it all just some form of anti-fat prejudice, and Myrna's awful legacy to me?

But all I can say is that I wanted to be a different sort of father to my children when my time came, an active father, one that could protect them, one that could run, a live father, not some distant memory. Running seemed to me to offer a thread, a thread that I could cling on to, and it was always obvious to me that my children would understand the importance of this thread and maybe one day incorporate it into their own lives. But I suppose it is a sort of religion with its own rituals and magic; rituals that can never be broken, no matter how hard you try.

So what really did I learn from my father? I learned to be strong because he wasn't strong enough in the end to stay with me. I learned to charge people for things because he didn't, to make sure that I got paid for any work, to always get the invoice to them, always. My mother always used to say to me, 'You're like a wee Jew sometimes, and, just remember, you'll never be half the man your father was.' And in many ways I suppose that's true. But I wanted to be a different sort of man anyway: a living one for a start, not a memory, not a saint, not the best and the most generous and the 'softest' man in the neighbourhood, the man they all cried over. I wanted none of that, and my wish weirdly came true; but sometimes it doesn't feel that good, and funnily enough the rituals, now firmly established, never left me, not once.

Eight years ago I woke up one day with an ankle swollen to three or four times its normal size. I had been hobbling along, trying to run the night before on a running machine in the gym, but on the Sunday I couldn't stand up. Carol drove me to casualty where they identified a stress fracture from running and potted it. But on the Monday when the consultant orthopaedic surgeon took the pot off and examined the ankle, he said that he didn't like the look of it. He insisted on a blood test, saying that he suspected that it could be septic arthritis, which is pretty serious and indeed can be fatal. When the results came back he called for an operating theatre immediately, right in front of me, for 'a trauma case', and in theatre they bled the ankle. I told him just before I went for the surgery that I was a runner but he said that sometimes things happen in life that mean that you have to change the way you think. He said, 'I think your running days are well behind you. In a year or so you may be able to run a mile on a treadmill but you can forget about marathons or half marathons ever again.'

Two weeks after the operation I couldn't walk let alone run, but I had to exercise. Carol gave me a lift to the gym (and was so bored there that she started running on the running machines and from that moment took up running). To get from exercise machine to exercise machine I had to go on my hands and knees and pull myself up to get some upper-body exercise. It was all that I could do – it wasn't running but it was something. It was as close as I could get.

I would go to the gym at times when I knew there would be few people there as I didn't want others to see my embarrassment. One day I was doing some bench presses on a particular machine and I could see this guy watching me with an expression that was a mixture of bewilderment and a little bit of anger, for some strange reason. Don't ask me where the anger came from but he looked puzzled and resentful.

'Can I give you a little bit of advice?' he said to me. 'I've been watching you for the last hour or so and this just isn't right. You can't even walk, what are you doing in a gym? Take my advice, mate, you need to go and see a bloody psychologist. Go to your local GP, I'm sure that he can recommend a good one. You need urgent help,' and he turned away and walked off, without any sympathy in his voice or in his demeanour.

I ran my next half marathon six months later; I limped part of the way while still running, but I got round in 1 hour 40 minutes. I wanted to tell both the guy in the gym and the doctor. But fuck both of them. What do they know anyway?

7

Room at the Top

September 2010

I like racing overseas; they have a different way of doing things. But within a few yards of the start of any race, wherever you are, everything becomes so familiar again. It reconnects you to the real you.

'Good job!' the stout woman with the red tortoiseshell glasses and the grey sweat top shouts at me in Southern California, emphasising the 'b' sound in 'job' as if she is surprised. It sounds to my running ears as if the 'b' is reverberating in my tired and over-heated brain.

I had been invited to the University of California at Santa Barbara to give a few guest celebrity lectures. There was a large turnout and the talks were extremely well received. I need this kind of affirmation; it tells you a little about my fundamental insecurity. My family were all back in Sheffield. I had timed my visit around some races that I wanted to run. I had stopped off at Chicago on the way there and run the Chicago Half Marathon. Stupidly, in retrospect, I had done a 5K the day before at Montrose Harbour. My time (1 hour 41 minutes for the half) was more than a little disappointing but my legs felt tired from the start of the race. But I had a few races still to go to make amends.

I left my hotel in Santa Barbara that morning at 4 a.m. to race in Malibu Canyon at 7 a.m. I drove down Route 1 in the dark, picking up the traffic heading to LA from San Francisco, out past Montecito and breathtaking views of the great Pacific

Ocean to the right. Dawn crept up slowly as I headed into the hills just before you get to LA. The engine of the automatic car that I had hired was pulling noticeably, as I turned right into Malibu Canyon Road where Mel Gibson had crashed his Maserati only a few weeks previously. I parked on the main road to save ten bucks – old habits die hard – and I walked down into the canyon in the dawn light. Runners were emerging slowly from their cars like caterpillars unfurling themselves as the light crept in. It was the Malibu Canyon Dirt Dash, a 5K, a 10K and then the Dirt Dash itself. I could see the organisers hosing the final stretch of the race to produce some lovely mud for the photographs. 'Hey, you only do 5Ks, I do 5Ks through mud, man, and this is the real deal. Do you want to see my photograph of some proper racing?'

The runners walked about in the half-light with cagoules and tracksuits. Some had blankets wrapped around them. They were registering, getting instructions, looking at the map of the course, trying to imagine the terrain and the route. The event was organised by the Samaritans, so before the race there was a prayer which was actually quite moving at that time of the day, and a marching band with two boys and a girl, who didn't look as if they quite knew what they were doing there.

The race seemed to be an out and back course. We lined up quickly and we were off. I could tell where I was in terms of position on the turn, but I lost count, top ten maybe. It knew it was called the Malibu Canyon Dirt Dash but there wasn't much sign of a hill until it suddenly emerged from nowhere, on a blind corner. It climbed and climbed and climbed, and my running shoes started slipping back on the sandy gravel. The runner in front of me suddenly stumbled and fell on the rough path. He got up quickly, but I could see the blood dripping from his knee. We climbed up to the summit and then descended abruptly; it felt like jumping off a cliff, all that work on the way up for no obvious benefit. Some tall American youth, impossibly blond and Californian looking, raced me to the finish. He went one way around a sign and some spectators, and I went the other way, but he had the advantage on the other side. The time was very slow – 23 minutes and something – but it was difficult to gauge given the hills, the gravel and the sharp, cutting terrain; however, I came twelfth overall, easily the first in my age category. It was much slower than my time, 20.52, in the 5K the week before on Zuma Beach, but I was still reasonably contented given the hills. The man with the bleeding knee recognised me from television and invited me the following night to a party to celebrate the opening of the West Coast office of his firm. The party was to be held in Soho House, West Hollywood. It was clearly a celebrity hangout, and Dominic, still bleeding away, told me to 'dress to impress'.

So the following day, on the way to the party, I packed my running stuff to have a run in Malibu Canyon once again. I planned to change after my run into my party clothes, having bathed in a pure canyon stream with fast-flowing, crystal-clear water. I had this great image in my head of me fit and healthy, tanned, dressed to the nines in LA for a party with all the celebs. The only problem was that the traffic was very different the next day and the drive took much longer than I had anticipated. I know that lateness can be fashionable but I am always notoriously late, unfashionably so, and I didn't want to be any later. I didn't really have time to make my way back up into the canyon so I just parked the car at the side of the road, put my running gear on with some difficulty in the back of the car, and had a run along one of the canyon roads, occasionally slipping in the dirt at the side as I tried to avoid the oncoming traffic.

After my run the traffic was even heavier, and there would have been no way of bathing or getting changed, so I drove in my smelly running gear into Mulholland Drive and then down Sunset Boulevard to the end of Sunset Strip. I spotted Soho House because of the small knot of paparazzi outside. I drove past them in my still-wet shorts and vest. There was valet parking at Soho House, so I joined the small queue of cars waiting to go into the underground car park only because I had no choice. Ideally, I would have liked to have parked opposite, dried myself with a towel and changed, but there were no quiet places and the idea of being papped as I stripped off didn't really appeal to me. Suddenly, I was in the underground car park at the front of the queue. A polite Mexican in a crisp white shirt came out of his booth and leant forward to talk to me about parking my car but I had to explain to him that I was not wearing any trousers. He looked puzzled for a second, so I pointed to my bare legs.

'No trousers on,' I said. 'No trousers on today.'

He looked alarmed for a split second, but it was a long split second, as if he had just seen something that he shouldn't have seen, indeed something in his years of working at this classy but slightly louche establishment that he had never seen before, and then he smiled knowingly in a way that I didn't like, as if the penny had suddenly dropped.

'No, no, no. Not like that. I think that you misunderstand, I'm a runner,' I explained. 'There's nothing dodgy about me not wearing trousers, honestly, I'm just a runner. It's normal.'

'Si, si!' he said. 'Si, si!' with a louder and more insistent articulation and a big, knowing grin, and I was sure that he was not convinced by my story in this lair of celebrities with all of their peculiar peccadilloes.

He led me to a dark corner of this underground car park where I got my towel out and dried myself, and then changed with the towel around my waist as if I were at the English seaside. He stood watching me from a safe distance with a small group of his colleagues. He pointed my way as if he was warning them to keep an eye on me. One or two of them looked slightly alarmed. They all had pristine white shirts, starched and neat, hardly any creases. I dropped my soggy shorts onto the concrete floor with a loud, wet splat. My shirt was crumpled but at least it was dry. I handed the car park attendant the keys and I noticed that he stretched out his hand to receive them rather than coming too close. I didn't smell great, even I knew that, and I was used to that peculiar runner's smell.

I walked into the scented reception where two beautiful girls in black dresses checked my invitation, and then I ascended in a lift to a dark room, lit only by candles, with magnificent views of LA sparkling at twilight. I passed the Beckhams on the way up and saw both Cameron Diaz and Kelly Osbourne on the way to the toilet. I didn't try to talk to anybody because that is not my nature. My mother used to tell me off about this, endlessly. I had been a very shy child when I was young. My brother was the opposite of me in this respect, as in many others: he was outgoing, entertaining and eager to meet strangers, never shy but without ever crossing the boundary into being 'too forward', charming in the extreme. He was perfectly positioned on the right side of being sociable.

'You can be a really odd boy, when you want to be,' my mother would say, where 'odd' meant socially awkward. 'When are you going to grow out of it?'

In some ways, I never did. I can talk to strangers easily and confidently these days – it must be all that psychology – but when it comes to greeting celebrities or somebody important in any social situation then I never introduce myself. I always hang back and let them make the first move, which is a bit disconcerting given that I do a series for ITV which involves taking celebrities out hunting for ghosts. It's odd having a reluctant psychologist who waits for the celebrities to come up to introduce themselves to him. I suspect it makes me seem a bit stand-offish. And why would the Beckhams go out of their way to say hello to the slightly unkempt man at the party? I could feel the grime of the run on my face because I hadn't managed to shower, but the skin on my face felt tight, so I felt relatively OK about my appearance. I noticed that Beckham aftershave was sitting out in the bathroom, waiting to be used, so I splashed some all over my face to disguise my stale, sweaty, bodily odour.

I hung back in this room full of well-dressed businessmen all talking shop. Dominic came over and started chatting about his excitement at working in LA. His work colleague told me that Dominic ran to and from work every single day in the City; 'more than regular, it's weird, it's compulsive with him', is how he put it. He explained that nobody had ever seen anything like it before in his firm, and then added, 'You're a psychologist, you might understand.'

I told him that I did understand for many, many reasons and in many, many ways, but I didn't elaborate. I just wiped my grimy face nervously once more and smiled quietly to myself.

8

Preparation, Preparation, Preparation

August 2011

It was a muggy sort of day. The sort of day that could catch you out, if you weren't careful; it was probably a lot hotter than it looked and this race already had an ominous feeling about it. The previous year Carol, who is an excellent runner for her age, had collapsed in the final few hundred yards because of the heat, and she did this in painful slow motion. She was leaning forward at an angle as she entered the track at the end of the race, and the angle of lean suddenly got sharper and sharper as her body curved forward, and then down into the gravel she went. We were all on the grass waiting for her to come in, and we could see that forward lean and knew immediately what it meant. It wasn't the first time this had happened. Ben was first there, of course, as he's the fastest, but he hesitated in helping her because, he explained afterwards, he was worried that she might be disqualified. Some local veteran runner with grey hair and glasses and a yellow running vest, whom Carol knows well, clambered over the fence and helped her onto her feet; her chest and her left arm were red and bleeding with gravel streaked into the cuts. Because Carol has one arm, it makes protecting herself in a fall that much more difficult, and it was the thin left arm, amputated above the elbow, that was most badly hurt. Carol was apologising, the sweat dried on her hair, streaks of saliva out of the sides of her mouth, elongating the mouth slits, like

Jack Nicholson as the Joker in *Batman*. Ben walked beside her as she was helped along.

'She can't finish now,' he said. 'She had better not cross the line; she's had artificial support in getting to the finish.'

That previous year had been a hot day as well, and it had taken its toll. The warning signs were already there.

The race started at 10.30 a.m. in Askern outside Doncaster, so I could either set off from Manchester where I now lived that morning at about 7.30, up at 6.45, or drive over to Carol's the night before, to my old house in Hollow Meadows, and have a more relaxed evening and morning. When I had suggested earlier in the week that I might come over the night before the race Carol had not seemed very keen on the idea, but on the Saturday she said that she thought that it would be very nice if I came over. She even sounded enthusiastic. So I arrived at about half nine, looking forward to seeing her. Sam, the son who still lives there, was away visiting friends in Bristol, and I felt quite sorry for her lying on the settee alone, holding her left arm presumably to stop the interminable pain, alone in that big dark house, some arts programme on the television, the sound quite low. I would have had all the lights on, and the television up full blast.

I'm not used to sleeping there now, and I hadn't managed to fall asleep until about half five in the morning so I woke up fatigued and resigned to not being at my best in the race; it always seems like this somehow on race days. Ben and his girlfriend Jo were going to make their own way to the race. Both were running. Last year I beat Jo although we entered the final bit of track together; Ben was cheering for her rather than me, that's all I remember, and being very competitive, though not quite as competitive as Ben, she was not happy that I had beaten her in the final few hundred yards. Ben knows not to wait for me; he says that my lateness just stresses him too much. On race days he can do without that kind of pressure.

We drove to the race listening to Radio 4; it was Carol's

choice, not mine. I prefer loud music, maybe *Led Zeppelin I*; sounds that will go round and round in my head while I run. 'Boom boom, boom boom, boom boom, boom boom, boom boom': there are five of those great booming noises, then into, 'In the days of my youth, I was told what it means to be a man.' I like that noise and even that sort of sentiment reverberating in my head on my lonely journey along the roads when I am running. Maybe even Faithless. Carol keeps Radio 4 on constantly in her car; she thinks my musical tastes are a bit juvenile. Paddy O'Connell was on *Broadcasting House*, talking about the possible causes of that week's riots in London, Manchester and Birmingham. Carol is a civil servant and she quipped that it was ridiculous that David Cameron was trying to blame the whole thing on greed and criminality.

'It's all about hope and aspiration,' she said, reasonably enough, I thought. 'I think that Paddy has got it spot on today.'

For some reason I was feeling argumentative, perhaps it was the lack of sleep in that house that I once thought of as my home, perhaps it was a little jealousy of how she was talking about 'Paddy'.

'The problem with politicians,' I said, 'is that they constantly confuse causes and explanations; I'm not even sure that they understand the difference between justifications and excuses. They just don't get it, conceptually.' I glanced her way but there was no response.

This just urged me on. 'Paddy O'Connell could have been a bit more explicit in his challenges. Psychologists have to differentiate these concepts all the time. You need a clearer terminology.' There was still no answer.

'What was the immediate cause?' I asked imperiously. 'What images were in people's minds this week about the Metropolitan Police? I'll tell you what: the senior policemen at the News International hearings all on the take, all with nice little earners from the *News of the World* after they left the force; the pompous politicians, sitting behind their big desks, firing questions at them with all of their little expenses fiddles;

Rupert Murdoch being hit in the face with a cream pie and that Mr Plod taking ages to get across the room to apprehend the stand-up comic who did it. Did you see the way that policeman waddled across the room? Human beings are designed to detect weakness when it comes to aggression, it's part of our evolutionary imperative, and just look at what they had been seeing in the weeks up to the riots and then after all this the police just held back. Human beings can be very imitative when there are only possible rewards and no negative consequences for their actions.'

There was no response from Carol; she wasn't rising to the bait. She was probably planning her race strategy. Paddy O'Connell was interviewing the Home Secretary, Theresa May, about the reactions of the police on the first three nights of the riots. 'Timid' was the word that kept coming up. The police objected, naturally enough, to this term. But the chat on Radio 4 was extremely civilised, as the word 'timid' was thrown this way and that.

I could see that Carol was now looking extremely irritated; I wouldn't have described her look as 'timid'.

'Why don't you go on the radio and put them right then?' she eventually said.

Funnily enough, I had been in London that Tuesday evening for a series of radio interviews the following morning for a campaign on how close we were as a nation. The campaign was funded by Nivea; my role was to talk about some new research that I had been conducting on how people signal their relationships in public using touch. A classic study published in 1966 had suggested that England was a 'zero touch culture', but our new research suggested that things had changed dramatically and we were now using all sorts of 'tie-signs' in public. It just wasn't the day to talk about this work on closeness. But, nevertheless, I'd had back-to-back interviews and when the riots were raised by the interviewers I simply talked about the aftermath and what this had demonstrated about closeness, and how the community spirit that had been shown in some areas reflected how we can come together especially in the face of adversity.

The stony silence in the car was making my race preparations even worse, so I thought that I would break the silence, to try to get things on an even keel before we got to the race itself. I mentioned that I had fairly recently (actually it wasn't that recent, but I just wanted to annoy her) been on a *Tonight* programme with Paddy O'Connell on detecting deception in those television appeals where relatives plead for information from the public when all along they are the guilty party. Their non-verbal communication, in particular their micro-expressions, often give them away. I like dropping names at times like this – well, I don't like it but I do it; some might say that it is a classic sign of insecurity. Carol, however, was not impressed.

'Did you say the usual then?' she asked, as the car turned off the M18 towards Doncaster. 'I can't imagine Paddy O'Connell being very impressed with that.'

'It sounds like you fucking well know Paddy O'Connell,' I said. 'At least I've fucking well met him. This is fucking typical on a race day when I stay with you. It always ends up like this. Where's my race number?' I asked.

'Same place as always, back seat.'

'Have you any pins?'

'You know where I keep them; they're always in the same place.'

'Have you got any big pins? You know I only like the big ones; they're easier to get through the number.'

'Oh, the big nappy pins. Is that what you want? For God's sake, you're like a child. Not a bit of wonder Ben doesn't like travelling with you on the day of the race. It's not just that you're late for everything; you just go on about nothing all the time. You distract everyone.'

The rest of the journey was made in frosty silence, except when we started passing the yellow signs on the side of the road, which read 'Keep to the pavement', indicating that this was part of the course itself. We saw a figure up ahead in a red top with long legs and a long, even stride. 'That's Ben, warming up,' Carol said, recognising him immediately. I was not so sure that it was him but I was pleased that I didn't say what I thought because it was indeed him. Carol tooted the horn and he waved back. We bumped into Jo immediately at the race-day car park, looking a little nervous.

'Ben is very relaxed today; it's me who's wound up,' she said.

It was the 'Askern 10', the South Yorkshire 10 Mile Championship, a hilly course on a warm day with a bit of a wind, the kind of race I hate. I always like to remind people that there are no hills in Manchester so it's hardly ideal preparation for these kinds of races. My preparation had been reasonably good, however. I had aimed for two glasses of white wine the night before, but Carol had topped up my glass for a third time before I could stop her. I had eaten alone at about 10.30, which was not ideal, but at least it was pasta; Ben would have eaten his pasta at 6. He always tells me off for eating so late the night before races. But I had not raced the day before, as I had intended to do, because Ben had persuaded me not to, so my last race, a 5K, had been three days before. I felt tired, slightly hung-over, but my legs were fresher than they sometimes are. I went to the toilet three times as usual in quick succession, going then almost immediately queuing again; funnily enough Ben does exactly the same thing, it's always three times. Like father, like son on this one.

The runners were starting to gather. I could see Ben on the start line on the very first row; I started a few rows back with Jo. The hooter went a few minutes late, and we set off quickly, but immediately I realised that I had a problem. There was something sticking into my left foot: it felt like a sharp stone or a nail or a piece of glass. I was running in some racing flats with hardly any sole at all, indeed just holes between the lattice frameworks at the bottom of the shoes. I ran for about 100 yards and then stopped abruptly to examine the shoe to pull the nail or whatever it was out. I had never done this before in a race. Jo looked surprised but ran swiftly past me. I swept the sole with my hand but felt nothing and nothing came off. I couldn't untie the shoe because I tie the knots so tightly that it takes ages to get the shoes off; I usually need help to untie them. Carol, with her one arm, often does it for me. I do this because once in the Belfast Marathon exactly 21 years earlier my lace had come undone at 23 miles and I couldn't bend down to retie it because if I had tried I would never have been able to get up again. I ran the last three miles thinking that I might trip over at any point.

That race was one of my genuine nightmares and it was the last marathon I ever did. My mother had never watched me run a race so I had said I would go home to Belfast so that she could watch. I had been on holiday with Carol and our three children, Zoe, Ben and Sam, the week before in Tenerife and after Carol and the kids went to bed I would go out most nights to the bars and clubs, which stayed open very late. I had got used to this sort of lifestyle, which Carol seemed to accept. On the day of the race, I was very tanned but poorly prepared. It was a beautiful morning and my mother said that she would be at the finish with my tracksuit and a towel. All I remember about the race was that there was a relay held concurrently with the marathon, and old school friends would run past me looking fresh, having run two or three miles, and say hello, and I would grunt back. I looked and felt very tired indeed. This was not lost on the spectators who were shouting out how tired I looked compared with some of those around me. Some were also shouting out 'n*****' because I was so dark. It rained the whole way round and then my lace came undone. At the end of the race they gave each finisher a pint of Guinness which I gulped down and then vomited back over myself. I looked for my mother but there was no sign of her. I hobbled along to Royal Avenue to get the bus home, shivering and smelling of vomit. I had no bus fare. I explained this to the bus driver. He looked at me without any real sympathy and told me to sit at the back of the bus away from everybody else.

'I'm only letting you on this once,' he said. 'Don't ever try this stunt again.' He didn't seem to know that there was a race on that day. I just looked like some bedraggled coloured person who smelt very bad and who had been sick all over himself.

When I got home my mother's only comment was, 'Look at the state of you. Thank God I didn't watch that and besides the rain was too bad. You wouldn't have liked me to stand out in all that rain, would you?'

The lesson that day, apart from not drinking Guinness after a race, was to tie your running shoes very tightly. So I had done this ever since.

I had two choices when my foot began to hurt: either drop out of the South Yorkshire 10 Mile Championship after 100 yards or continue with a foot that I could hardly bear to put on the pavement. I prayed that endorphins would kick in and I would cease to feel the pain, but this never happened. Jo was in front of me, Carol was somewhere behind and my only goal was to get round without Carol catching me. My gait started to change to protect my left sole but the whole 77 minutes, because that's how long it took, was excruciating. Ben clapped as I entered the final bit of track and looked happy, partly, I suspect, because he had come 5th in the race in 56 minutes, and 3rd in the South Yorkshire Championship, but partly, I think, because Jo was in front of me. I wasn't humiliated just by him but by his girlfriend as well. Carol came in a few minutes after me. I lay on the grass in the heat and slowly untied my shoe to display the hole in my left foot.

'It's your own fault,' said Ben, 'always buying the cheapest running shoes. You've got the money; you're loaded, so why don't you spend some of it?'

I lay on my back and closed my eyes to shut everything out, but my foot was throbbing and I could hear Ben and even Carol being congratulated. Nobody knew who I was, lying there in my green Sale Harriers vest, although on the way round I did hear somebody shout '*Big Brother*' at me but I was in such pain I couldn't even do that slight smile of recognition.

'Stuck-up celebrity bastard,' the man had muttered to his wife loudly enough for me and everybody else to hear.

After his warm-down, Ben got presented with a bronze medal and I am embarrassed to admit that I was pleased that, for once, Carol got nothing. She always gets first prize in her category in the ladies' vets. She looked surprised at this as some other name was called out instead of hers and she tried to cover her emotion, but I could see one of those micro-expressions emerging from beneath a masking smile that I have been studying ever since my Cambridge days.

Perhaps the oddest moment of the whole day was that Ben got himself a pint of Guinness to drink while he was waiting for his prize. I have never seen him drink Guinness before and I bent forward as far as I could and took a sip out of his glass. Jo laughed, but Ben looked slightly annoyed.

'This reminds me of something,' I said.

'When you could still run half decently?' he asked.

'No not that. I was just reflecting on the fact that some things never change.'

'Things do change,' said Ben. 'I knocked two minutes off my time but you seem to be running backwards.'

'But what about my foot?' I held up my sock with a neat little circle of blood indicating where the hole was. It was a pathetically small circle.

Ben gestured towards his mother, standing there with a black sock covering the stump of her left arm; he didn't say anything at first. Perhaps I didn't look guilty enough; perhaps I should have pushed through the pain barrier.

'You know, some people complain and some just get on with it. I think I know which group you're in. I've seen you racing. Last year Jo tells me that you were chatting away to her all the way round. If you're racing properly, you shouldn't be able to talk like that. I don't think that you're really trying. We all push it in this family, except you.'

Then we left this old miners' hall and walked into the bright sunlight. Carol was chatting away to all the fell runners that she knows, Ben was being congratulated by small groups of strangers, and then there was me limping after the two of them with a hole in my left foot. I learned later that day that if I had done the 5K the day before then I almost certainly would have won it, and that would have been a first for me in a running career of maybe forty years. That was probably the hardest thing to bear about the whole weekend.

But only probably.

9

The Elephant in the Room

Ben

I suppose the question everyone asks me is, 'Why do you run every day now? What changed? Why bother?' And they're never content with any answer. 'Don't you ever get sick of it?', 'Take it easy', 'Put your feet up', 'Relax.' I want to ask them why they're so lazy, but I'm too polite for that, far too polite for that. That is my nature.

But I am aware that there must be a reason. It's more than a hobby to me, it's a compulsion. It dominates my thoughts every day. Every decision that I make in my life is considered based on how it will affect my running. Running is always there in my mind, at the front or at the back.

Running has always been a part of my life, off and on. It has always been a part of all of the lives of everyone in my family, directly or indirectly. I have always been aware of its importance to my dad. When I was young I didn't understand it. I just never saw the point. You venture out into the cold and rain, you run around for a bit and then you come home. You are tired and wet and miserable. There was always a feeling in our house, although it was rarely articulated, that there was something wrong with my dad, perhaps very wrong, that he was strange in some way. He had to run every single day and it didn't make sense to me or to any of us. I was always under the impression that running came first. It took priority over everything else, including the children. There were countless times that appointments were missed because of his running.

We were kept waiting for meals every night because of this running thing. My mum's patience was worn thin a long time ago. Everything had to be put on hold in our family because my dad had to go for his run.

When I was very young I used to dread him asking me to go out for a run with him. I felt no enjoyment in running. I was tired and cold. I longed to stop; I longed to be back home. I once threw myself down into the snow on a long run with my dad in order to rest. I pretended that I had fallen over. It was the middle of winter in the middle of the moors by our house; it really is the middle of nowhere. But even then he just helped me up with a few words of encouragement and we continued. It didn't occur to him that we should turn back. My hands were blue and sore and I felt like crying, but I stopped myself. I remember visualising for a few seconds our living room and the big warm fire roaring in the fireplace but it just made matters worse. I focused on the figure in front of me, in the blinding snow: two lone figures in the wilderness, father and son against the elements, crossing the Rockies; that's what he would have been thinking. I tried to feel heroic in this kind of way but I was too sad and too miserable for that; I was far too sad for that.

Even if I took no enjoyment from running at this stage, I knew it was something that should be done. I remember the feeling of guilt when I didn't go with him. It sat like a weight on my mind.

We used to go and watch the Sheffield Marathon every year. It was a family trip, a family day out. We would get the Sunday papers on the way there. We would park in the same place every year and walk to Hillsborough or later Don Valley Stadium. The main thing that I remember about the day was the sheer boredom of the whole thing. We would sit there in the same spot for over three hours for the marathon, or an hour and a half for the half marathon, and wait for him to come in. My heart would sink when he told us that he was planning to do the marathon that day because that went on forever; he often didn't make his mind up until the last minute, which looking back strikes me as being quite bizarre. I've never heard of anyone else doing that. It just proves that he didn't really do any specific training for either of the events. I think that was part of the challenge for him: just turn up and do whatever he felt like. I know for a fact that he did several marathons when his only training was months and months of runs that were no longer than five miles. He may have been dedicated enough to do some running every day but he often didn't seem to be that bothered about getting the big runs in, the way you have to if you're serious. My dad would always ask me to join him for the last mile of the race. He wanted me to jump over the barriers and finish the race with him. As a painfully shy child, I couldn't think of anything worse. We would go to the church pantomime every year (without Dad, of course) and all the other children would go up onto the stage for the final song. I would never go up. The idea of being up there in front of all those people filled me with terror. So I would sit with the rest of the adults and watch the pantomime, or I would stay well behind the barriers and watch him finish the race. It was his moment of triumph, all alone, although he never looked particularly happy.

At some stage, however, I started to do the fun runs associated with the bigger races. To be honest, I'm not exactly sure how this started. I don't remember ever asking to do one or indeed getting much pleasure from competing, but at the same time I can't imagine being entered in a race against my wishes. But I would do a fun run and my dad would watch me and shout encouragement. He never seemed embarrassed. I have a few snaps of these races and I do look as if I was really trying, despite all my misgivings. He told me that I was a natural runner; all I needed was some dedication. But I never wanted to end up like him, with that weird compulsion.

One year when I wasn't doing the fun run my dad had what we all call 'his big wobbler'. The Sheffield Marathon and Half Marathon used to be run right at the height of summer. This particular year it was absolutely sweltering. We took our seats as usual that day in Don Valley Stadium and I started to read the *Funday Times*. I still remember the heat to this day, which is very unusual, but there was just something about the heat that day: it felt dangerously hot. I remember that it was too hot even to sit in an uncovered stand out of the shade, let alone run. We waited as usual as the elite runners came in at about 70 minutes; it was always a tough, hilly course. I expected to see my dad about 15 minutes later but there was no sign of him. Eventually, he entered the stadium around 25 minutes after the guy in first place. It was instantly clear that something was wrong. He was staggering and stumbling down the home straight (something I was to mimic a few years later). We rushed to the edge of the track just as the medical crew were getting prepared. He crossed the line – I remember him vomiting on the guy in front, who looked really pissed off – and then he collapsed, just straight down into the dirt. He didn't even have time to collect his medal. He was rushed into the bowels of the stadium, to a medical room near the indoor warm-up track. The sight I remember most vividly was the bathtub filled with ice. He was packed in ice in order to bring his core temperature down. He was also hooked up to an intravenous drip to combat the extreme dehydration he was suffering from. We sat outside that room for what felt like hours on end. I was probably the most scared I had ever been in my life. I saw my father as being immortal; he was strong, fit and clever, and I had never seen him in this kind of state before. At one stage I went out to collect his medal. The slower runners were still finishing so the volunteers were still handing out the medals. I went over to explain the situation to them but at first they wouldn't give me the medal. I became more and more frustrated. By the time they gave me the medal I was weeping and shaking uncontrollably. I was probably upset by all of the things that I had just witnessed. I heard later that one of the runners died that day because of the heat. His kids were waiting for him as well.

I don't remember the point at which my dad and I started to spend time together again. I do know that for a long period of time, more than months, maybe years, I wanted nothing to do with him at all. I mean at all. I remember that I used to tell people of my greatest fear of all, that I would somehow end up like my dad. I had moved to Macclesfield in order to live and work in a pub. I was supposed to be the deputy manager of this new place but I ended up running the whole thing. It was a huge establishment and I had far too much responsibility at such a young age. It didn't seem like it at the time but looking back I suppose that subconsciously I was trying to take the path most disparate from that of my father. He was a career academic; I had dropped out of university and immersed myself in a world far away from that of universities and running. I vaguely remember a couple of runs while in Macclesfield but nothing serious so it still surprises me that I agreed to do a race with my dad in Rochdale. We had started to have some sort of a relationship again. I had started to make the short train journey over to Manchester quite regularly for shopping and a meal in a city-centre restaurant, usually in the Gay Village for some reason. It was on these visits that my dad started to notice that I was looking increasingly not well. Not ill as such, just not very well. I was losing weight and had bad skin due to the stresses of work. I was also drinking quite heavily and was desperately unhappy. I knew from the beginning that the move was a mistake but I felt like a fool for wanting to quit and go home. I was a prolific quitter, a serial quitter. If at any point the going got tough, I would simply give up: university, relationships, you name it. In hindsight the invite to the race was probably my dad's attempt to get me back on the right track, a bit pathetic really but presumably that's all he could think of at the time. He evidently believes, as I do now, that running is the greatest natural cure there is for all ailments be they physical or mental. The chance to try to reignite my interest in running and fitness overall must have been too good an opportunity for him to ignore.

When the race started some long-forgotten competitive streak must have kicked in and I set off fast. I knew that I used to be a pretty decent young runner and thought that there was no way a man 30 years my senior would beat me. I was wrong. After about 7 kilometres of the 10K race I had nothing left. My lifestyle caught up with me and I slowed to what felt like a walk. Sure enough my dad overtook me and I came 2nd in the race of 2 in a time of 45 minutes.

I truly believe that this was a watershed moment for me in my running and for my life as a whole. I said to myself that night that I would never again be beaten by my dad. At that stage I wasn't setting my sights particularly high. I wasn't aiming to beat his personal best for the half marathon of 1.26 when he was at his peak (and going out the night before, as he likes to remind me). I just didn't want to be beaten by the current version that seemed to be well past its peak. That thought drove me forward.

10

A Weekend Away

October 2010

I can't actually remember whose idea it was but I knew that it wasn't mine. The idea was that just the two of us would go off together for a weekend to Cardiff to run the half marathon. Ben had studied the form book carefully. He had worked out that he could do very well in this race; he hadn't checked to see where I might be placed.

'You'll be OK,' he said. 'You always are. You're not very focused but you'll get round OK.'

What was surprising was that his mother wasn't involved in the plan. Carol hadn't been invited. It would just be the two of us with no buffer and no antidote, nothing to stop any friction. I was nervous about the whole thing. I hadn't been away with Ben on his own since he was about six years old, when we had travelled from Sheffield by train to Leeds for a live daytime show. Then, I was going to talk about body language and coincidently I was going to do my first live television interview. Ben had taken the day off school and at Sheffield station we boarded the train carefully. Boarding a train, especially at Sheffield station, is always done carefully in our family for obvious reasons.

We had arrived at Leeds in the snow. Ben was wearing green wellies and I was wearing an aqua-blue thick shirt and a patterned red tie. I have a clear image of how I was dressed that day because I have watched the television excerpt many times, mostly in horror at what I was wearing. I was nervous for more than one reason that day: I had been trusted with looking after Ben and, of course, I was talking on live television. These two things interacted and made the whole feeling that much more intense. My interviewer was Adrian Mills from *That's Life!* I remember how friendly he was and how nice he seemed before the interview, which was quite disconcerting. Ben hovered on the edge of the set. He was nervous for me, which in turn made me more nervous. I could see Ben's face just behind Adrian's left shoulder. I thought that Ben might need to go to the toilet. Adrian smiled my way.

'We'll be coming to you after the break. Let's have a go at the first question. OK, here goes. Why are first impressions in interviews so important?'

I glanced at Adrian; Ben moved slightly in the corner of my eye. I thought of first impressions.

'Well,' I said. But it didn't come out like that, it came out: 'W – We – We – We – We – We – We.' Then an 'um' and then an 'ah'. 'Well,' I said, getting the whole word out this time. Ben looked terrified. Adrian held his hand up.

'Excuse me for a second, Geoff; I'll only be a minute.' He vacated his seat and Ben walked slowly over towards me.

'Is it over already? That was really quick.'

I could hear Adrian talking to his producer: 'Nobody told me that he had a stammer. This guy can't talk.'

I could feel myself reddening. The producer told him to try anyway, it was too late for anything else, my presence on the show had been announced. Ben moved back to his first position, still in my line of vision, while the floor manager counted down: 'Three, two, one . . . action.'

Adrian smiled but I could read his fear; it was written all over his face. 'Right, Geoffrey.' I could hear a slight tremble in his voice and he started the question for the second time, this time live. 'Why are first impressions in an interview so important?'

'Well,' I said, 'because research suggests that we make up our mind about another person in a fraction of a second and then for the rest of the interaction we look for evidence to back up our preliminary conclusions rather than looking for any evidence to contradict or change it.'

This all came out fluently and without any hesitations whatsoever and with no hint of a stammer. Adrian's jaw dropped for a second time. My fluency astonished him; I could see Ben smiling still out of the corner of my eye. The interview itself lasted for seven or eight minutes and there was no sign of any anxiety in my voice, only in Adrian's. At the end of the live interview Adrian stood up and shook my hand.

'That was really good. But can I ask you something. You weren't taking the mickey out of me earlier, were you? Because I wouldn't appreciate that, it wasn't that funny.'

I explained that I wasn't taking the mickey and that I had an occasional stammer that would come and go of its own volition. I was not its master, it was mine. But it wasn't a joke on my part, I assured him of that. Ben ran up to me and we hugged as the studio cleared. This was a long time ago and here we stood at Sheffield station for a second time to board a train.

Ben can be quite moody before a race and to compensate I can be a bit too chatty. He always has to tell me to shut up. He wanted to plan this race, to think about it. I just wanted it to be over with. He meticulously planned the two days away for us both in Cardiff.

'We can walk to the hotel from the station and then it's a very short walk from the hotel to the start of the race.'

It was a bright autumn afternoon on the Saturday as the father and son strolled through the centre of Cardiff. I knew that he didn't like to train on the day before a race and he doesn't even like to walk about that much, but nevertheless I insisted that he accompany me to the shops to find a new running vest so that I would look good on the day. He did this without any visible reluctance or annoyance. It would have been easy to find a suitable running vest but I wanted the best, and a bargain. So we went into the shopping arcade and then out the back and down some narrow streets and down into basements looking for a running vest at a bargain price. I was amazed at his patience. I expected some sort of row but there was none. I couldn't find what I was looking for and we went back to the hotel empty-handed. Even though it was a fruitless journey, he still showed no annoyance. Part of his planning for a big race is to eat at a certain prescribed time on the day before. He likes to eat very early; I, on the other hand, like to eat quite late, which he says is indicative of either lack of planning or great stupidity. But I had already explained that there was no way I could eat dinner at 6 p.m., so we compromised and we found ourselves in a modern Italian restaurant, all glinting glass and black marble floors, at about 7.30 p.m. We could sense many of the diners staring at us – two men together. Ben commented that he thought that everybody imagined we were a gay couple.

'You can see it in their faces,' he said. 'Two good-looking guys dining alone, one older guy and one younger. They all think we're a couple, they're wondering what's going on here.'

And sure enough, as I glanced around I noticed that we were getting a lot of attention. I ordered wine, Ben ordered some water and we both sat there relaxed in our own way.

On the morning itself I woke up early, not because of any alarm call, but because of Ben loudly munching his porridge, bolt upright in bed. He likes to digest food three hours before the race, whereas I'm happy to gulp mine at the very last minute. We walked out of the hotel with our little bags over our backs past the sorry-sighted hen parties having one last smoke before making their weary way to bed.

Ben was disappointed that he wasn't allowed to start in the very first pen. It seemed to be only Kenyans or Welsh runners allowed into that particular area. The Welsh international footballer, Craig Bellamy, started the race. Some half marathons seem to last forever but this one didn't; there were lots of changes of scenery that made the time pass very quickly. In many races I have four or five thoughts that I can't get out of my head, but on this day I had only one. It concerned the role of emotion in directing intuitive thought, which is something I need to understand but feel that I currently don't. And that day, even after 1 hour and 36 minutes I felt that I was no nearer a resolution. I was almost disappointed to find myself crossing the line at the finish. I hadn't sorted out this idea. Ben wasn't there to watch me finish and I was disappointed at this because I was relatively pleased with my time, but when I did find him I noticed that he could hardly stop smirking. He had run the race in 1 hour 14 minutes. This was much quicker than I had ever managed. I mentioned my time to him and asked him what he thought of it.

'Not bad,' he said, and then he added laughingly, 'but you're no competition for me any more. I'm not even sure that you'd give my girlfriend a good race even over a half marathon!'

And we both laughed in a way that had more of a hint of attack and defence than ideally I would have liked.

11

Just Father and Son

Ben

I'm not sure why I chose Cardiff. To be honest, at first I wasn't even thinking about going with my dad. It was only after I'd asked him and he had agreed to go that I realised the significance of the trip. My last trip away with him on my own was probably about 1988. I used to go with him as he travelled the country appearing on TV. I definitely remember a couple of trips to Newcastle but the one that really stands out is Leeds in the snow. I only had a pair of green wellies with me. This caused great amusement among the presenters and production staff of the programme. Indeed, my commemorative script of the programme features the legend 'nice wellies' among the autographs.

I have an unusual relationship with my dad; hence the 22-year gap between trips away. Our conversations are more like those of two friends than a father and son. It's a lot better than it was, however; we went through a period where we hardly spoke. I disagreed with a lot of things that he did and I thought it was more productive to not speak to him at all rather than constantly argue with him. Recently our relationship has improved immensely. The fact that this has coincided with my taking running more seriously may be more than a coincidence.

Physically, I felt that I was fit enough to run fast. I read that it was a fast course and obviously this had something to do with my decision to do that race. My training was pretty much perfect: lots of steady miles and tempo runs, not much speed work but the reps at the track sessions tend to be short and fast, so I was getting some speed work in, at least in certain sessions. I managed to keep my mood in check in the days leading up to the race. This is one unfortunate side effect of my improvement in running. I get progressively tetchier in the week leading up to the race until I peak on the day before. It's best to say nothing to me at all the day before a race as I take any comment as a personal insult. This time I was fine. I think it was because I knew I had prepared fully. It's like an exam: if you do the revision, you go into the examination itself calm. If you haven't studied properly, then you panic. The main thing that I worried about in the run-up to the race was my dad.

One thing about my dad is that he is always late for everything and I mean everything: family meals, church and most worrying of all races. What I didn't realise as a child was that he was often late because he was out running. As my mileage has increased I have started to prioritise running over everything else. This means that now I am the one that is reliably late. This isn't true of races, however, where I like to arrive there at least an hour before the start. This gives me enough time to stretch, warm up and go to the toilet three times. I also like to spend some time alone before each race. It allows me to think about the race – split times, tactics, goals, etc. I enjoy this period as I can focus fully on what I have to do. My dad, on the other hand, turns up five minutes before the start and bombs off!

My preparation routine actually starts the night before the race. I have the same meal at the same time and go to bed by 10.30 p.m. at the latest. I've known my dad for 28 years and I have never seen him go to bed before 11 p.m. In fact, when I was a child I never saw him before 10.30 in the morning either. My worry was that my dad would want to eat late and then go out the night before the race, whereas I would want to be tucked up in bed. Initially I suggested six o'clock for the meal.

I knew this was never going to happen but I thought if I went in with a low bid, we would have some room for compromise.

As it turned out, after the meal at about 8 p.m. and the two glasses of wine, my dad wanted to go to bed at 10 p.m. I think the fact that he knew that I had set my alarm clock for six the next morning frightened him.

The weather on the day was absolutely perfect. It was sunny and still and cool. I managed to have my little focus period in the morning in bed. I didn't work out my splits exactly but I knew where I needed to be at key points. I knew the start would be fast and I went off well. I ended up in a group of 3 and we went through 5K in about 16.30, which would have been a PB. After about five miles I got dropped by the group. I realised that it would be hard to run the remaining seven miles on my own so I worked really hard to get back to the other two. I got back to them at about six miles but instead of going past them I stayed in behind them to let my legs recover from the effort. We weren't going particularly fast at this point and this was confirmed when I heard a group of about seven come up from behind. I tagged on to that group as they went through and we worked really well together. I took a couple of turns at the front and when the group broke at about 11 miles I was ahead of the rest. I knew then that I was going to run a big PB. I actually started to enjoy the race in the last two miles. As I crossed the line, a great sense of relief washed over me, which I think you can detect in the finish photos as I'm smiling at the end of 13.1 miles of hard running. This was tempered somewhat by the discovery later that the course was 193 metres short and the race, therefore, wouldn't count.

12

Worlds Apart

December 2010

It was New Year's Eve and I was sitting on a large bed with pure white sheets in a hotel on the Singapore River. I had just had my run – that is always the noun, as if I had just had my medicine or just had my dinner, as regular and as restorative as that and just as necessary. I sat on the bed to take off my running shoes. My feet hurt, or to be more exact, the base of my toes on both feet hurt. My suspicion was that my new running shoes were a little bit big for me but I had bought them anyway because they were discounted. This is one of my many foibles. My psychological understanding of this is that because my family were poor, I always look for a bargain and the passage of the years has not dampened this psychological pressure one iota, even though I have become moderately successful and could afford any running shoes I desire, a shopful of running shoes, if I wanted. The Saucony running shoes were size 9, US size 10; I take 8½. They felt comfortable, almost too comfortable, if that makes sense. They had a soft, cushioned sole, and I felt that I could run in them for miles but as yet I hadn't tried. The weather back in England had been too bad for them; the warm winds from the west that keep Britain relatively warm in the winter seem to have stopped and England was now frozen. I had been running in trail shoes on crisp snow on top of black ice that felt just like glass but without ever cracking. The trail shoes had, however, stopped me from falling and the Saucony road shoes lay untried except for short five-mile runs.

I stood up and I noticed that I had left a wet mark on the bed where I had been sitting. It was the exact shape of my behind. I had left the cold behind and run out along the Singapore River, past the bars and restaurants with the Alaska white crabs, the champagne crabs, and the Australian and New Zealand lobsters scurrying along the bottoms of the glass tanks at the front of the restaurants, the carp swimming delicately in the tank beside them, as they waited to be killed and eaten. I had passed a bar filled with men in pink shirts with loud voices in the banking district as I ran towards the Fullerton Hotel, the bankers having a few snifters before the night's festivities. I got as far as the parliament building before the skies opened. I would have said 'it was bucketing' when I was a kid, and that's how it seemed, as if the water were being tipped out of a bucket. Indonesian families hurried by in their sodden sandals and Chinese girls in tight hot pants, showing sheet-white thighs, stepped gingerly between puddles, carrying polka-dotted umbrellas. Two Sikhs in grey shirts and blue ties hurried along as the traffic sloshed past, and then stood there with me, where I was sheltering at the edge of a shop with raindrops cascading off my shoulders, my running shorts smoothly stuck to my thighs. Running along in my oversized shoes, the noise had been like a plunger that was being stuck to the floor with each step I took. One Indian man, with dyed black hair turning a vague orange, tried to engage me in conversation as the monsoon rain continued to fall.

'Have you heard of the Singapore Running Club?' he asked. 'I ran with them for 25 years. I was a guide for them.'

He had a gap in his front teeth and a notable paunch that drew my eyes naturally towards it. I wanted to ask him why he had stopped running. An inescapable feature of running is that you cannot disguise it. You could show me a photograph of myself from any day in the last 35 years or so and ask me if

I had had my run or not when the photograph was taken, and I could answer with absolute certainty and complete accuracy one way or the other. That's how dramatic the effects are. He couldn't draw me into a conversation about his great running history with that paunch. Not a conversation about running. It wouldn't have felt authentic. I suppose that's the point about real running: there's no way out; you can't retire and just move on with your life. This is your life; there's no escape. I shrugged in a wearisome way while simultaneously issuing a polite nod, more a signal that I had heard what he had said than anything else. I waited for the rain to lighten and then followed the man with the orange hair out from the shelter and down through the puddles. I passed him, saying nothing, trying to find the river again in the Lion City, so that I could find my way back to my hotel with that satisfied feeling inside, so that I could say, 'Yes, I have had my run, for today at least.'

The run the next day was slow but hard; it was far too hot for running. I ran along the Singapore River again, down by the parliament buildings and the statues of tall Englishmen carved in white marble, towards the hotel with the top floor in the shape of an ocean-going liner. Sweat was dripping into my eyes. There were no other runners about. Some people say that running gives them a great sense of communion with at least a section of their fellow men. A connection, shared experiences, shared suffering and knowing looks as we cross on our separate paths. But more often, it seems to me, it's about separation, vague looks of incomprehension, this heat, New Year's Day, so many other things to do. Why?

The following night I was on a plane again, in business class of course, thinking about running. Sometimes I think that it's no big secret, no great mystery. It's like we were made for this when we moved across the plains of Africa; this is what we evolved to do, not walking, not shuffling, not tiptoeing or driving or being ferried around. Running after things or running away from things, that's what made us. It's as simple and as complex as that. But I have known this for a very long time. I like to run in the evenings, at dusk, maybe when the animals from my evolutionary past were most vulnerable. I hate running in the mornings; that's why I would run all races at night if I were in charge of the world. I am simply not a morning person. I can talk in the morning but I prefer not to. It takes me a while to wake up and to become alive or to run. For me and for many others, one of the most truly unpleasant experiences is running first thing in the morning, before I am awake, before I am alive, but I do it when I have to.

I thought about my recent appearance on early-morning television. I need to feel that tightness in my face that comes after a run, so that when I laugh, which I do often, nothing moves. Lorraine Kelly, my host, introduces me: 'Well, Geoffrey, nice to see you again . . .' That was one of the first lessons I learned about live television: you have to feel comfortable in yourself. You have to be prepared and you have to feel ready so that when you see those fingers counting down 3-2-1 you don't feel as if you are ready to run. Smile, nice and tight, smile; feel that tightness. But that means that you have to get up around two hours before. So there I'd been in London, in December, when it was still dark with frozen pavements, putting on the Saucony running shoes and stepping outside the hotel without a word or a smile to anyone. In the mahogany-clad foyer of the hotel, the concierge smiled my way.

'A bit early for a run,' he said in a strong Eastern European accent. 'You must be keen.'

'Or stupid,' I said to myself quietly. I stepped out into the greying light; the traffic was already getting heavy. I made the first step. Was it Mao Tse-tung, quoting the philosopher Lao-tzu, who said that 'A journey of a thousand miles begins with a single step'? Perhaps Chairman Mao (or maybe Lao-tzu) was a secret runner, perhaps he was referring more widely than to the people's revolution, perhaps he meant the journey of life, a life of habit, maybe addiction and the ties that bind us. That first step that drove me here. That first step is always the most painful when your body isn't yet awake; you need to express that commitment to move, to run and to energise, ready for Lorraine, ready to smile.

'Don't rush me.' That's what my mum always used to say. It was always about drinking, and here I was, sitting alone in business class on a flight from Singapore to Brisbane, sipping champagne, with the stewardess hovering by my shoulder. I'd already had my run, of course, before I boarded the flight, down along the river again, stepping carefully between the remains of the streamers and the fireworks, the morning after New Year's Eve. One old Indian man was sleeping in the shade below a narrow bridge. I ran in a detour around him, being careful not to wake him.

I had no real hangover to get rid of, but if I had had a hangover, it would have been no great surprise. I've never tempered my social life for this life of running, rather the reverse: I drink because I run and more or less vice versa. Running purges the body, that's how it feels; it's the cheapest detox in the world. Last night it was just a few beers in Singapore, the high prices in the bars saw to that. Then 40 minutes into my run I could feel that my face had stopped wobbling and it felt tight again. That is the reward and the reinforcement I look for, the first hit, that tightness.

Now I sat sipping Moët & Chandon while the Indian air stewardess stood waiting impatiently for my glass. 'Don't rush me.' I could hear my mother's words. When I was a boy, drink was the great relaxer, the great reinforcement of the working class in the mill streets of Belfast, but only at the weekends. But as the '60s gave way to the '70s and then the '80s, and the fate of the common man and woman seemed to improve, the aspirational goals never seemed to change, rather they stayed exactly the same. People could now afford to drink during the week as well as weekends; they could drink and smoke to their heart's content. After all, you only live once, and for quite a short time too it seemed. My running, compulsive even then, set me apart.

'All that sweating,' my mother would say to me, 'it can't be good for you.' How would she know? As a child I had a dream that recurred in many forms and on many occasions. The dream would always involve me trying to introduce her to some sport. All the dreams had the same basic narrative: she was sitting in a haze of smoke and fumes, fumes of alcohol evaporating out of glasses, sitting with her friends on a Friday night, Big Minnie, Lena and Lily, Sadie Snoddy, and I would walk into that fug-filled room. My mother and her friends would all look my way, as if waiting for me to say something. There would be a pause, a long dream-like pause, full of unnecessary detail and objects with no apparent significance except that they were here, here in the dream, in this anticipatory build-up, in this pre-punchline position. In the dream I can almost feel the anxiety building up inside me and then my mouth opens and I say something, I make a suggestion. The suggestion is always something to do with sport: I am suggesting she take up some sport, and I am carrying something with me – a tennis racquet, a bat, running shoes, a squash racquet, a badminton racquet, swimming goggles (she couldn't swim). Sometimes it is very specific and at other times it is more generic, but I show them what's in the bag that I have brought with me and they all laugh at me.

'My Geoffrey wants me to start playing badminton. What the hell would I be doing running up and down a badminton court?'

And all these middle-aged women cramped in this tiny front room laugh loudly and physically, with their drink in one hand and their cigarette in the other, so that their great heaving laughter leaves a temporary pattern in the air, the trajectory of smoke stationary for a second or two in the ether.

I am enough of a psychologist to know that it is probably an anxiety dream, most are, with a bit of wish fulfilment (after all, I get their attention, which is better than being ignored). I wanted my mother to be fit and healthy, to live long, maybe to live forever, and that's where the anxiety comes in. But it was never going to be this way in real life, in the life beyond dreams. I did my sport (running, badminton, squash) and my brother, Bill, did his (rock climbing, mountain climbing, skiing, canoeing), and we assumed that she would never understand where our compulsions came from, or what the motivations were, or whether it was a good thing or a bad thing. She thought that running and rock climbing were both dangerous things, not natural, she would say, not natural. Why do you want to do that? They could both damage the body in different ways; that's what she felt. She was certainly right half the time, in Bill's case.

So I sat there on the plane sipping champagne, the stewardess still standing there to my left. 'Don't rush me,' my inner voice was saying. 'Don't rush me.'

The next day I woke up late. It was early evening in Auckland, 7 a.m. according to my body clock. I was staying in the five-star luxury of the Langham Hotel. As soon as my head had hit the soft, downy pillow early that afternoon I was asleep. I had spent the previous night on a chair in the business-class Emirates lounge at Brisbane airport. There are many worse ways of spending a night, sipping champagne until 4 a.m., with the champagne on tap, as much as you like, free of charge. But there are also many better ways of spending a night. I had stuck a pink Emirates 'Do not disturb' sticker to my forehead to amuse myself. But I was quite alone. The flight from Singapore had dropped me off at 1 a.m. and the flight to Auckland wasn't until 8.25 a.m., so I had a longish night with many snoozes. It felt like falling off a cliff and then a sharp awakening. I dreamt I was at an awards ceremony with Dermot O'Leary and Louis Walsh, when the host psychologist (not me) was attacked by a member of the audience, another psychologist, for selling out. I was just passing the stage. I had been washing my hands and they were still covered in a pea soup-coloured goo. Louis saw me and asked me what I thought of the comment from the member of the audience. So I started the defence of the psychologist, which turned out to be my own defence. I went on and on and on and on until Louis had to grapple the microphone from my hands.

And then I woke up with an abrupt shock, as if I were falling again. By the time I got to Auckland I was exhausted. It had taken five days to get here from the UK with only one day off at Singapore and more or less non-stop eating and drinking. Business class the whole way. I felt fat, semi-drunk and exhausted.

So I put on my running shoes and set off at 7 p.m. in that bleary-eyed state to find my way to a park, the Auckland Domain, with short sharp hills and Middle Eastern children playing baseball. My legs felt leaden, especially on the hills, but my face needed to feel tight again so I persevered for nearly an hour.

There was a 5K race the day after tomorrow in Hamilton near where the conference I was to speak at was being held, and I must say I was very tempted, but how long does it take to get over extravagant living like this?

13

Back Home

Ben

Running becomes an awful lot harder during the winter. Anyone can go out and jog around on a warm, bright summer's evening. It's when it's dark, raining and cold that your will to run is really tested. I was introduced to someone recently who is apparently 'a decent runner'. I asked him what his training was like through the winter months and he replied, 'I don't run during the winter as it ruins my trainers.'

I used to struggle hugely with the motivation to run when conditions were difficult. I think this has become easier as I've increased my training. If you're working to a set number of miles or a set number of sessions per week, it takes away the option of missing training. Everybody has that internal dialogue where you set out the reasons for and against going out. If you are committed to a training plan, it makes that dialogue irrelevant. You must go out so you just do it. If you don't, the 'runner's guilt' kicks in. This state of mind will be familiar to all runners. It's that heavy feeling in the pit of your stomach when you know you should have run but haven't. It manifests itself no matter what the situation. This is why so many runners train on Christmas Day and also why so many runners train through injury even if it exacerbates the problem. For the record, I always train on Christmas Day with the whole family because I enjoy it, and have caused many injuries to get worse due to my unwillingness to take a day off. Famously, Seb Coe always trained twice on Christmas Day as he assumed that Ovett would be training twice as well. This is another useful tool for motivating yourself to train. If you can convince yourself that your rivals are training twice as hard as you, it gives you that little extra kick up the backside. This works whether you are an Olympic champion or a local fun runner.

This winter had been a particularly hard one due to the weather. As Britain was basically frozen for most of November and December, it made conditions underfoot rather tricky. I managed to go out every day over the winter though, and although I've had a few injury niggles and fallen over a couple of times I've come through it relatively unscathed.

The new year started with my standard 'off work' two runs a day. My first run on New Year's Day was at about 9.30 a.m. I had a small hangover that I was trying to shift. I didn't see a single person on this run but when I went out for run number two later in the day people had finally roused. I ran past one couple and the man said, 'Running on New Year's Day, that's dedication!'

I wanted to stop and politely inform him that this was just a leg stretch and the real work had already been done when he was still in bed, but I didn't. You have to get used to a lot of comments from passers-by as a runner. I think in this country it's still seen as a deeply uncool hobby. In December I was running on a day when the snow was at its deepest. There was never any thought in my head of not running. On this one particular run I was called a mug (fair enough); a Paki (?); and a cunt (again fair enough). I was also snowballed mercilessly. I think it's seen as strange when a person willingly puts themself through pain to achieve something. People will often ask me why I do it. My answer is that I really do enjoy the running itself. I enjoy being on my own and I like the fact that I have time to think. Also there is no reliance on others for success. A friend was once trying to explain to me why his football is more important than my running (he's a Sunday league footballer). He said that if he plays badly, he lets the rest of the team down whereas if I run badly, it's only me who's let down. What he hadn't considered was that he could play badly but the rest of the team might cover his mistakes and so he would still win with the team, but his point was sound. I enjoy the fact that every aspect of my running is controlled by me. If I don't perform, it's my fault entirely. I have no coach, and any improvement I have made is down to the fact that I voraciously collect information on running performance and training in order to become a better athlete alongside the obvious training every day to exhaustion.

I don't just run to become a better athlete, however. A big reason that I train as I do is due to vanity. I am a vain person, I always have been. I like to be slim and I like the cheekbones that running has given me. If I don't run for a couple of days, I am convinced that I'm getting fatter. As a vain person, this is reason enough to train every day.

14

Types of Fear

January 2011

It was 7.35 p.m. on 4 January and I was sitting in a luxurious lounge looking out at Whale Bay on the western side of New Zealand. I had in front of me a pint of tap water, which I was sure was more or less pure New Zealand rainwater, and a Tuborg beer which I had dipped in the freezer. I intended to drink the water first and then the Tuborg, but at that exact point in time my will was weak. I had been back from my run for five minutes, maybe less. I ran down to Whale Bay to briefly view the surfers clambering over the black volcanic boulders for their evening waves, but the path stopped abruptly so I then turned back up to Wainui Road and the twisting, turning route into Raglan. The edge of the road was slanted and angled, and there were short, sharp climbs as I emerged from each blind turn. Camper vans loaded with surfboards, hand-painted in thick orange and black, and Toyota saloons from the 1990s brushed past me dangerously. I was the lone runner out at this time, as I ran past stationary campers with long-limbed girls brushing their luscious black hair in the evening sun, the men out for one last ride on the sonorous waves as the dusk threatened. The run was hard. I ran for nearly an hour but it couldn't even have been eight miles. I could almost feel an ache in my knees from driving the car down here, but more than that, I ached from the sun from my rooftop pool the day before. I never burn, but here I was, my feet, shoulders and arms reddened in odd angular patches where my enthusiasm to spray the sun cream obviously evaporated. I felt patchy and fat. I needed to run.

I had intended to do a 5K in Hamilton that night at 6 p.m. but although the distance from Raglan to Hamilton might have looked OK on the map, in reality it turned out to be very different. I was happy with my slow, restorative plod running past small unruly wooden huts, irregular and haphazard, the baches of Raglan sitting near the entrance to Whaanga Road Harbour on the west side of Te Ika-a-Maui (North Island). This place, it seems, has been inhabited for a thousand years by the Tainui people but many centuries later by the white missionaries, the settlers and the farmers they brought. It was a beautiful, quiet place and in the last century these people came and built their own houses, many out of crates, like tree houses or children's playhouses. Some were from the late 1940s and early '50s but some dated from much earlier, home-made beach huts in styles that defied regulation or convention, boat baches, a moon house, caravans without wheels. The moon house was owned by an ex-sailor who thought that it looked like Hugh Hefner's house from a '60s *Playboy* magazine. A hand-crafted *Playboy* hut, out on the bay of the whales, but with no bunnies.

I took in the scenery but moved steadily through it, this little hippy colony in this most mesmerising of places. I was the outsider. I kept moving as the middle-aged couples and the young romantics and those in-between sat watching for whales at dusk. Nobody even glanced my way.

There is something about running that is heroic. The young gardener from Tipperary was weeding around the red-hot poker flowers as the tui bird with the white fluffy spot on its neck picked delicately.

'You're not going for a run in this heat, are you?' he asked. 'Sure, it's the hottest part of the day. Have you seen those hills? I'd leave it till later if I was you and I'd run down the road; you can always run back up if you feel like it.'

I smiled back bravely and quietly.

It did feel heroic for a moment or two as I started my run. I stretched into my stride quickly and the momentum pulled me up the gravelly path, on Whaanga Road in Whale Bay. I climbed and I turned, blinded by dust from the four-by-fours, their drivers surprised to see anyone out on foot in the heat of the day, let alone running up here. I picked my way carefully across a cattle grid, tried to jump across a small river that crossed the road, and then there were sharper climbs and turns. This was the Te Toro gorge. I glanced to my right and I saw the Tasman Sea glistening in the sun. I climbed higher and higher. I'd got my first 5K next week and a half marathon the week after, when I got back to England, in York. It's called accurately the Brass Monkey. I had intended to run faster but was in a relaxed frame of mind that made me want to climb to the summit. The heroic explorer of how many centuries back, how many millennia, how far back? I was sure that this was the speed that we evolved to travel at and it felt comfortable. There was a lot in reserve for any eventuality. This was probably the speed that we ran at across those plains, carrying our spears. I felt like I could have gone all day like this but I'd got a 5K the next week and I didn't want to tire myself unnecessarily. My head overruled my gut instinct here, the great dissociated mind of the modern runner, maybe of the modern man, pulled in two directions at the same time, every temporary decision the transient conclusion of this push and pull. A major part of me wanted to get to the top of the gorge to see what was there, just over the horizon. This is the stuff of our deepest psyche, the deep-seated part of the brain, the hypothalamus and the ventricular formation. Our forebrains have grown up around these. The fulfilment of the hunt, first contact, first blood, then enshrined in more literate times in biblical legend, the promised land, the land of milk and honey, the land of plenty, just over the horizon, the end of the hunt. One of our most deep-seated instincts is to explore, but I have that modern mind with fragments of coaching manuals and good advice from a range of sources. I turned back down the gravelly track, and the gentle rain started to fall and the tui chirped in the trees, singing for ancient reasons that I will never understand.

The next day I ran up Whaanga Road again, staring out at the rippled blue Tasman Sea. The hills on the other side of the sea were still bathed in sunlight even though it was touching 8 p.m. I saw the odd flash of white, some small boat disturbing the endless blue of the bay. I climbed higher. A dog was lying in the middle of the road, rolling in the sandy grit, cooling itself, playing. It saw me and scrambled to its feet like some old servant caught out by its master, and moved towards me, head down and wanting to be patted, tail wagging. I stroked its head briefly then continued running. It followed me; or rather it led me up this twisty-turny road, checking that I was still there. It was old and thirsty, and one of its legs seemed a bit lame but its pack instinct forced it up the path this way. A four-by-four came hurtling down towards us, and instinctively I grabbed the dog by its collar and pulled it to the side of the road. I worried about my new friend's safety. I ran only half the normal distance so as not to tire the dog too much. I decided on doing 'efforts', as they called them at the club, at the bottom of the hill. The dog and I turned round; he looked grateful. I met some people at a gate and asked them if they owned the dog; they said they didn't and they were not sure who did.

'It lives somewhere on this sandy road,' they said. 'It lies in the middle of the road and all the cars go around it. It's very old.'

I went back down the hill and did four five-minute efforts. I had a 5K in two days and I needed to remind myself what fast running consisted of. Then it was back to my apartment and the cocktail hour.

When my children were young I would go for my run in Ibiza Town or on a Greek island or somewhere in southern Spain, and then I would sit out on the hotel balcony drinking maybe three, maybe four Bacardi and Cokes before drinking any water or soft drinks. It was my way of signalling what it was to be alive and enjoying myself. Part working-class Belfast, part the man who ran away, way beyond his roots. My children always called it 'the cocktail hour'. It was a lesson that was never passed on to Ben (until very recently). He is far too disciplined for a cocktail hour like this. Here in New Zealand I sat on a sunbed sipping a Tuborg. I could hear a wedding party from down the hill and the clatter of bottle bins full of empties being moved. The hubbub of intoxicated talk got louder and louder, the odd shriek coming from nowhere. I was in a good psychological state, almost tipsy, but not really from the beer, like a man who has had his drug, contented, alive and even happy.

I had a 5K race two nights later on the North Shore of Auckland. I had aimed to return my hire car that morning but apparently no pedestrians are allowed on the bridge to the North Shore, so it was either a two-hour bus journey or a fifteen-minute drive; so I kept the hire car and got nervous. I don't know what it is. People have often asked me whether I think that I could ever win a race, and when they do I wince slightly; there are few ideas further from my thoughts. Coming last in a race has always seemed like a distinct possibility, ever since I was a boy, but never winning a race. In those days I would gaze at my competitors with their thin white legs and their long shorts and think, 'Maybe today I'll come last.' In the school cross-country races there was always a boy like Solomon who would be last. Corpulent, rich, not bothered about running through nettles or mud. I sometimes wonder how many millions he's worth today. But, unlike Solomon, I was bothered, I could not feign indifference. In those days I started slowly enough to make coming last a real possibility. These days I start like a frightened hare; I have led the field in Chicago, California and Manchester, at least for the first 800 metres; fear drives me. I never think optimistically about running.

I was in New Zealand to talk about the individual psychological barriers to climate change and, coincidentally, I

Ben and Sam on a boat trip
on a family holiday to Turkey
in the early '90s.

Ben just after a race in South Yorkshire:
hard lessons early on.

Ben has just finished another race with a slightly worried look,
as if desperate to please.

A great running stride from the very beginning.

Father and sons – the hand on the shoulder says it all.

Ben aged ten in the Sheffield Fun Run (1993).

A caravan holiday with my mum in Wales. I'm stripped and ready for my run.

The cross-country team at Belfast Royal Academy. I am back row, second from the right, looking as miserable as the rest. I, however, had good reason: my father was not long dead and my life had now changed.

My first marathon (Sheffield, 1982), ten or so miles in.

Father and son just after the Sheffield Half Marathon (May 2011).

Just finishing the Sheffield Marathon (1986). I look as fresh as a daisy, but that's not how it felt inside.

Wilmslow Half Marathon (March 2011): the finish at last. (© Mick Hall)

Ben in the Horwich 5K (June 2011).

Ben in the Yorkshire Cross-Country Championships in Wakefield (January 2012). It never becomes easy. (© Susie Whitelam)

Ben in the Percy Pud 10K in Sheffield (December 2011). It was freezing cold. (© Susie Whitelam)

Getting used to the heat in Santa Barbara (September 2011).

Training in Santa Barbara for the Pier to Peak Half Marathon (September 2011).

Beach front, Santa Barbara: getting ready to set off on the hardest half marathon in the world (September 2011). A little bit too relaxed.

Crossing the finishing line of the world's most difficult half marathon. (© Mike Bauffard/Santa Barbara Pix)

Lining up for the Chicago Half Marathon (September 2011). The smile would soon fade.

Father and son warming down after the Sheffield Half Marathon.

had been researching whether optimism might be one of them. It had been claimed that optimists, quite literally and unconsciously, look on the bright side of life. Show them images of skin cancer on a slide with other images of the same size and similar patterns, and their eyes unconsciously move away from the melanoma to something with a better feel to it. Of course, for the past ten years or so there has been a boom industry in optimism training because optimistic people seem to live longer, they have better immune function, they are more responsive to health advice, and they are more likely to be careful about diet and exercise. But has it all gone too far? Do optimists refuse instinctively and unconsciously to contemplate the negative? In the case of climate change, do they refuse even to consider the awful possibilities? The polar bear stranded on the ice floe, the droughts in India, the tropical islands submerged under the seas. This was the subject of my new research as I monitored eye movements 25 times a second towards negative images of climate change, or positive images of nature, or towards everyday household objects. Optimists may have been blamed for missing the warning signs of the economic bubble about to burst and even 9/11; however, when it comes to negative images of climate change, their eyes seemed to fixate on them much more than do those of pessimists. Here they have it all, the right focus and the right mindset to do something about it. This could be important research because it might mean that we should be trying to make people more optimistic to get them to think about their individual contribution to climate change.

I focus on the negative too, but not in that sort of optimistic way. My ankle hurts and my shoulder. I may have lost the pounds from my business-class flight but I can feel where the paunch has been, a reminder of over-indulgence. I felt nervous. I scanned last year's times for this race. It was a small and select field; the winning time was sub-16. I scanned for finishers between 20.20 and 21.59 but there weren't any, and few after that time; I could be last.

I don't want to be a rose-tinted-glasses optimist, I want to be realistic but hopeful and I am in many domains of my life, but not when it comes to running. I just have this terrible fear of failure when the talking has to stop and you stand there exposed publicly. And I clearly do care because otherwise I wouldn't bother in the first place. But here I am, in my moments of anxiety and in my anxiety dreams imagining myself with a placard around my neck saying: 'His time was over 22 minutes for a 5K.' Optimism and pessimism are probably not a single dimension: you can be optimistic about some things but not about others. The psychologist Martin Seligman says it is all about how you explain the small events of everyday life. Put the good ones down to yourself and you stay optimistic, put the good ones down to chance or transient things, then you stay pessimistic. I don't think that I have ever put a good race down to my inner self, down to my skill and determination, down to my soul. Any good races, I have always assumed, are easy, short or both, or alternatively they took place a long time ago when I was young and life seemed easier. The problem with comparative youth is that it is transient; it is no good as an explanation because it leaves you with nothing to hang on to except fear.

I got a little flustered crossing the bridge from Auckland centre to the North Shore. Pedestrians looked surprised to be asked for directions and nobody was able to give me very good directions. One man said it was like Spaghetti Junction. One woman said to me, 'Hey, you're Irish, they're all like you. We went there last year. They preferred to stop someone rather than read a map.' I didn't know whether to find this flattering or insulting.

I found the race venue in good time, even though my car park ticket hadn't to begin with let me out of the hotel car park. I sprinted back to reception and got my ticket validated. Ben would have been appalled. Racing along the thick carpet of a five-star hotel foyer in a bit of a panic would not have been his idea of a warm-up. This hotel, the Langham in Auckland, by the way, is listed as one of the best hotels in the world: exemplary room service, more or less continuous folding down of crisp white sheets every time you leave the room. This is a setting not really conducive to hardship and pain. The previous weekend there had been a famous Bollywood wedding in the hotel. They had rented most of the rooms, and the groom, whose initials apparently began with a 'V', had helicopters flying in a V-shaped formation over the hotel and down into the grounds. It was that kind of hotel.

I was early for the race, however, very early. I had never been this early in my life before. It was just after 4.30 p.m. and the race didn't start until 6.15. I'd got nearly two hours to wait. I sat in the car sipping a bottle of New Zealand water and got very excited every time I saw a runner in a vest. My hopes rose as the runner approached and then fell as they continued on past the Northcote Tavern, which was where the race was to start from. Eventually I walked down to the tavern. It was just after 5 p.m. and the bar was dark, and full of men drinking and talking excitedly. The racing odds of horses were pinned up around the wall.

'I'm sorry to bother you,' I said to the waitress, 'but I'm looking for a race. Is the race on tonight?'

The waitress was friendly. 'As far as I know,' she said. 'They gather in the Rose Garden and then they run off and do their own thing. As far as I know, it's going to happen.'

I went outside and hovered just outside the Rose Garden. Two large New Zealand women sat in the sunshine drinking pints of lager, and they eyed me suspiciously. It was slowly dawning on me that the race might not be about to happen on this particular night, and it was almost too painful a thought to bear given that I had spent most of the day thinking and worrying about it. I refused to accept this intrusive thought. I walked around and around the building expecting to see some sort of gathering form, but I saw nothing except the odd lone runner mid-run, sweating profusely, and a few men walking their dogs. On my final circuit of the hotel, I saw a car with an old man with a pale-blue vest, and we made eye contact.

'Are you here for the race?' I asked delicately.

He nodded. It turned out that he was a regular at this particular race – indeed, he was to be next week's organiser – and he was as surprised as me that there was no race on that night. So much for the information superhighway; so much for the Internet. I had travelled across the entire globe for this race. He got out of the car slowly and his skin was stretched and saggy as if he had spent too many years lying about in this hot New Zealand sun. He suggested that we should run around the course together.

'But you are probably a bit too quick for me,' he said, looking for reassurance.

I was not, however, in the mood to give him any. We set off. He ran like a crippled dog, breathing heavily.

'I get this oxygen depletion very early,' he said.

His knees, it seems, had gone; all those New Zealand hills. As we ran along, between gasps he told me that he had been running for 55 years and that at one point in his career he could run a 10K in 35 minutes; now, he said, it was closer to 60 minutes but he was not prepared to give up.

'Perhaps I should become a walker,' he said, 'but I can't. They do a walk from this tavern every Monday as well as a run. The walkers go 15 minutes earlier but I can't bring myself to join them.'

The course descended quickly and we climbed up some rickety steps. If this had been the actual race, I would have hated those steps, but now I was looking for an opportunity to slow down to keep with him. I was now running on the spot at the top of the steps waiting for him; he was still breathing heavily and deeply.

'This has only happened in the past three years,' he said apologetically. He told me that he was considering the New Zealand Masters Championships in a few weeks' time; he was considering running in the 1500m.

'I don't actually think that there will be much opposition or competition in the over-70 category,' he said, and I could see him planning his race strategy as he hobbled along behind me.

We ran for a quarter of an hour, 14 minutes and 36 seconds to be precise, before I felt that I had had enough. I turned to him and shook his hand. I explained to him that I had to let my adrenalin out. I had come here for a race, not this. I sprinted off heroically – that word again – and I could feel him watching me and praying, maybe for a second, that time could maybe stand still. He would still like to run, he wasn't prepared to be a walker just yet, he was still quite prepared to just hobble along that course like an old dog, kicked and beaten by its cruel master who took enormous pleasure out of inflicting unlimited pain.

The next day there were some parents around the pool in the heat of the day. One wore a 'Dad we salute you' black T-shirt. What child bought him this? Parenthood is a weird concept. There were women with bodies ravaged by childbirth covering up until the last moment before dropping their bathrobe to the marble floor and submerging themselves in the pool. Fathers were chucking their kids about in a gleeful state before returning to their sunbeds, their job temporarily done, and then they would sit back and eye the talent around the pool.

I used to play a regular game with my children: I would give them a scale from 1 to 7 and they had to locate me on it. It was a scale measuring how good a father I was (their mother, by the way, always got a 7, invariably and without deviation). On this scale, '1' represented Fred West, the serial killer and rapist, indeed the father who raped his own daughter, and '7' represented my daughter Zoe's best friend Joanne's father, apparently the very personification of the caring, sensitive father that I never was, and a man whom I had never met. My children would put me on this scale somewhere between Fred West and Joanne's dad. Zoe would always place me somewhere between 1 and 2 and we would both laugh. It was our little safety valve, my little signal that I knew that I wasn't as good a father as I should have been. I was always out too much at the time, where 'out' is a state where the imagination of those left inside runs wild. Often I wasn't that happy when I was out, even when I was doing things that should have made me happy. But my children weren't to know that. I was away having fun, living it up, self-centred, selfish, out. And when I returned I would play with them for a short while, but then it was always time for a run. This run represented me going out again. Perhaps it wasn't that surprising that both Ben and Sam eventually came with me. If they wanted to be with their father, they had to run. But even when they came with me I still had to have 'my' run, one that tired me, otherwise it wasn't worth doing.

Ben told me only last year that once in the winter in the Peak District he had physically thrown himself into the snow, pretending to fall over, because he couldn't keep up with me but he didn't want me to leave him. And, of course, on another occasion I lost him. That night, I felt ashamed to my stomach, but I still wanted the two of us to run home, down past the grazing sheep, down through that dip in the hill with the gurgling mud that fills it and down through the coarse heather, back down to his mother who had always good sense. Ben got to do the ratings that night. I got a 1 that night from Ben. Me and Fred West both. Rapist, murderer, child abuser, addict.

Sometimes it amazes me the way that guilt can force its way to the surface at any moment (and I don't just mean the guilt about losing my son on a run). I store guilt the way that some runners store energy or others store fat. I think it is the emotion that drives me and controls me; perhaps it's my Ulster Protestant background. Carol is the same. When we were students sipping our *vin ordinaire* in the backstreet cafes in St-Tropez, I could see how she was desperate to be French. I would sit there toying with my wine and my Disque Bleu, with the soft feel of the packet, the smell of the cigarette, redolent of backstreet philosophy and the sophistication of

134

the cafes on the Boulevard Saint-Michel in the late afternoon, the smell full of existentialist glamour. I watched *The Roads to Freedom* on television long before I ever read the books and I was surprised when I did read them at how badly written some of them were. But the TV series gave me the feel of French life: the pursuit of the rational mind, the limits of rationality, and long, lazy afternoons of sex, talk, and physical and emotional bonding in an oddly existentialist, guilt-free time, together with the dreaded (to an Ulster Protestant) Catholicism with all that forgiveness thrown in. But for Carol and me, every time we thought of living a life like this the guilt-ridden, gnawing thoughts would commence, trying to chew their way to the surface. If you're a runner, however, guilt can be a good thing; it keeps you on the straight and narrow, on that long ledge without room to turn, without any space to change direction, to go back.

I glanced back at the man in the black T-shirt. He was still sitting there by the pool, engrossed in conversation with another man with spectacles and a grey beard. I realised that I had read his logo incorrectly. It did not read 'Dad we salute you'; it read 'And we salute you' – it was a tribute to AC/DC, not a Father's Day gift from a son or a daughter, from delighted grateful children, the sort of tribute that I would never get.

15

Even More Nervous

January 2011

I was nervous about another no-show. I caught the shuttle bus into central Auckland by the Customs House and walked down towards the viaduct on a bright, sunlit afternoon. Tonight it was O'Hagan's 5K run from an Irish bar on the viaduct itself. It had all the characteristics of the race of the night before. Show up on time, pay a few dollars and run along an unmarked road. I was not optimistic about the run actually taking place. I got there in very good time and there were no signs of any running vests, just serious drinkers in the late-afternoon sun. I got nervous. Am I racing in an hour or do I have to go on a solitary run along a viaduct in this busy, heaving place? But then I saw two runners walking along. One was blonde and clearly thin enough to be a runner. A short, pink cropped top, an exposed abdomen and rippling muscles. I went up to the two of them and politely said, 'Hi. Excuse me, but you look as if you could be runners. Are you here to do the race tonight? And do you know where you register?'

The blonde said that she was a runner but it was her first time here. I pointed out O'Hagan's to them and then I made my own way there. I went into the bar and saw all the runners registering in the far corner; and then I noticed something else. All of the runners looked incredibly fit, even the very thin one in the pink top. I moved quickly from anticipation to fear in an effortless slide. Was this the race that I would come last in after all these years? My anxiety wasn't helped by the organiser explaining that the course wasn't really marked: 'Just follow the runner in front unless you're first.'

I'm not so worried about being first as being so far behind the runner in front that I get lost. I enquire about this possibility.

'You can't get badly lost down here,' he said. 'You're in the centre of Auckland, for goodness' sake.'

The runners started to gather and my fear was not allayed as I watched the girl in the pink top warm up with some stick-thin man in a running vest emblazoned with 'New Balance'. Their strides were like those of galloping ponies. I felt that I had to run to warm up, so I shuffled off behind them and felt their long strides pulling them away from me, effortlessly and tirelessly, even in the warm-up. My fear level was rising. I went to the bathroom four times in the ten minutes before the race. I had been living the high life for the past few days or so. My expectations of a good time were very low. I would be happy with anything under the dreaded 22 minutes. I would be ecstatic with anything under 21 minutes. I enquired about the possible winning times to get some idea about the quality of the field and was dismayed to hear 15 minutes being mentioned. I think, 'This is a run from a pub, for goodness' sake; what's going on?'

We lined up and it was explained to us that we must take care because we were going to be running through Auckland traffic. The hooter went and the two galloping ponies headed off in the middle of the road, in the face of heavy oncoming traffic, weaving in and out of the cars without any apparent fear. I followed them desperately. It felt weirdly like a frantic club run, having to cross roads with cars whizzing past so that you didn't get lost, almost like Sale Harriers on a Tuesday night, except here we were running in bright white sunlight. I had no idea of where I was going, so I desperately clung on to the man in front. Then I passed him and got even more worried. The girl in the pink top was already out of sight, in every sense. The final 600 or 700 metres were even worse than the start. A car nearly hit me, the driver tooted loudly, I made an obscene gesture back, and then I turned the corner. I was not exactly sure where I had to stop running so I just guessed, but then I glanced at my watch and it read 20.46. I was delighted. The girl in the pink top ran the course in 14.59, a new female course record.

Then it was back to the pub for the prizes. The girl in the pink top was presented with three bottles of New Zealand wine and I wondered how long it would take her to drink all of it. On my current form it would probably take me three nights, maybe less. It turned out that the girl in the pink top was Kimberley Smith, the star of New Zealand long-distance running, Olympian, and record holder for the 5K, 10K and the half marathon – and I had said to her, 'You look like you could be a runner . . . ' Funnily enough she didn't say anything back about this.

After the prizes, I went for dinner on the viaduct itself, overlooking the yachts. The buildings had a pale sheen in this white light; the colours were vibrant like in a magazine, as if doctored to fool the senses. It was as if I was on a high, all senses heightened, like some great blinding trip; it was all white light, white heat. My body had managed to manufacture all of this quasi-psychedelic experience from its own natural resources with no unnatural stimulants or psychotropic substances. I talked quickly and excitedly. It was a feeling like mania. On the way back I helped a Korean woman carry her pram onto the shuttle bus; I was in that sort of mood to help my fellow man and woman, my empathetic sense primed. All of this because of 14 seconds (below the 21-minute mark); it was a very peculiar thought. How can such a short interval produce such a dramatic change in mood, perception and character? What emotions are tied up to this great desire maybe not to run faster, but at least not to slow down? What emotions indeed? It was a weird and wonderful thought. The whole thing was like discovering the doors of perception,

without Aldous Huxley as the guide. I was finding it myself –
me and millions of others, that is.

It was now the morning after my latest race. I sat by the
rooftop terrace pool basking in the sun. As soon as I sat down
the friendly young man in grey polo shirt, black shorts and
grey cap brought me some iced water and a small tray of fresh
fruit. To say that I felt spoiled is an understatement.

I had just done a telephone interview with the *Wall Street
Journal* on the subject of handshakes. Chevrolet had asked
me several months earlier to come up with a formula for the
perfect handshake. It was purportedly done to train the sales
staff to execute the perfect handshake, but in reality it was
just a PR story to draw attention to the brand and a new sales
package that they were introducing with a longer guarantee
on their cars. I had already been reading the psychological
literature on handshakes for my new book, *Get the Edge: How
Simple Changes Will Transform Your Life*, so all I did really
was to combine all of the factors that contribute to the
perception of a handshake into one neat formula for optimal
effect: the vigour, the firmness of the hands, the completeness
of the grip, the dryness and texture of the skin, etc. The
formula that emerged came out something like this:

$$PH = \sqrt{(e^2 + ve^2)(d^2) + (cg + dr)^2 + \pi\{(4<s>2)(4<p>2)\}^2 + (vi + t + te)^2 + \{(4<c>2)(4<du>2)\}^2}$$

where PH is perfect handshake; (e) is eye contact (1 =
none; 5 = direct); (ve) is verbal greeting (1 = totally
inappropriate; 5 = totally appropriate); (d) is Duchenne
smile – smiling in eyes and mouth, plus symmetry on
both sides of face, and slower offset (1 = totally non-
Duchenne smile, i.e. false smile; 5 = totally Duchenne);
(cg) is completeness of grip (1 = very incomplete; 5 =
full); (dr) is dryness of hand (1 = damp; 5 = dry); (s) is
strength (1 = weak; 5 = strong); (p) is position of hand
(1 = back towards own body; 5 = in other person's
bodily zone); (vi) is vigour (1 = too low/too high; 5 =

mid); (t) is temperature of hands (1 = too cold/too hot; 5 = mid); (te) is texture of hands (5 = mid; 1 = too rough/ too smooth); (c) is control (1 = low; 5 = high); (du) is duration (1 = brief; 5 = long).

I had devised this formula one Sunday night back in Sheffield and checked it with my son Sam and one of his friends. I wanted to be sure that all the scientific notation made sense, so I made them execute one handshake after another until I felt like I had got it right. It seemed like a very informal way to come up with a scientific formula, but it was really my check on everything that had been produced and published so far. The inclusion of pi was a little bit over the top. I thought that the variables 'strength' and 'position of the hands' needed multiplying by some constant of around 3, so to dress the whole thing up, instead of saying 3, or approximately 3, I came up with pi. It was one of those things that you regret almost immediately after you have done it, especially when someone in an interview asks you how scientifically you came up with the exact figure pi in this precise formula. But it had done the trick. The story ran around the world and I got to talk about the science behind the whole thing with any journalist who was interested, and again draw attention to the power of non-verbal communication in everyday life. The rest of the journalists who had picked up the story just quoted the formula or said that a formula had been devised.

The *Wall Street Journal* wanted to talk to me because some people in New York were going for the Guinness World Record on the longest handshake ever produced (something like 15 hours). There were no breaks allowed in this handshake, including toilet breaks. The journalist sounded incredulous: 'And they're not even allowed to wear diapers,' she said.

It had never occurred to me that someone would want to wear a nappy while engaged in the longest handshake ever recorded.

'But,' she added, 'they are allowed to wear latex gloves.'

It was going to be hard to weave the formula into the story. My suggestion was that the perfect handshake has approximately three shakes, so how many shakes would have to be shown in a 15-hour marathon handshake? Or, if we make up our mind about another person on the basis of the minimum of human physical contact, like three shakes, what happens to interpersonal perception when you have 15 hours to look at the other person, think about them and then draw your conclusions? I wasn't optimistic about the connection being made but the journalist thanked me profusely.

A 15-hour handshake might seem like a pointless activity, but was there any more point in what I was doing? The 10K that I did the previous night was very informal; they only recorded the times of the first 3 runners. I was 10th in 44.28, but it was surprisingly hilly and incredibly hot. The course was not marked, yet again, and I got lost for short periods of time on all three laps. My concentration does wander, I'm afraid. My legs were tired that day. But that night, as if to celebrate, I went back down to the viaduct to recapture the mood of two days previously and drank a lot of wine, but without success; 44 was OK but I was hoping for a lot better. It didn't feel like any kind of a trip that night.

I was contemplating the Wild Turkey Off-Road Half Marathon on the Saturday, but every runner had to carry a knapsack with them at all times packed with essential first-aid and emergency supplies. It would have been a spectacular race, but the idea of buying all of this stuff, bandages, aspirin and malaria tablets, just put me right off. I had settled instead for a 5K or a 10K on the Sunday. I had a half marathon the following Sunday back in England with Carol and Ben. So, as usual, my training was neither particularly focused nor directed. As long as I do something, I feel OK; I don't keep a running diary in the way that I once did. It all seemed too OCD then. I had even started tidying the cushions in those days in the front room of our house looking for symmetry and order; I couldn't leave the house until all of the cushions were perfectly straight and in position, the very roots of obsessive compulsive disorder. Years later, when I became the most untidy person in the world, I tried describing this early inclination to others but it always seemed unbelievable to them. I had broken the spell. Maybe that's why I'm not obsessed with weekly mileage the way that some runners are, or why I don't even possess a running diary. Maybe it reveals more of the kind of person I have become. Maybe the idea of the diary reminds me too much of the person that I could have become, somebody locked in obsessive ritual who needs to draw protection from the orderliness and the sameness of their actions, time and time again, instead of someone who likes to risk everything by throwing pi into a formula even when it's not necessary, even when it's not called for: Mr Risky, Mr Unpredictable. What time would I run the 5K or 10K on the Sunday? Who knows? Maybe that's the attraction. Maybe I like surprises.

16

Winners and Losers

January 2011

How good would it feel to win a race, to actually win a race, to beat the field, to destroy the opposition, to be first? I'll tell you how good it would feel: it would be indescribable, better than anything else that has ever happened to me, like giving a single short talk for tens of thousands of pounds, or winning a major prize for my work, or hearing myself being described as 'brilliant', 'a genius' or 'a visionary thinker'. It would be the best thing in the world, but could it ever happen to me without me having to cheat? Perhaps if I picked my race carefully enough, it could happen. That's what many runners seem to do, they pick their race carefully. They study the results of hundreds of races to see where they would have finished. I am no exception and neither is my son, Ben. He wanted to run the Kassel Half Marathon only because he thought he could win it. But there's always the danger that others have spotted that this particular race has a relatively slow winning time and so have decided to enter it as well.

I studied the form book in New Zealand and realised that there was one race in which, if I did do a great time, then I could be placed in the top three, maybe even better. The winning time in 2010 in the first race of the series was 20.29 for the 5K and 36 for the 10K. The 10K would be too fast for a top-three placing but, fingers crossed, assuming that others hadn't noticed, the 5K might not.

So I entered for this race and early one morning I found

myself crossing the bridge to the North Shore of Auckland for a second time, and glancing back at the steel-grey colours of the Sky Tower and the shimmering greyness of Auckland at dawn. I was nearly the first there, that's how keen I was, in a secretive and quiet sort of way. The running nobody who, nevertheless, held secret aspirations that he would never discuss. I weighed up each of the competitors as they arrived, like a prizefighter. This was going to be a race with only one winner. I had never been in this psychological state before. I wasn't going to be running against the clock, I was going to be running against them. And every time I saw the sinewy, muscular build of a good club runner my heart sank until I reminded myself that there was a simultaneous 10K. There were quite a few fun runners and that made me happier. The bigger the bottom, the better, I was thinking to myself.

We were called to the start, which was going to be on a narrow bridge across a lake. A good start was crucial so I asked the man from the Mizuno tent which direction the race set off in. He told me that it went up the hill at the start, so I walked slowly behind the fun runners waiting to be instructed to turn round at the last minute. The call never came so I panicked and tried pushing my way through the crowd on the narrow bridge, which was completely congested.

'Introduce yourself to the person next to you!' screamed the announcer. 'Wow, give yourselves a pat on the back! Wow, this is going to be a great race! Wow!'

I was panicking, and then we were off. I crossed the mat a while after those in pole position and started my watch, but nothing happened. I was going to be racing blind without any timing instructions. The course undulated with many sharp turns but my heart was also racing. I didn't want to lose sight of what I could achieve here. I passed some runners, and then some others. I counted maybe 10 or 12 in front on the turn but this, of course, was a simultaneous 5K and 10K. There was no need to panic. I came running down the slight hill at the end and I could see the white finishing post. In bold, dark letters it read 'FINISH', clear and unambiguous. My heart was pumping. I could hear the announcer: 'Here comes the leader of the 5K, Geoff Beattie.' It was a lifetime of dreams fulfilled in just one moment. I dipped under the finishing arch, like Emil Zátopek, like Gordon Pirie, like John Walker. I had done it, after all these years. I had actually done it. I was the hero.

But the race organiser ran up to me, red-faced and puffing. 'That's not the finish,' she said. 'You have to do that little loop around the lake.'

I stood there, my mouth open. 'What?' I exclaimed.

'You haven't finished yet, you have to run round that little loop; you need to get going.'

To say that I was stunned would have been an understatement. I was shocked, bewildered, I couldn't get my legs to move at first, and then I did. I could see in this loop several other runners, now in front of me. I ran, swearing, cursing, and finished bewildered and forlorn. I was hardly able to talk.

When they read out the results, they read out my name in first place and then corrected themselves. I was put down as 6th with a time of 21.31, presumably my clock time because I had gone over the mat on my shorter course. That could have been my day. I felt emotionally flat for at least one week afterwards. After all, when you have a dream, a dream that you might not even like to admit to, and you can see it materialise right in front of you, and then it's taken away from you at the last minute, you do feel flattened. That's the right descriptor. I was flattened by it.

When I told Ben about this afterwards he just laughed, but not in a cruel way. I think that he may have really felt for me. At least, I hope he did.

17

Dedication

Ben

I keep a training diary and record everything in it: the miles, the weights, how I feel and any distractions. This is one week of my life as a runner. This week was abnormal only because I went over the 100-mile mark. Throughout the year I ran over 10 weeks of 90 miles plus and many, many more of 80 miles plus. These figures are not huge for a distance runner but at the time this was new territory for me. This particular week was immediately preceded by one of 80 miles with a race on the Sunday and followed by a week of 83 miles, again with a race on the Sunday. This means that the mileage was significantly reduced on the days leading up to the races on both occasions.

> 21–27 February 2011
> Monday
> **a.m.** 2.5 miles to work easy with heavy rucksack. Legs OK.
> **p.m.** 10 miles @ 7-min. mile pace. Lighter rucksack, legs had stiffened and got a bit cramped. Took it easy and loose stride.

If you want to be a distance runner and run decent mileage, you must run to work. Otherwise you have no time to do anything else.

Tuesday
p.m.   4.5-mile warm-up to track.
Session   Bondarenko session of 4 times 2 km with Hallamshire Harriers.
5-mile warm-down.

Wednesday
a.m.   5.5 miles to work easy with rucksack.
p.m.   9.5 miles @ 6.58-mile pace. Kept it nice and easy, faster than I wanted but legs felt good.

Thursday
p.m.   5-mile warm-up to track.
Session   1,000 metres, 900 metres, 800 metres, 700 metres, 600 metres, 500 metres, 400 metres (recovery 200 metres).
5-mile warm-down.

Friday
a.m.   2.5 miles to work with heavy rucksack.
p.m.   8 miles easy @ 6.57-mile pace.
Gym   Arms, stomach, chest, squats (sore).
p.m.   2.5 miles home with heavy rucksack.

Saturday
a.m.   8 miles @ 7.34-mile pace. Was going to do hill reps but legs were too tired.
p.m.   7 miles @ 6.02-mile pace. Form was good.

Sunday
a.m.   18.65 miles @ 6.48-mile pace. I got home from a party at Bradwell after 3 hours' sleep. My left glute was very tight.

My girlfriend Jo and I had been to a party in a converted barn in Bradwell on the Saturday night. We had a few drinks but went to bed at a reasonable time. The DJ at the party played his terrible music all night to the one person who had enough drugs to want to dance. Our dormitory was directly below the party room. At one stage I tried to convince Jo that I was sober enough to drive us home at 5 a.m.

After getting three hours' sleep, I woke up before the rest of the guests and decided to run home. It was hilly, windy and hard but was far preferable to staying at the party.

Week total   101.85 miles

18

First and Last

Ben

I've travelled to almost a hundred races with my dad over the years. At every race we have ever been to together we've had exactly the same conversation. As we arrive at the start he will size up the competition, turn to me and say, 'I could be last today.'

He would rather see rotund middle-aged women in deely-boppers shuffling around than a group of primed East Africans warming up and raring to go. The fear of coming last has always been at the forefront of his mind. It consumes him. It's easier for me now. I still get the fear even now, but I know it's unlikely. In road races I'm always up towards the front; in the first couple of per cent of finishers. However, I can now say that it was me and not my dad who finally succumbed. It was me who came last. It was my first ever track race.

I was travelling with a group from my new running club, Hallamshire Harriers. There were four of us in the car. I'm the slowest but was not overly worried. I had quit a club where I was comfortably the fastest runner to join a club where I was only just inside the top ten. I knew that I had to train with faster runners to become a better runner. This is especially true of sessions. Easy, recovery runs are fine on your own; in fact they are better on your own. If you run your easy workouts with someone else there is always the temptation that you will want to push the pace, to test yourself against your partner. Runners by their nature are super-competitive. You have to be. You must have this burning desire to continue to improve, to never be happy, to always find fault. By running your recovery runs too hard, you simply don't recover in time for your next race or session. Sessions are far easier in a group, though. Of course, it is easier to pace yourself against other people; however, the real benefit of sessions in a group is the shared sense of pain. The feeling that if other people are going through the same agony, the collective will can drive you to finish what you started. The rest of my training group had decided to do an open 3000m race and asked if I wanted to join them, so we drove to the BMC meeting at the Stretford track in Manchester.

There was an A and a B race with the A race aimed at sub-9-minute runners. I knew I wasn't in sub-9-minute shape. At best I was hoping for 9.15. I knew I could hit 3.05 minutes per kilometre on the track but that was not going to get me round 3K in under 9 minutes. I told the rest of the group that I was planning to do the B race, but they wouldn't hear of it.

'They'll be loads slower than you in the A race,' they said. 'Everyone lies about their time.' They were very persuasive and they all seemed to agree that it was vital for me to get into the faster race. I was persuaded that it would drag me round to a faster finishing time.

We arrived at the track and the first person that I saw was Andi Jones. Andi Jones has earned a large number of GB vests and competed in numerous major championships. He was the first English finisher at the 2010 London Marathon. I actually read his blog every week; he's a bit of a hero to me. This made me incredibly nervous. We entered the stadium and registered for the race. As instructed, I entered the A race. We went out to the track to change and warm up, and it was then that I saw GB international number two: Jenny Meadows, Great Britain's current number-one 800m runner and a world-championship medallist. At that point, I went to the toilet. I came back out to the track and then saw Tom Lancashire – Beijing Olympian and top 1500m runner. I went to the toilet again.

Eventually we were called over by the starter. He had a list of the runners for the A race. I silently prayed that I would be missed off the list. At that stage I didn't just want to run in the B race, I wanted to run away! The starter went through the list and I heard the name of Andi Jones plus a number of other top domestic runners. In all there were 27 names. Mine was read out last. It had to be more than a coincidence. We toed the line and I stood at the back of the pack. This wasn't pessimism or defeatism; this was common sense, self-preservation. I knew at that point that my aim was just to not get lapped.

The gun went and immediately I was last. My training partner was just in front of me but it was clear that it was going to be a hard night. I can honestly say I have never felt so exposed in my life. The crowd was small, maybe a couple of hundred people, but I felt that every eye was on me. It sounds ridiculous – why would anyone watch the back of the race rather than the real athletes at the front? – but I couldn't shake the feeling. I felt like a fraud. I was off the back and running completely on my own.

I didn't find the race itself that hard; 3000m is only 7½ laps of the track. It flew by. I just couldn't shake off the feeling that I shouldn't have been there in the first place. These were people that I look up to, these were people that I read about, I copy their training schedules, I idolise them. With about three laps to go came the sudden, beautiful realisation that I wouldn't be lapped. The gaps thankfully weren't getting any bigger. I was no longer focusing on my time but just aiming for the one runner in front of me that I thought I could catch. He gradually seemed to be coming back towards me as the laps continued. Finally, with just 300 metres to go, I caught him. As we went round the bottom bend he looked round and saw that I was on his shoulder and he promptly . . . stepped off the track. My only chance of not being last was gone. To give up with 300 metres to go made no sense whatsoever; I can only think it was the shame of losing to me that drove him to it.

There was no sense of shame at the finish. The time was probably about 10 seconds down on what I wanted but you could put that down to the fact that I ran the whole race alone. I stepped off the track and that was it. My greatest fear in athletics had materialised and I was none the worse for it.

Out of interest, I would have won the B race.

19

Success in Germany, but Relative

Ben

A lot of people would think it strange that a man approaching 30 years of age would willingly go on holiday with his parents. But I am such a man. I can't remember where the idea came from for me to go to Kassel. My mum and dad had been for the last three years with Sale Harriers. They arrange an exchange with a German running club every year where a group comes over to run the Wilmslow Half Marathon in March, and then the return leg takes place in May at the Kassel Half Marathon. I had taken a sneaky look at the results from previous years and knew that I would feature quite high up in the race.

I hadn't been away with my mum and dad for about 12 years and had never been without my brother and sister. In the intervening years I had been on lots of holidays with friends and girlfriends but there was always something different about holidays with my dad. Like many self-made men from a working-class background, my dad is what you might call careful with money. As children we never missed out on anything but if ever there was a chance to save money, my dad would take it. Indeed, he used to boast that he had never bought anything that wasn't in the sales. We had a foreign holiday every year as children, usually to Greece or Spain; however, we would always go for allocation on arrival. This money-saving technique led to some very interesting holidays.

The one that I remember most vividly was to a resort called

Perama. It would appear that I have at least managed to repress the memory of where exactly Perama is although the other details remain etched on my consciousness for all time. We arrived in the middle of the night and fortunately the darkness masked the true horror of the place. Unfortunately, when the morning came it was all too clear that we were in the middle of nowhere. There was literally nothing for miles around but a huge power station. As is his wont, my dad decided to go for a run to check the lie of the land the first day. This was pretty standard on a family holiday. My dad would go off on his own on the first morning. He would run around the resort and find the beach, the nice-looking restaurants and any other points of interest. Perama certainly had at least one point of interest: my dad returned from his run to inform us that he had found a dead body! While he was running he had entered a dried-up river-bed and come across some large shape under a white sheet with the unmistakable sight of blood seeping through the white linen. He immediately rounded up not only us but also the staff and most of the guests of the apartment block that we were staying in. There is something in my dad's character, some infectious quality that makes people want to follow him and listen to him. Within 5 minutes he had rounded up a posse of about 20 people. We decamped to the river-bed and sure enough there was the sheet with the shape protruding from underneath. There was no doubting either that it was blood that was seeping out. That metallic reddish-brown colour, like a deep rust. My dad had a self-satisfied look on his face as a murmur went round the group. He had indeed found a dead body in the middle of nowhere. Nobody seemed to know what to do next. Finally, my dad took charge of the situation, as he tends to do. He picked up the longest stick he could find and walked slowly over to the sheet, and the completely motionless shape that lay underneath it. Slowly, very slowly, he manoeuvred the stick under the sheet and gradually lifted it away from whatever it was concealing. The silence was deafening. After what seemed like minutes, he finally flicked the sheet away and there was a huge dead . . . dog, a Rottweiler with a broad back, almost identical to that of a human being.

This story was to be repeated a number of years later in slightly more worrying circumstances. I visited Barcelona for a long weekend with a friend, and by this point I had taken on the mantle of the running reconnaissance man. It was early evening and I was going for a run to get our bearings as to where we were in the city when I literally tripped over another shape under a white sheet. Once again the sight of blood seeping through was quite unmistakable. However, this time it wasn't a dead dog but a young immigrant man who had been stabbed to death just minutes before. At that moment I decided that running in Barcelona might not be the best idea and that the Lonely Planet guide to Barcelona may have been overly kind with their description of our hostel as 'authentic'.

The trip to Kassel was far more relaxing. In fact, my worries of being forced into vigorous sightseeing activities the day before the race proved completely unfounded. We were staying with a host family in a huge rented house, and they left us alone to do what we wanted the day before the race. This consisted of sitting in the sunshine in the garden and going for a short run. It really did feel like a holiday!

My main worry the day before a big race is food and drink. I have a certain nutritional regime that I like to stick to – PSP: porridge, soup, pasta. Make these your three main meals the day before a race, don't eat until you're overly full, and drink as much water as you can, and you won't go far wrong. In fact, it's a pretty good system to stick to all the time. As a distance runner running between 80 and 100 miles per week, I am always hungry. The temptation is always there to stuff your face. Not necessarily with bad food; in fact, I don't really like junk food any more, but just huge portions. The motto should be: 'Never hungry, never overfull'. The evening before the race we went to a traditional German bar to receive some traditional German hospitality. This consisted of the majority of the travelling party sampling the local beer in vast quantities and a German buffet. This, it turns out, consists purely of fried meat and bread, which wasn't ideal, but as I wasn't particularly hungry anyway, I had a small plate to be polite.

The build-up to the race was pretty much perfect for me. We arrived early thanks to the punctuality and efficiency of our hosts. As someone who hates to be late and likes to be organised to the nth degree, I found this particular national trait very comforting. I managed to find some time and space to complete my warm-up on my own. This time is very important to me. I like to try to focus my energies and mentally run through the plan for the day. When I got to the start line I noticed for the first time how warm it was. I was only in a vest and shorts and I was sweating just standing around. It was before 8.30 a.m. and the start line was shaded by trees. I was glad at this point that I had done a lot of training in the hottest part of the day during the mini heatwave that we'd experienced in early spring. There was a lot of media walking along the start line, interviewing the local runners. I started to panic as they made their way along the front row towards me. I weighed up my options: drop back and lose my place in the front row, or try to conduct an interview in German with the only phrase I knew that a friend had texted to me: 'In Sheffield man kann ins Kino gehen.' I wondered to myself whether the public of Kassel would be interested in the location of cinemas in cities in the North of England. I thought maybe not, so I went for option three: keep your head down and don't look up. It worked and we were ready to go.

The gun went off and I started fast as usual. I was in a group of four with three runners from the local club, PSV Grün-Weiß. We went through the first kilometre ridiculously fast in about 3.05. My theory was that they couldn't maintain that pace but they were just trying to break me early to get all three podium positions for the club. This was backed up by the fact that they had a coach with official accreditation on a pushbike following them and shouting instructions. He seemed to be shouting at me at different points but I just gave him my patented blank look in response. I got dropped after about four kilometres. The pace had slowed but it was still too fast for me. I knew it was going to be a long, hard slog on my own. It was very hot by now, in the high 20s, I think. We were in an industrial part of town. I remember thinking how nice and clean the town was. Even in an area of heavy industry, the road surface was lovely and the buildings were spotless, unlike the filthy, charred, abandoned steelworks that I run past daily in Sheffield. I had been told by our host that there was one long hill at about 5K. I couldn't identify it, though, as we seemed to be climbing constantly. I had been told that the crowds were huge around the course but at this point I was literally alone. The group ahead were fast moving out of sight and there was nobody around; not even marshals.

I got to halfway on target. My plan was to run two 35-minute 10Ks and then I would have 4 minutes to run the last 1.1 kilometres. As the first half had all been uphill, I thought a negative split was not only possible but probable; however, although the second half was mainly downhill, it was all run on huge, wide roads with no respite from the sun. I realised I was starting to overheat as it was now absolutely boiling hot and I couldn't get a drink because it was sparkling water at all the stations. Now, I don't like sparkling water at the best of times but when you are running at your limit in 30-degree heat for 13 miles it is absolutely disgusting. My pace had definitely dropped and I had stopped looking at my kilometre splits. The intense heat continued until we got back into the park where the race had started. I was still in fourth and hadn't seen another runner for about three miles. As I got back onto the flat in the shade of the park, however, I saw a shape in front of me. It was the third of the PSV runners and he appeared to be struggling. Whether it was cramp or an injury, he seemed to be coming back and I was reeling him in fast. I went straight by so he didn't have a chance to latch on. I tried to give him some encouraging words but my bone-dry mouth would only stretch to a barely audible grunt. I knew then that third was mine and I really enjoyed the finish as the crowds, and the noise they made, were incredible.

As soon as I finished the race I went back to the finish to watch my mum and dad come through. Hindsight is a wonderful gift but I had an ominous feeling already that something was not right. My dad came through and for a while I calmed down. He looked exhausted and dehydrated but he was OK. I knew my mum shouldn't be far behind. As the time ticked closer to 1.50 the ominous feeling in the pit of my stomach turned to all-out fear and despair. I knew something was wrong. Other members of the Sale Harriers party continued to filter through the finish and told us that they'd seen my mum out on the course and that she looked fine and was running well, etc. They told us we must have missed her coming through. I knew this wasn't the case. All I could think about was her out there on the course on her own. Eventually, after using one of our hosts as a translator, we managed to track her down to the first-aid area. She looked incredibly frail and weak but the look on her face was one of shame rather than self-pity. By this point I was visibly upset and all she kept saying was how sorry she was.

I had seen this happen to my mum before. In 2004 she was running the Sheffield Half Marathon for the first time. I was living in a shared house near the halfway point of the course. I was not running. I wasn't capable of running. My lifestyle had got out of hand: I was spending most of my time going out drinking and all that comes with it. I woke up on the morning of the race and I wasn't alone; this wasn't unusual. I had no idea who the person next to me was. All I knew was that I'd met her the night before and she was now in my bed and I had a race to watch. I asked her to wait there as I lived very close to the halfway turnaround point of the race and I had estimated what time my mum would be coming through. I got down to the roundabout where the race turned, just before the leaders came through. (If you had told me at this point that in a few years' time I would be one of those leaders, I'd have thought you were insane.) I'd noticed the heat as I was walking the 400 or so yards to my vantage point. It was boiling. A few people seemed to be struggling even at the halfway stage.

My dad came through as expected. He may not be the fastest runner in the world, but he's very consistent and his times are embarrassingly predictable. There was no sign of my mum. I waited and waited until I was almost alone. The only runners coming through now were a trickle of the overweight 'fun' runners, and all the other spectators had left. Even my friend from the previous evening had got bored with waiting and had started the walk of shame, flashing me a dirty look as she walked past. Eventually I saw the sweep bus. The sweep bus follows the race in order to pick up any runners that are not going to finish within the allocated time limit so the council can reopen the roads. The sweep bus at a half usually picks up people that would finish outside 3 hours. Even with this being her first half marathon, I knew my mum was quite a bit faster than that. When the bus arrived I got on just to reassure myself that I had simply missed her coming through. I got on and looked down the length of the bus towards the gloom at the back but didn't see her anywhere. It was then that I noticed a small figure in the first row next to where I was standing receiving medical attention. At first I didn't even recognise my own mother. She was so pale and gaunt and when I chokingly tried to talk to her, there appeared to be no flicker of recognition in her eyes. It was truly the worst experience of my life. We then transferred from the bus into a waiting ambulance as she was in a bad way. She still didn't seem to know who I was.

Here in Kassel she came round as she had in Sheffield with vows to 'take it easy' and 'not push so hard next time'. It will never happen. There is an innate competitive streak within my mum and within all runners that can never be satisfied. You can always improve, always achieve more. This, I believe, is the problem with running as a sport: it is more of an obsession. Talent is not the same limiting factor as it is in most other sports. You can achieve a huge amount on hard work and training alone. I believe that this is what makes it so addictive. You look at the great distance runners and see somebody with the same body as you and you think that if you could just train more or work harder you could achieve the same results. The fact that all those years of training have fundamentally changed the elite runners' physiology is not apparent from the outside. You can't see why you shouldn't be able to run like an elite athlete, so you push your body through a hundred gruelling miles every week in order to improve. This in turn can make you very aware of your own mortality and, in my case, that of those around me. The incidents with my mum served to remind me how she may look and seem physically weak but is so mentally strong that she is able to put herself in real physical distress – for a hobby.

I had been in this position with my dad before at the very same race, the Sheffield Half Marathon. He had collapsed at the finish and was in such an extreme state of dehydration that he was packed into an ice bath and put on an intravenous drip. My dad always liked to mention that this had once happened to the great Alberto Salazar in the Falmouth Road Race in the United States. He obviously got some vicarious thrill in comparing himself to one of the greatest marathon runners of all time. I always found it amusing that this proud Ulster Protestant was willing to compare himself to probably the most devout Catholic distance runner of all time. (In fact, as Salazar's form and career began to slide after his Boston and New York victories he sought help in various Catholic holy sites around the world, literally hoping for a miracle. This is in stark contrast to the space-age scientific techniques he uses today.) The strange thing was, I was never as worried about my dad as I was about my mum. He was so strong, I just knew that he would be OK. He had done far worse things to his body over the years willingly that it must have been used to the stress that it was put under. There was always a feeling that was shared by the family that whatever happened, he would always be OK. Whatever scrape he got into, he would always seem to come up smelling of roses with just another funny anecdote to keep us all amused.

20

Contentment?

June 2011

I suppose that this was what I had always aspired to. I was sitting on white, golden sand in Jebel Ali in Dubai on my way to an interview in Australia for a new post as head of school. Now, I was internationally known and internationally desired; headhunting agencies with gleaming offices just off The Mall in London invited me to apply for jobs all over the world. It felt good to be this wanted. A citizen of the world; freed from my background and my roots in Presbyterian Ulster with the red-rust swings chained up on a Sunday lest we enjoy ourselves, pushing ourselves up higher into the rain and the sleet on the Lord's Day, with that smell of rusty metal on your hands for the rest of the day, but not on the day of rest. I watched the speedboats gently swaying just off the beach. Girls in pink bikinis but with small, sexy pot bellies, with the low, guttural sound of the Moscow suburbs and the confidence, or front, of Russian entrepreneurship, filled the silence of the sea. My opening sentences for the job talk were running through my head:

'I was asked to start my talk by telling you what kind of leader I am. Well, if you ask a psychologist you expect some kind of analysis so according to Kurt Lewin, I am a "participative leader".'

Expect some laughter.

'I wouldn't have told you that, of course, if it didn't sound good.'

Expect another faint murmur of laughter, maybe slightly more embarrassed this time because they're going to realise they are being played.

'Basically, I invite comments and opinions but ultimately I make the final decision.'

Me, you understand, me, not we, not you; I make the final decision. That's what I would tell them. I could just hear silence at this point in my imagination. I could see their looks, first the instant appreciation of honesty, but then changing, as if they were now trying to work me out. The silence grew a bit and I smiled. It is sometimes a little constraining being an expert on body language because I could feel myself smiling as I imagined it, and it didn't feel quite right; that smile (the one I was now imitating in my head) could have been misconstrued, it was a bit too deliberate, a bit too manipulative. So I decided to tone it down a little. I noticed that the speedboats had stopped rocking for a second. I thought that it might sound a bit over the top, hinting at a little bit of megalomania perhaps, telling people that I alone want to make all the decisions and have ultimate control. But somehow I wanted their blessing in this whole process by calling myself a 'participative leader'. I wanted them all to participate in me feeling important and building myself up at their fine institution.

But what else could I say? Every university wants leaders. They ceaselessly complain that they are wounded by all that endless democracy and the never-ending range of details that have to be considered at every level – the layers of staff meetings, executive committees, board meetings, senior executive meetings, senate – so that all the academics can somehow feel actively involved in the whole decision-making process, and then in the end someone still has to go and make the final decision. So the question I was asking myself was simply, why not be honest, why not just say it as it is? But how honest should you be? And how honest should I be about my intentions? They were paying for me to fly business class to Australia; they wanted to know, quite reasonably, how serious

I was about the post in question, but in my head I had turned this question around to how serious they were.

'Do you have my level of ambition?' my inner voice was asking them. 'What support would you offer to achieve world-class research in this field?'

I knew what I was now worth and I had worked out that I could no longer be shy about it. But was I serious about leaving Manchester and my children, even my grown-up children? Was this ever remotely conceivable? I had been offered a post at another British university months before and had not accepted it because it was too far from Sheffield, so what was I doing going to Australia for an interview? Was I running away, maybe, looking for a fresh start without messing up this time? In how many ways can you chase lost times?

I had been training at Sale that previous Tuesday. They call them 'efforts' at the club and I can understand why. I was nearly sick with efforts that night, finishing with runners with much better 5K and 10K times. I am usually around those with 18.30 for the 5K and 38 minutes for the 10K. Why can't I race like this? Don't I have the stamina, or is it because I don't have any belief? Do I have too much fear of embarrassment? Do I dread crossing the line looking half-dead? I had competed in the British Masters Championship 5K the previous Sunday and the Dunham Massey 5K on the Friday. I had enjoyed Dunham Massey. There is a slight incline to go up three times. Of course, it feels like a hill on the race itself but the downhill section that you run across twice is grassy so you don't actually make up much time; other than that, it's a nice course. I had finished in 21.22, below the dreaded 22 minutes. I had beaten quite a few quite capable runners who probably had an off day so I was fairly pleased with myself, I felt good. But Sunday was a different matter: it was the British Masters. This is, of course, a big national event, maybe one of the biggest in the annual calendar for vets. I had gone for a meal the night before, so that was half a bottle of white wine before I even started, then the manager sent over some champagne cocktails, and I couldn't be rude; then there was some more wine, and then an early start. Any hope that I had on the morning itself was focused on my single can of Red Bull, which I clutched tightly. I was relying on this to wake me up. Even my driving was a little shaky that morning, a little bit hesitant, which is just not like me. It frightened me a little as I drove up the motorway. Any sensible man would simply have stayed in bed and called in sick.

Horwich is a suburb of Bolton and I arrived there on a slate-grey morning with old, thin, grey-skinned men emerging from their cars, smiling and cheerful. There were runners in their 70s and 80s. They all seemed to know each other, all regulars of this particular race. Given that the Masters category has been extended down to 35 for men and women, there were a number of what were clearly top athletes there as well. I did not feel good; indeed, that, if anything, is an understatement. I was just pleased that Ben wasn't coming to watch. He was running the Horwich 5K later that same afternoon. I knew that there was a group of runners coming from Sale and it still hadn't occurred to me why none of them had been running at Dunham Massey on the Friday evening. Of course, I soon discovered that it was because they'd been resting for the premier 5K in the country, and were shocked that I hadn't. It seemed so obvious now but it hadn't occurred to me before, it genuinely hadn't occurred to me. I warmed up with a few of them, but they turned a corner and I lost them, and then I had to sprint to the start because I was now lost. I wasn't even thinking well. I made a joke to one of my friends from Sale because I noticed that he was trembling slightly before the start. I said that he was shaking with nerves but that I was shaking from all that alcohol the night before. He didn't laugh in quite the way I had hoped and I felt oddly out of place. I didn't really want to be there because I felt that I had let myself down.

Suddenly, things got a whole lot worse. I bumped into someone whom I hadn't seen for 25 years. John used to be

Carol's boss at Heffers Booksellers in Cambridge. Later he became a publisher and published my first book on the psychology of language and non-verbal communication in the early 1980s. That was a long time ago. I remember listening to the Sex Pistols at his wedding and I have an image in my head of his beautiful new wife twirling and singing along, 'V-A-C-A-N-T'. In the meantime he had sold his publishing business for millions, and now was semi-retired, dedicating himself wholly to running. We were shocked to see each other there that morning because neither of us knew that the other one even ran. When I asked him what time he was hoping for, my heart just sank; I heard the number 18 and failed to process anything else. He was out of my league. And then he started asking me some questions.

'You've always been very competitive,' he said. 'What about you?'

I made some stammering comment but declined to answer. 'I'm not very quick,' I said instead. 'I'm not really serious, I was out on the piss last night, I'm only here for a laugh, I'm far too busy for this sort of stuff, I still have to work, you know.'

I was even making myself cringe; these, after all, were just words that hardly captured my complex relationship with running. I couldn't work out why John had made this comment about my competitiveness until I suddenly remembered that Carol had once set John and me up for a squash game at some point during my Cambridge years and he hadn't taken a single point. I obviously had wanted to humiliate him: 9–0, 9–0, 9–0. This odd little memory, buried for years, ricocheted around my head, like a small black ball in a hollow-sounding reverberating space, as I watched him nervously wait on that start line, focused and now even more determined. He reminded me a little of Carol in his determination and focus. I wanted to crack a joke but I thought that he would just disapprove, and I couldn't bear any more disapproval. Not only was he a better runner than me, he now had something to prove.

The gun went and I pressed my stopwatch but it wouldn't start. I was fumbling, just standing there with a hangover, not going anywhere, and shaking slightly. Nearly all the runners left me, especially John who just shot off, and I stood there fiddling with my watch, half-drunk, pressing and pressing a watch that stubbornly refused to budge. Eventually I set off on my own. I couldn't time any of my kilometre splits because I never did get the watch going. All I remember about the race was running up the same hill four times, and all that greyness, and this crippling despair, and wishing that it was all over, looking at the backs of runners, and green Sale vests, and wondering how I'd got there.

As I finished, I heard the time from one of the timekeepers but I pretended I hadn't. It was past the dreaded 21. It was 22.01 to be exact, but when you hear that number 22 your heart just sinks. To say it ruined my day would be an understatement. James, whom I beat every Tuesday at training, had clocked 20.25.

'Did you really expect anything different?' he said to me afterwards. 'You need to take it more seriously. You can't race after a night out.'

'But I do take it seriously,' I said. 'I do. I just don't know how to do things differently.'

He went around telling other runners about my cocktail hour the night before. I could hear them all laughing.

'What time did he do?' somebody asked. I couldn't see who it was because I wouldn't look.

'What's all that about?' somebody else asked.

I waited for Ben to arrive to do his race, on my own. I hung about for three or four hours on that grey day in this boring little town. I walked up and down past the burger shop, which was the only shop that seemed to be open, and when he finally arrived with a friend from his running club, he just ran straight past me with a cursory wave. It was more a hand flip than a wave, almost dismissive in its form.

'We need to warm up properly,' he said on the way past,

without slowing down. I stood on the pavement waiting for his race, again on my own. He did the race in 16.28.

'That's my son,' I said as he went past, without even glancing my way, to two women from the earlier Masters race. 'He's the good-looking blond one.' I didn't ask them what time they had done because I was too embarrassed that they might ask me back.

Ben, of course, did ask me about my time that day but I just shrugged.

'I was shit,' I said. I had stopped shaking and I was now feeling stone-cold sober and very contrite, perhaps as contrite as I have ever felt, and that might be very telling, but I knew that things wouldn't change.

So here I was, sitting in Dubai, a world away from that Sunday. I was happy again, or so I told myself. My aspirations were pulling me ever upwards until I had hardly any time to reflect on my core values or what I really wanted out of life, or even to train properly, or to think about what I might have missed with my family. I was that proverbial man on the treadmill. Could I really abandon all of my family to chase those dreams that I once nurtured in the dull streets of Belfast, to make sure that I never returned to the ghetto, as predicted by my chemistry teacher and all those others who just said it with their eyes? I felt that perhaps it was becoming time to take stock, to re-evaluate my life, maybe to change, maybe even to train properly. But I felt instinctively that this could be far too dangerous. What would happen if I started to train properly and then was still at the same sort of level? What would happen if I was still no good? What would this runner do then?

I dipped my toes into the warm water of the Persian Gulf, ordered another cocktail (I'd had my run) and sat with a bit of paper on my knee, half in and half out of the water, planning the interview meticulously. This was going to be all about talk and self-presentation, about me and my career, about what I had achieved in so many domains, the prizes, the big grants and the accolades, and I knew one thing for certain: I was good at talking about these things. But I also knew that there were many, many things that I could simply never mention, otherwise the man in front of them would not be a sparkling participative leader, the kind of leader who can make decisions and spin on a sixpence, the kind they all wanted – or indeed any kind of leader – but just a man laden with frailties and deep, deep regrets. A man who had turned up for the premier event in the running calendar prepared to fail, indeed over-prepared to fail.

A week later, I was in Australia and crossing the Hawkesbury River on the train from Newcastle to Sydney. I could see the white sails of the boats on the river and the wooden verandas of the houses down by the edge of the water, with couples sitting out in the sun on a Sunday, with their skinny lattes and their crisp linen clothes. It was a sign of the good life. Then the train swept back out into the bush and past sharp, tall cliff roads with dangerous, precipitous falls, the rocks shining in cream-coloured stone. The interview was now over. It had been amiable enough. I was a little bit over the top at times but, then again, I think that you sometimes have to be.

'I'm no shrinking violet,' I had said to the interviewing panel, which made me slightly embarrassed, and the panel all nodded back in agreement at the violet who sat there right in front of them, clearly not shrinking. The outcome was currently unknown but, of course, the uncertainty gave me more time to wrestle with my conscience. Would I really leave all of my family ties behind to come to live here – without any of them? My daughter Zoe had talked in the past about living in Australia after her gap year, as did my son Sam. I was always horrified at the prospect of that degree of separation. Perhaps it was now payback time; I was getting in first. I was the first to apply for a job in Australia, first to be interviewed for a job, but then what? Newcastle was not how I had imagined it to be. I had sat that morning in my hotel dining room, watching the whales head north up the coast for warmer waters. I sat looking for their spouts emerging out of the choppy sea. Closer to the shore I counted 22 surfers on the July rip tides, and out past both the surfers and the whales there were these endless coal boats ferrying the coal from the Hunter Valley to the coal-fired power stations of China and Japan. Newcastle was the biggest coal port in the world. And every night on the television news the opposition MPs spoke vehemently and emotionally against carbon tax for the coal-based industries. The debate was highly polarised and you could just read the emotion in their faces as they spat out the words. They invited me on to the *Kerri-Anne* show to talk about my research on sustainability and how to spot a 'green faker', somebody who espouses environmentally friendly attitudes but whose deep-seated values are at odds with this. They asked me to analyse the body language of the Prime Minister of Australia, Julia Gillard, to see if there was any evidence of her being a green faker. I felt slightly set up.

A daily run took me out over the cliffs above Newcastle and down onto the next sandy beach along the coast, past Merewether and some good-looking, cheery and optimistic houses in various pastel shades. It was a stunning early-morning run, a beautiful bit of coastline. I would look forward to the view each morning as I climbed to the highest point. Then one morning on a whim I went down to the edge of the cliff top just to look at the rocks underneath and the crashing frothy sea. After my brother's death I found that I didn't like looking down from great heights any more because I found it hard to stop imagining a body tumbling and twisting on the way to quietude. I climbed over a small safety rail and the view from the edge was both beautiful and frightening: sharp rocks with their tips protruding out of the froth, like spikes waiting to impale you. I felt slightly dizzy and stepped back. Then to my left I noticed some flowers left out on the cliff top, then some more flowers lying there, withering and dying, and then I noticed a plaque which read:

Yvette Fries, 1985–2005
You came up here and spread your wings
And flew to the place that happiness brings
God called you home, his plan for you
To be an angel and this came true.

It took me a second or two to realise that this was not the normal kind of commemorative plaque which you find on a park bench, and then another second or two to realise that 'spreading your wings' was not really figurative language about the personal development of a young woman embarked on a flourishing career. This was where this young woman had come to kill herself. Then I stopped and counted, and realised that there were nine different plaques in all, nine different suicides on this dramatic and very beautiful cliff top with a great view of an arcing golden beach and white surf, and whales with their spouts on their journey north. If you are not happy in this place, what hope is there? Was that the logic that drove them to climb over that low fence and to step off into air to feel nothing? I used to time how long it would have taken for my brother to hit the ground from the summit of Nanda Devi and embarrassingly I would try to work out his final velocity; all of those years of physics training and the laws of motion, I suppose. Newton and I had gone to the same college in Cambridge so I had learned something from all of this. And then I would try to imagine how it all might feel to him in those seconds. The organiser of the expedition had offered to show me photographs of Bill's dead body but I declined to look at them. I felt like a wimp, but I don't think that Bill would have wanted me to see him like that. I have his photo from the day before his death in my mind for eternity.

On that night I sat in the dining room of the hotel watching the surf. I watched this girl with long dark hair in a white dress walk down to the edge of the water on this deserted beach, and walk quite alone straight into the sea. My eyes were straining to follow her; it was very dark. For a moment she seemed to disappear. The workings of my mind were being directed by my morning runs past the cliff top with its dead flowers as a reminder of turbulent grief and the charged emotional significance of that sorrowful place. What should I do? Should I run out and try to talk to her to save her life? Should I tell her what a great psychologist I was and hope that she might listen? But then I picked her up again, this white ghostly shape, walking parallel to the shore, but still in the choppy surf. I thought that I saw a black shape to her left; perhaps it was her boyfriend finding her after an argument, trying to persuade her to come back to shore and back to life. Both shapes then disappeared.

I had been a little down after my first 24 hours in Newcastle. It was a strange town; it reminded me a bit of Sheffield, heavily industrial and very ugly but set in some beautiful scenery. I felt a mixture of guilt, I suspect, and the fact that this citizen of the world, who could go wherever he wanted to, had ended up here, in a place that was both beautiful and ugly at the same time. But I had managed to lift my mood by going for a run and I had managed to find myself quickly again and feel connected to both myself and my surroundings. Running was the thread to guide me back to who I am. Even finding the words about the young woman on the cliff top, which I would not have found without my run because running takes you to strange, unexpected places, connected me to the sadness of my past. And this is something which I don't want to forget or repress, and can't, because it is a major part of who I am. This reminder makes me feel content. I always think that it really is a shame that others don't have this thread to hold on to. I was happy, indeed more than happy, that Ben had found the thread for himself and that he could hang on to it whenever he had to, whenever it was necessary, to be himself.

A few days later, I was travelling on the bus from Darling Harbour to Bondi Beach through the trailing suburbs of Sydney. The bus went down a slight hill and then stopped. I wanted to be struck by the vista but all I saw was a little beach.

It was July and, of course, their midwinter, but it was still 62 or 63 degrees, except in the wind, which on that particular day was biting. I travelled there in my running gear because I knew that I had to get my run in before 5 p.m. when it would get dark. This was the main thing on my mind. Where was I going to leave my bag and my camera case while I ran along the beach for 40 or 50 minutes? Would I hide it in the rocks? What would happen if someone found it? What would I do then?

At the beach the ice skaters were out in force, skating to 'White Christmas'. This seemed strangely incongruous, the white ice against the white sand of Bondi Beach. One lone middle-aged, well-muscled man ran up and down the white sand. He was the only person who appeared to be undressed but I soon joined him.

'Get the sun on your body,' my mother would say when I was a child. She, my brother and I all had dark skin and in the summer we would all go 'black', in her words, in the tepid Belfast sun. They used to say on our street that there was a touch of the tar brush about our family. My grandfather had served in the army in India and somehow the street had got confused about our Indian roots.

'Have you got a bit of the darky in you,' they would ask, 'or is that just fake tan?'

It was hard to know what to say.

So I sat on the sand for a few minutes with a towel wrapped tightly around me with sand in my face and between my teeth, before seeking shelter from the wind in the rocks around the far side of the bay. Bondi Beach was not how I had imagined it. It was a lot smaller than I had thought, and I couldn't help noticing that the paint was peeling off the beachside apartments, and the metal on the side of the balconies of these beachside apartments was rusting. I had expected the whole place to just gleam.

One old man with thin grey hair and a tired, colourless shirt came up to me on the beach. I was huddled on the sand in front of him. His nose was painted in the Australian colours of green and gold. He had some Chinese writing on his surfboard but I hadn't noticed him surfing. His tone was friendly; he asked me if I was about to go into the water because 'you're stripped and ready'. I told him that this wasn't really my plan but rather I was just trying to get a wee bit of sun.

'Oh', he said, 'a fellow sun worshipper. Do you not want to know why my nose is painted in green and gold?'

I shook my head in a sad and pensive way. 'Is it to protect you from the sun?'

'No, not really,' he said. 'It's because the Chinese girls on the beach stop me and ask me why I've got it painted that way, then they read the Chinese writing on my surfboard and then we start chatting. Simple. I tell them that I live up there on the hill above Bondi Beach and they say to me, "You must be a millionaire," and I say to them modestly, "Not really," and they like to joke and argue with me, telling me that I'm far too modest for my own good. "You live on Bondi Beach, the world-famous Bondi Beach, you must be millionaire." I used to be in the air force, you see, and I suppose that I could have saved up quite a packet if I'd wanted to, but I didn't really save the way that I should have done, and to be honest I'm just an old-age pensioner who gets by with a little walk on the beach.'

The old man seemed happy enough; he obviously liked to talk. There were not many Chinese girls about the beach that day, so I was going to have to do. I noticed the melanoma on his face and the skin pink and sore around it.

'I'm of Irish descent,' he said, catching my direction of looking. 'We burn quite easily.' And then he turned it back to me. 'You've got a good colour,' he said. 'I wish I was your colour.'

I hadn't the heart to tell him that I was Irish as well, but one of the darker Paddies. He noticed my running gear.

'There are some great runs around here but you have to be quick, it gets dark very early.'

So there I was sitting on the rocks with only one thing on

my mind: how to get a long, slow run in. Instinctively and without any thought I picked up a pumice stone and started scraping the hard skin off the soles of my feet. I hadn't done this, or experienced this feeling, for years. The action, the noise and the feeling brought back memories of the past. My mother was obsessed with her feet. Regular visits to the chiropodist would be one of her few luxuries in life, and at night she would rub the hard skin of her feet and then mine with a pumice stone, and then tickle my feet with a rolled-up newspaper.

'My father used to do this to me when I was a little girl,' she liked to say. 'Everybody loves having their feet tickled.'

Carol had come down to see me one night when we were first going out, and she noticed me sitting in the front room, in front of the electric fire, with my feet up on my mother's lap and her tickling my toes with a rolled-up newspaper. She looked horrified. But we were more casual about these sorts of physical contact than perhaps her family was.

'That's just not right,' she said. 'You shouldn't let your mother tickle your feet like that.'

After I became a professor of psychology, my mother liked to tell anyone who would listen, 'He's a professor, you know, but you couldn't tell by looking at him.'

I could see the old man with the melanoma looking at my running gear carefully. Perhaps I needed my mother there to talk to him about life generally. She would have loved to have had that opportunity. She loved attention from men of a certain age. I can imagine what she would have said: 'He's a runner, you know, but you couldn't tell by looking at him.'

21

Paradise Islands?

July 2011

I was standing on the corner of Market Street and George Street in the middle of Sydney as it juts down to Darling Harbour, waiting for the lights to change. Standing there on the street corner in a heaving pulse of pedestrians, but I was quite alone. There was an invisible bubble around me, a bubble of perspiration and hot, dripping sweat. I caught pedestrians glancing my way and then they left an extra six or nine inches just in case my sweat landed on them when I turned round. They were dark-suited with their skinny lattes and sushi for lunch. I was impatient, twitching nervously, waiting for the lights to change. Then I arced out around the pedestrians waiting in the queue, standing on my own, the man on the endless mission. I had been out for 1 hour 30 minutes today, by accident mainly, because I got lost. Up into Sydney and down through the Royal Botanic Gardens, dropping down Macquarie Street and then along the path to Sydney Harbour. I tested myself up the steps back into the Botanic Gardens and then dropped down to the harbour path again. There were hundreds of runners all out for their lunchtime run.

With running, it has always been a case of us and them. People used to shout at me as I ran along in the Belfast of my youth. It was always the same sort of thing: 'Keep those legs up, keep those legs going.' As if those legs could ever stop. Young boys would run along beside me before they would stop abruptly, winded, as if they had managed to make some great point. I would sometimes speed up as they ran beside me, just to make my own point. Sometimes men would shout from cars or toot their horns to make you jump in that quiet somnambulant state. But now in most cities they seem to understand running much more. Back in Belfast I used to sneak out of the house for my run. My mother would be shouting after me, 'Don't you be getting all sweaty; I'm not washing all of that stuff again.' But it was never washed mid-week because we didn't have a washing machine. It was just left to dry, somewhere in the vicinity of the electric fire. I liked to get onto the hills around Belfast in those days, with minimal human contact, afraid that the people might laugh at me or shout at me. On a Sunday I would run 12 times around the park. An old woman asked me once if I was trying to lose weight. I felt hurt because it suggested to me that she thought that I might need to. But I shouldn't have worried. People need to understand the behaviour and actions of others in terms of how they think. Running was always going to be torture from that woman's point of view. Why do it unless there was a good reason like, for example, losing weight? But I had no simple explanation for running; sometimes I wish I had. Running makes you a strange kind of tourist. I had managed a tour of the harbour, Sydney Opera House, Sydney Harbour Bridge, the Royal Botanic Gardens, the shops, the cafes; the external environment of the city was now interwoven with the internal environment of my thoughts. The day before on the ferry to Manly Island I had seen an Indian father and his child play with a hat for 40 minutes or more. A child's game with absolutely no point to it, but the father showed a great deal of patience and love for his son. Perhaps I was too busy for these pointless little games with my own children, far too busy, keeping myself separate, protected in my own invisible bubble.

Before Australia in July and New Zealand in January, the last big trip had been to Mauritius and another international conference, with runs that took me out of my five-star complex and around this poor island. Again it was a strange mix of new sights and old, familiar thoughts that I couldn't get away from. Mauritius was not what I had expected.

There, I had found myself slowly walking back to my hotel room, stepping carefully around snails with large, almost comical heads, and brightly coloured shells. They were the size of small, rotund sparrows. It was 1.30 a.m., the end of another day in paradise. I was staying in a beautiful hotel with manicured, verdant lawns that swept down to the white sand and clear warm waters of the Indian Ocean. I was attending a sustainability conference in Mauritius to present some research findings on the psychology of sustainability and why people claim to care about the environment but actually do very little. I had spent the day in various plenary sessions listening to the latest views on environmental sustainability. I had presented my work on the implicit attitudes to carbon footprints and the response was very favourable; many productive possibilities emerged; and I discovered that few researchers interested in sustainability seemed to have thought about this issue before, but I could see that many were thinking about it now.

I had chosen a hotel close enough to where the conference was being held just outside Port Louis, in Pointe aux Sables, but really miles apart from the chaos and patchy squalor of that town. I was guided to my room by the sound of the *crapauds*, the Creole name for the little frogs crying out for a mate in the ponds dotted around the hotel. These ponds were artificial, with slate waterfalls, the water emerging out of the mouths of golden lions, and goldfish swimming under the gentle, sparkling falls, but the tropical nature of the island had invaded the interconnected ponds to give them new life; the whole thing pulsated like a membrane. The croaks sounded like the raspy death rattle of a human being, that terrible Cheyne–Stokes sound and rhythm, but with the opposite emotional significance. This noise was all about life and the celebration of libido rather than the celebration that Thanatos had finally neared the end of its fateful journey. I timed the interval between the croaks: almost exactly one per second. The whole hotel was pulsating with this incessant noise that seemed to be getting louder. The volume bore no relation to the tiny creatures from which the noise comes. I picked one up to examine it, and it sat quietly in my hand before I released it back into the lush pond life.

I had travelled halfway across the world to be here. One and a half hours to Charles de Gaulle airport and then eleven and a half hours to Sir Seewoosagur Ramgoolam airport. Then, I had to travel another one and a half hours across the island in a private taxi, sitting there with its engine running so that the air conditioning would make it nice and cool for some Westerner like me. Of course, I could see the extraordinary irony in holding a conference on sustainability in Mauritius with academics reluctantly travelling from Minnesota and Harvard and Manchester to be there. But then again, it does not pay to be too ethnocentric when it comes to academic debate. Sustainability is a global issue and Mauritius is much closer to Africa, India and Australia than many other possible locations. And Mauritius did give me a sharp reminder, with its corrugated-iron huts with hardboard walls and buckets on the ends of rope for toilets, of the sheer economic significance of premier tourism in countries like this, with hard-working Western executives with lots of air miles in need of air-conditioned taxis and hotel rooms. If, and when, we cut back on air travel to Mauritius and other jewels in the Indian Ocean, either voluntarily or through some kind of prohibitive legislation in the future, these places will suffer greatly. And this is a real possibility in terms of the current ethos, with air travel often being singled out for particular criticism in terms of global warming. Sustainability is all about choice but many of the choices are not easy.

The next afternoon I lay in a hammock overlooking the sea watching a weaver bird pick at the bread that I had dropped,

dropped carelessly rather than intentionally. Two small, familiar-looking sparrows approached to nibble the bread beside the weaver bird; a red-crested, red-bodied serin walked arrogantly towards the other birds and stood in the middle waiting his turn. A water vole with pink feet ran through the scene and appeared to squeak. Two tiny grey doves arrived and walked around each other in what looked like a dance. This small part of earth, covered in luxurious thick grass, was fully alive and perfectly harmonious. The sea lapped the shore and I started to drift off. This was as close to a tropical paradise as I had seen or I could imagine. Somewhere in the blue distance two fishermen a half-mile out from the shore cast their lines. On this gently sloping shore, they looked as if they were walking on water. But the perfection of the whole scene made me worry in the way that things do when they are too good.

I went for a run that afternoon and soon saw, more starkly this time, that this paradise that I was now inhabiting was something of an illusion, a mirage created by unconscious forces, driven by images of white sand, palm trees and glamour in a desert of crippling poverty, where generations of African and Indian slaves that had worked on the sugar-cane plantations now provided an impeccable service culture, in which dark-skinned waiters and waitresses in sailor suits and Nehru jackets appeared to be naturally obsequious (but that was a dangerous conclusion, although their smiles did fade naturally and slowly as they turned away from you as if they were genuinely pleased to serve you). I was suddenly overcome by an ill-defined and unfocused guilt. I feel guilt about the beauty of the world, or that part of the world that I was now privileged to inhabit, and guilt about my position in it, in that I still did not appear to be doing too much to help even some bits of the planet (as if you could choose to help just bits of it rather than the whole natural thing). I kept passing squashed dead rats just outside the sugar-cane fields; rats who had gorged on the sugar cane and were now so big and so heavy that they were unable to dodge the trucks that hurtled past. The dead rats were enormous and very frequent, and I tried to jump over each of them to avoid the mess.

The next morning the sun was shining again, it was high in the sky, brilliant and intense, and my spirits lifted immediately. In front of my veranda grew a panoply of palm trees with their heavy yellow coconut burden. Incongruously, a rose bush sat to my left bearing pink roses, presumably for the honeymoon couples that come here. The palm trees were thick and luxuriant and spaced at a pleasant distance but with no obvious pattern, as if nature had been tamed and improved by man's intervention. They had even made the spacing seem random and natural but it was far too pleasing to the eye for that.

At midday suddenly everything started to change again. The rain was coming once more but now it felt different. However, this was also the day of my first sailing lesson and I did not want it to be spoiled by the wind and the rain; after all, sailing needs wind, doesn't it? The attendant in the sailing office advised me to leave my powder-blue Armani sunglasses in the kiosk, 'In case you capsize or are knocked unconscious by the boom, monsieur,' he said helpfully in his Creole.

I also offered up my grey Nike Pegasus running shoes, stained with clay and reeking of sweat and effort. He motioned to the step below the kiosk. 'Leave them there, monsieur, they'll be quite safe.'

He obviously didn't want to touch them. The instructor stood forlornly on the small Laser sailboat.

'The rain,' he said, 'it is coming. It is a cyclone.'

I put on my yellow life jacket carefully, fastening each of the three poppers in turn; I didn't want to miss this opportunity.

'Cyclone is good,' I said. 'Lots of wind.'

'No, no, monsieur, too much wind, cyclone blow, blow, blow.'

He obviously wanted to go back into the kiosk to play cards

181

with his friends. His facial expression was telling me everything that I needed to know.

'Do you suffer from panic?' he asked.

'Pardon?' I said.

'Do you have panic? Because if you do have panic, we can't do sail, if you panic we drown. We might as well go home.'

I shook my head slowly and mournfully, eyes wide open like a small but determined puppy. 'I don't do panic,' I said. We walked slowly together to the slightly built craft and I clambered in clumsily, which only seemed to worry him more.

'Cyclone is very bad,' he added, allowing me one last chance to back out.

We sat on the little boat facing each other as he explained what each of the small instruments did. The rain was definitely getting harder. There was a thin nylon rope, blue and white, for tightening the sail, a light aluminium rudder for steering the boat, and a boom that shuddered unpredictably and violently across the boat.

'You must sit hunched up and duck when the boom comes otherwise you will be knocked out,' the instructor explained.

We set off into the silver-white bay, now grey from the rain. I was gently guiding the boat. He was standing on the bow holding on to the sail, the pelting rain streaming down his face, looking miserable; he would clearly rather not be here at this moment in time but I had been insistent. He looked past me towards the shore, wistfully.

He tried one more time. 'The rain,' he said, 'it is coming. It is *très mal.*'

We were picking up speed and the small boat was gliding through the waves. I wanted to take in all of the stunning scene, but the driving rain was forcing my eyes into narrow slits so I was just focusing ahead.

'Where are you from?' he asked.

Soon we were talking about Ronaldo and Alex Ferguson, and the way that Manchester United always seem to start slowly in the Premiership but nevertheless always seem to end up on top. We were making contact at last. He asked what I did for a living and when I told him I was a professor of psychology he became animated.

'My mother do psychology, too,' he said. 'She reads the Tarot cards and she reads the rice grains. I have seen her with my own eyes cure a man in a wheelchair using the Tarot cards. She found out what the matter with him was and then fixed it by sacrificing a hen. Can you cure the man in the wheelchair?'

I shook my head sorrowfully. 'Unfortunately not,' I said, 'but I once cured a student with a fear of public speaking by forcing her to talk to a lecture theatre full of 200 students – but that was about it.'

'You very cruel man,' he said. 'My mother can walk on coal and she can do sacrifices, just small sacrifices, chicks, hens, goats, nothing too big. She just cuts their head off and reads the Tarot. Can you walk on coal, monsieur?'

'No,' I replied 'but I did walk across the beach this morning and it was very hot indeed!'

He didn't really get the joke but I laughed anyway, which he seemed to find uncomfortable. He had a professor with him in his small boat in a developing cyclone who appeared to be laughing at himself.

'Turn left, monsieur, left, you must dance with the wind, not fight it. You must learn to live in nature, not fight against it all the time.'

The wind was now much stronger and the boom was being shunted abruptly from side to side. I could see no pattern in the changing turbulence. He, however, was standing on the bow reading the direction of the waves. He clung on to the sail, delicately balanced in the driving wind and rain. Suddenly he shouted out a warning but it was too late: 'Duck, monsieur, duck!'

And the inevitable happened: the boom struck me with some force in the back of the head giving me an instant headache but simultaneously waking me up. I suddenly had the first clear thought of the day. What was I doing in the middle of the Indian Ocean on a tiny boat (almost like a lollipop stick) with the son of the local witch doctor? The rain was torrential.

'What you think of black magic?' he suddenly asked.

'It depends upon how it is used,' I replied.

'Sorry,' he said back, sounding as if he assumed that I hadn't heard his first question. 'What you think of black magic?' he asked again.

'Good,' I replied this time.

'You like?' he said, smiling with large white teeth.

'I really like,' I said. 'I would love to meet your mother. Could we perhaps go back to the shore now?'

'No, not yet,' he said, his smile temporarily leaving him. 'Your lesson is not up yet. I want to learn more about your psychology. Turn the other way.'

'Towards the cyclone?' I asked hesitantly.

'Yes, that way,' he said, gesturing towards the cyclone but without actually mentioning it.

I sat in silence for a moment just listening to the rain bouncing off the boat.

'Have you met Ronaldo?' he asked and looked disappointed when I failed to answer. 'Would he like a sacrifice? What about Alex Ferguson? My mother would sacrifice a large goat for him for Manchester United to beat Chelsea. You tell me what score you want, two nil, three nil, my mother arrange it.'

His mind was racing away with him, thinking about all of the commercial possibilities when East meets West. I just wanted him to keep focused and get us back safely. I was trying to put all that I had learned in this lesson, which was not very much, into practice and the small white sailboat responded well, sprinting back towards the land like a dog trying to get out of the storm. I shook hands with him when I half fell out of the boat onto the shore. 'Thank you,' I said.

The rain was torrential now: torrents fell through the trees, torrents raged through the rivulets and drains. There was a large cyclone off Rodrigues Island, maybe heading south-east, maybe turning towards Mauritius, but it had still sent all this rain here. I stood sheltering with the rest of the beach boys who hired out the pedalos and the sailboats to the tourists. They told me that the cyclones were far more frequent and more intense than they had been in previous years, and that the beautiful manicured grounds of this hotel that sweep down to the lapping waves of the Indian Ocean were now often the victims of flash floods. They also told me that the temperature was rising; they had seen this with their own eyes. Even though they were all in their late teens and early 20s, they said that they personally had seen the change: each summer now the temperature climbed to 37 degrees rather than peaking at 32 degrees as it had when they were younger.

'It's getting too hot for some tourists,' said one dark African boy with a fashionable goatee.

'And much, much too wet,' said another. 'One day the tourists may not want to come.'

I knew that they were right from some recent studies that I had read. But it is one thing reading it in a paper, and it is quite a different thing to stand there feeling the new intensity of the cyclone on the horizon.

I climbed back off the beach and saw that the palm tree outside my room now appeared to be emerging out of a deep pool about two metres across. It was an odd sight, like an island that had been drowned – maybe like a vision of the future. A little bird, flame red in colour, called a red cardinal, hopped towards the pool of water around the base of the tree to pick insects from the soft, wet ground around the new pond. The heavy patter of rain through the leaves was everywhere. It was such an evocative image, an image that I knew would prove to be indelible, and it pushed one clear thought my way. It was such a cruel thought. The thought

185

was that we helped make this Eden. We tamed it, we structured it, and we imbued it with our unconscious desires and our symbolism of tropical-island beauty and romance and sanctuary and aspiration, but then our choices – one at a time, linear, sequential and unconstrained – may already have helped to bury it.

22

The Birdman

July 2011

My home in Manchester for the past 11 years had been on a canal basin near the city centre, just by the Manchester Ship Canal and a stone's throw from both the Imperial War Museum North and Old Trafford. Salford Quays was on the rise, with the building of MediaCityUK and the moving up from London of many of the BBC shows. But it was still an odd place. One minute, not a soul, the rippled waters of the basins whipped by the wind and the driving rain, grey water merging into grey concrete and grey sky. The solitary toot of the tram and then silence; if you were awake through the night, a dawn cacophony of swans, ducks and moorhens; and then more silence. But on match days you couldn't move, with the burger vans and the souvenir stands on every bit of pavement and the crowds all pushing towards that theatre of dreams and the smell of burgers. I could run around the basin and then along the narrow canal into the centre of Manchester, through Castlefield, down towards Canal Street and the Gay Village, and back. There would be whistles as I went up Canal Street in tight shorts and vest in summer, and then had to turn at the top and run back down. Men sitting outside the bars, commenting, 'Ooooh, he's back. Nice legs.' Or I would take a detour out along the dual carriageway and back down past Old Trafford, onto the road to avoid the congestion, the late drivers inches away.

The canal banks were fairly quiet regardless of the season.

There was the odd runner about, one obviously fearless elite female runner from Salford Harriers running in her knickers, but mainly I would just see silent fishermen with long rods and landing nets, contemplative and forlorn in their lonely occupation. I would skip past apologetically, hopping over the long rods before they got the chance to move them. On autumn nights it felt dangerous going down along the banks at dusk and one night I did see two young men dressed in black, their hoods up and fastened tight, running towards me, then pushing past. They were laughing and shouting as they hurried along. Further along I could see the dental consultant's that I used to go to, in a blaze of flames, just as I approached Castlefield. I turned off the canal path and into town but didn't cut the run short. That kind of event was rare; it was usually the rats, rustling and hidden in the rubbish at the side, that would frighten me.

I usually saw the birdman at the top end of the canal or around one of the basins. He was like clockwork. He had become an old and familiar sight. He wore the same Lonsdale sweatshirt every single day even in the summer and a grey beanie pulled down over his ears. In winter he would wear a hoodie over the sweatshirt and a black jacket. It was always the same clothing. In many ways he looked like a typical Salford lad, thickset with a fleshy face, a bull neck and broad shoulders. I always thought that he might have been a boxer, maybe retired. But day after day, run after run I would see him with two carrier bags on his bike, one on each handlebar. They were full of bread for the birds. He was always feeding the ducks, moorhens and swans, invariably the babies first, in a careful and systematic way. I suppose that I would never have spoken to him if, coincidentally, I hadn't timed my efforts to finish on that side of the basin. On the way past I merely commented that he seemed so regular in his habits.

'I feed them every day,' he said. 'They need me. Everybody thinks that if they throw a few crumbs into the canal on a hot summer's day that that will be enough for the birds, but what about the rest of the year? Who's looking after them then?'

I mentioned the moorhen that had been sitting in its nest on the basin in front of my house with its partner ferrying twigs in its beak, hour after hour, to it. I told him how I would drop bread down around the nest, but the moorhen would never move to get it. And I then described how I had seen it weeks later lying face-down in the water with its neck at an odd angle. There was one solitary egg left in its nest. The birdman, I am sure, almost cried.

'I didn't see it, luckily,' he said. 'I don't know how I would have reacted. The ducks around here can be proper bullies when they want to be. I've heard that if they're in a fight, they drag birds under the water to try to drown them. I think that's what happened to the moorhen.'

I stood there perspiring. I wanted to finish my warm-down but it would have been hard to pull myself away at that point in time, in the middle of the discourse. That's the thing about running: you can leave yourself open to strangers, almost exposed.

The birdman told me that he had lost his mother six years ago to cancer and that his world had fallen apart. 'I never worked again,' he said. 'I had lost my sister to leukaemia but then my mother went. It was too much to bear. I would be talking to people and it would feel like I wasn't there, like I was in some parallel universe. My father was an alcoholic and her death hit him badly. He said that he wanted to burn the house down with all of us in it but I said that my mother might have gone and we all missed her badly and we might not want to be here some of the time – but you can't take people's personal choices away. We have to make a decision about whether we stay or go.'

So this was now his life. 'I spend all my money on bread – even the cheapest bread in Sainsbury's has gone up to fifty pence and I buy at least four loaves a day – and I buy monkey nuts for the magpies. When they see me they tap on the branches, they know me, they can see me coming.'

I was now the travelling therapist. The birdman stood by the water's edge throwing crumbs of bread in a regular pattern, over towards the ducklings and then out towards the right for the ducks themselves. 'I know I talk like a woman. I see some guys' faces when I talk to them and they're saying, "Why is he talking to me about personal stuff like this?", but if I didn't talk about this stuff, then I don't know what I would do.' He paused and put some bread back into his Tesco bag. 'I get so much pleasure from the birds. People ask me what I'm up to and I explain to them that birds give you love. I need my routines and they need it too; I keep them all alive.'

I could feel myself getting cold. I told him that I would have to go.

'I see you most days,' he said. 'We keep similar hours. I bet you watch the ducklings and the goslings grow as well. It's amazing what you can see around here, if you just keep your eyes open.'

The next Sunday, the rain was coming down in sheets and it was so grey it was impossible to tell where the street stopped and where the sky started. It was a typical late-autumn Manchester day, but unfortunately it was July. The trail race was due to start at 11 a.m. I was running a little late. It was just after 10 a.m. and I had still to get to there. If there were any delays getting off the motorway, I would miss the race. I was nervous for many reasons. The first car that I saw when I climbed the hill was Carol's. I could see the sheen of her yellow running vest inside through the car window. It was too wet to get changed outside so she was struggling to get her vest on. I stood outside looking in with the rain bouncing off my head; I was too wet to move. Carol emerged into the damp grey air and we both jogged down the hill to the community hall where the race headquarters was. I needed the toilet but there was no toilet roll. I had taught Ben many years ago that this often happens so always take some toilet roll with you, but today I was ill prepared.

We lined up in the middle of the street. Andi Jones was the organiser and starter, and he made a few quips, mainly about the weather and the traffic. Most runners had club vests; Ron Hill had a vest with Dr Ron Hill MBE on the back. At the start we had to go up a hill and then down onto a trail path, which was flooded with deep, dark, muddy pools. The obvious line was to run right through them, which I did, so I found myself slipping and sliding in my flimsy race shoes. Carol was better prepared; she was wearing trail shoes. There were no kilometre or mile markers so I couldn't make my usual calculations. The slanting rain stopped on the way back and I felt like a bedraggled, mud-splattered dog, but strangely happy. On the turn I could see Carol behind me and during the final three miles I had only one goal: to increase my distance from her. My happiness was suddenly interrupted by a feeling of genuine sadness that hit me unexpectedly. A feeling of melancholic longing, rooted in our joint past. I pictured Carol back in university, trailing along after me on the way into the department. She had followed me to England, she had followed me into psychology, and here she was following me in the mud in the middle of nowhere in the pouring rain. I have always felt a little guilty about her accident. What kind of husband lies in bed while his wife runs for a train? A busy husband? Is that any justification? Her parents never forgave me for what happened to her. I don't think that I have ever managed to forgive myself.

I crossed the finishing line and looked back to the mud-soaked figures hurrying along. There was no sign of Carol, not yet, but that, of course, was a very good sign. And then that sadness erupted again. We sat afterwards in the community hall. Carol got first prize in her age category from Andi Jones; I got nothing, except a chesty cold the next day. It might have been the unwanted emotion rather than the rain, that's what my professional brain was telling me.

I hate what I call 'back to backs': a very late run the night before and then a very early run the next day. But it had to be a back to back. Out at 9.30 p.m. for a run and two timed 5Ks around Salford Quays. This particular course of mine is flat and full of litter. Oddly for an inner city, it is also full of rabbits that scatter in all directions as I run through them, and I occasionally see thin, ragged foxes that eye me suspiciously. But also on this particular course, I don't see many people, except on match days, though I do see masseuses leaving the run-down sauna at the 10.15-minute mark (my time in minutes on my first 5K, not the time of night). Occasionally they give me a cheery wave as I run past them. Strangely, I have never seen a customer go into the establishment which either means it is the world's worst massage parlour with no customers, or the customers are more cunning than the ragged foxes passing me on the patch of grass on the other side of the road and they know how to avoid prying eyes.

I had to work late and neither 5K was fast. My back hurt, my hips hurt and my knees ached from all of the leg extensions that I had been doing in the gym. Sometimes I take a fancy to a particular exercise and then I overdo it. I felt slow and tired, and I knew I had to get up early in the morning to train in order to get to the university graduation ceremony on time. As head of school, I was due to present the graduands and afterwards to make a speech to the students and their parents before being whisked down to Essex to film *Ghosthunting with . . . The Only Way Is Essex. TOWIE*, as it is known, was the new reality-TV show that had just won a BAFTA to many people's extreme irritation. I didn't really know the show but the 'cast' were famous for their surgically enhanced faces and bodies, their love of tanning, vajazzling, their stupidity ('So who's the prime minister, then?'), and their endless catchphrases: 'shut up', 'I'm looking reem', 'out of order'.

I expected to be filming until around 4 a.m. because we have to keep going until something happens; ghosts and ghouls can, after all, be extremely unreliable. I had once run the Sheffield Half Marathon after *Ghosthunting with . . . the Dingles (Emmerdale)*. We had filmed until 5 a.m., I was back at the hotel for 5.30 and up at 6.15 a.m. to get to Sheffield. In other words, I had 45 minutes' sleep before I had to get up. I did the half marathon in about 1.39, which is not a great time but I was exhausted. I lay down on the grass at Don Valley Stadium after the race, and fell asleep more or less immediately, perhaps in a matter of seconds. Ben said that he heard some ambulance man say that I had collapsed and was unconscious, then one said, 'No, he hasn't, he's snoring,' and they left me there sleeping and having wild and extravagant dreams.

So I was up early the morning of the graduation and the Essex shoot, but my legs were so tired I could hardly make them run. I usually break into a running pattern within the first two or three strides but not that morning. I had to walk for 50 yards or more before I could will my tired legs to start running. It was uncomfortable and almost painful. When I got back everything was a rush: a rush to my office, then a rush to the Whitworth Hall to go through the list of names as I donned my academic gowns, then a rush to join the academic procession, then onto the stage. I had to fight to keep my mind focused on one name at a time. There were a lot of exotic-sounding names but I didn't have time to check the pronunciations beforehand, so I had a window of two to three seconds before announcing each name to mentally rehearse the pronunciation. Then I had to rush to the group photograph, then rush to the marquee to hundreds of students and their parents waiting to hear from the head of school. I had nothing prepared. I felt like telling them about my running, my tiredness, and this strange, endless obsession, maybe as a metaphor for life, but I managed to push this thought aside and spoke instead about their possible and probable futures and why they should remain incredibly optimistic even in these tough times. It went down well but I was incredibly late for my driver and now very stressed as we hurtled down the M1 in the driving rain of a British summer towards some haunted fort in Essex.

I am supposed to be at the shoot at the very start of

Ghosthunting with . . . to do some psychological profiling – I use some basic tests of extraversion/introversion, neuroticism and sensation seeking – but they had to start without me. They were filming the cast in some dark tunnels under a fort so that it would seem as if they were exploring a haunted location on a very ghostly night. By the time I got there they were already quite scared. I had to talk them through the questionnaires and explain what many of the words actually meant. I had to explain what 'initiates', 'highly strung' and 'miserable' all meant. I had always thought that their stupidity was an act, part of the Jade Goody representation of Essex, but now I wasn't so sure. But I was taken aback by how nice and cooperative they all were. Each was allocated 30 minutes with me, but they all wanted to run over their allocated time to talk about their lives and their 'issues'.

Mark Wright wanted to talk about his relationship with his fiancée. 'I love her to bits but we're always rowing. Could you give me some advice on what to do? She's very possessive and when she has a few drinks she can just kick off.'

I asked another cast member, Harry, who is extremely camp, whether he was highly strung or not. And at that very moment, a very squeaky fart emerged from underneath him. It was accidental and he was highly embarrassed but I couldn't stop laughing.

I couldn't believe how plucked and pampered and perfected they all were, both girls and boys. In the test they all came across as highly extrovert, which I expected, and extremely neurotic, all exceptionally concerned and anxious to get things just right. Of course, reality shows probably attract people who are a bit neurotic to begin with but I suppose that when your whole career depends on the perfect pout of your lips, your exaggerated breasts or a whole string of meaningless catchphrases, you have every right to become a little bit more neurotic in the process and prone to all sorts of irrational anxieties. But I liked them in a curious way and felt a little sorry for them. The executive producer kept telling me that things were going extremely well in the dark recesses of this old fort. I went to explore some of the maze-like tunnels with one of the sound men but felt nothing inside. He was excited about the odd sounds as the wind whistled around the old tunnels, but he has an ear for that sort of thing. To me it just sounded like the wind.

The night passed very pleasantly and ended very early, between midnight and 1 a.m. I had to record eight pieces to camera, where I analysed the cast's non-verbal behaviour, to explain why they reacted the way they did, but they were all first takes and it felt easy and comfortable. We started to get ready to leave but suddenly there was a bit of a problem: the paparazzi had arrived. The first one arrived on a motorbike, followed by many more. We were told that we couldn't leave the fort just yet. Three security men were posted at the gates of the fort, now under siege. The people carriers lined up and we were first to go. We were given detailed instructions about what to do: we had to make our way steadily to the speed ramp and then accelerate as fast as we could until we were out of sight. We were going to be the decoy car. It felt very odd driving out of an old fort in the middle of the night and suddenly seeing dozens of cars parked down a side road, all with their lights on, like some sort of traffic jam in the middle of nowhere. We hurtled past them into the dark Essex night. None of the paps followed us; I couldn't work out how they had realised that there was nobody of any note in our particular blacked-out people carrier.

Back to the hotel, emails kept flying in with new work to be done before 10 a.m. the next day. I sat in the deserted hotel bar with a large glass of white wine going through them. It had been a long day, and it wasn't over by any means. I had a 10K on the Sunday in Middleton and now I was dreading the race because of the intensity of my work life, even though it didn't really feel like work, or sound much like work either. But it was still draining.

23

A Twenty-four-hour Race

Ben

When I was first asked last year if I wanted to compete in a 24-hour race it seemed a long way away. I instinctively said 'yes'. I always say yes. I like to say yes; I think it is a need to please. My stock answer is always 'yes', and I think about the consequences later. This need to please is a trait that I share with my father. He constantly needs reassurance. For somebody so successful, he is incredibly insecure. He needs to know that you are content. He will constantly ask if you are happy, if you really like the gift he has got you. I remember as a child forever being asked, 'Do you love me?'

As the date loomed closer I started to become anxious. I like to run high mileage in training; in fact, my long run of between 16 and 20 miles is more suited to a marathon runner than someone who mainly runs 10Ks and half marathons but I had never raced more than a half marathon in distance. The captain of our team had calculated that in order to win the actual race we would need to cover 70 kilometres each, that's something like 43 miles. I didn't increase my mileage but did do a number of workouts that were designed to replicate the conditions of the Thunder Run.

The first of these specific workouts was completed a fortnight before the race. I did three runs totalling thirty-seven miles within twenty-four hours over a weekend. These were three tough runs with the longest being nineteen miles over Stanage Edge in the Peak District in foul weather. The following weekend I came third in a low-key trail race in Manchester with my mum and dad. We waited an age for the prize-giving and the only thing I could get to eat and drink was a slice of fruitcake and a cup of tea. On the way back to Sheffield I decided that this would be a perfect way to test my resolve. I was tired, hungry and dehydrated but went for a hard 11-mile run as soon as I got back. I was nauseous and woozy but I made it. This reassured me that I was ready for the challenge of the Thunder Run.

The Thunder Run is a 24-hour endurance race. It can be completed as a solo runner, in a pair, in a team of five or a team of eight. We were competing in a team of five. The race is run over a 10K cross-country loop in the grounds of a country house in Derbyshire. You must have a runner on the course at all times and the winners are those that can cover the most distance in 24 hours. Basically it's Le Mans but with no cars.

The race was due to start at noon on Saturday and go through to the same time the following day. We arrived early on Saturday morning having no idea what to expect. None of the team had done the race before and I was shocked on arrival to see the sheer scale of the event. The campsite was huge and it seemed that we were the last to arrive. The experienced people had clearly been there overnight and were enjoying a leisurely breakfast on sprawling camps that were set up at regular intervals. We set up our own camp and then went off to register and receive a pre-race briefing, which went without a hitch. The fact that the event was sponsored by Adidas meant that the set-up was very impressive and professional.

Our captain had worked out a schedule that meant that we would all get one long break at some point rather than doing a straight five-man rotation. I was to run leg three. I noticed on the schedule that we were aiming for 45 minutes per leg. I was a bit disappointed as I wanted us to try and run harder than that; I wanted us to win the race.

The hooter sounded at noon and the runners set off. I was amazed at how fast some of them flew round the opening bend when they still had 24 hours to go but the anticipation and excitement must have been the cause. To be honest, early on, it was great fun. The sun was out and I was running around with a couple of thousand other like-minded souls. By the time I went off for my first leg (the team's third) we were in the lead. It was a tough cross-country course but I flew round my leg. I had a short rest after my first two legs, when I had some pasta and a protein recovery shake. One of my teammates had had the foresight to invite a massage therapist along to give us a rub-down after every lap. She did an amazing job of flushing out all the waste and without her the challenge would have been far harder.

Heading out for my fourth leg was one of the strangest experiences of my life. It was 1.15 a.m. and pitch black. I had had no sleep and was struggling to eat as well. The site was incredibly quiet but occasionally you would see a hint of movement as a fellow competitor readied himself for another leg. As I made my way through the camp, I felt like a miner dragging myself back to the coalface, especially as only the light of my head torch cut through the inky blackness. As I made my way to the start area I passed other runners returning to camp after a 'shift'. They had the blank, expressionless look of those that had put themselves through extreme effort, especially when illuminated in the light from the lamps. I exchanged a nod with each and every one of them. They understood without words; there was a connection.

Leg five was by far the hardest. I had returned from leg four still running well but exhaustion had taken a hold on me. As I received treatment to my swollen, aching muscles I was falling asleep. In Haruki Murakami's book *What I Talk About When I Talk About Running* he talks about envisaging himself as a machine built only for running, with no feelings

198

or emotions. This was his way of blocking out the physical pain. I, on the other hand, became if anything more human and more frail at this point. Although physically I still felt strong, emotionally I was struggling. The lack of sleep was leading me to become melancholy, almost mournful. In fact I started leg five in tears; I just couldn't work out why. By the time I had got to this leg I could no longer stomach any real food. I was getting terrible stitches and cramps. The only thing I could rely on for sustenance was Jacob's Cream Crackers with jelly babies on top. It had stopped being fun.

Throughout the night I came across solo runners slowly shuffling towards a goal that must have seemed impossible. I made sure I gave words of encouragement to every one of them.

The other members of the team were surprised by the consistency of my speed and my willingness to continue to push myself even though it appeared the competition was already won. There were runners there that on paper were faster than me and ran faster individual legs, but it wasn't a pace they could sustain and they lost a huge amount of time later on in the competition. Our physiotherapist, Catherine, asked me how I knew I could sustain my pace; how I knew I wasn't going to 'blow up'. I knew because I've blown up before. Your brain will lie to you. It will tell you that you can go no further, no faster. It's wrong: you can. Your body has huge reserves of untapped strength. The reason I knew the level that I could go to without blowing up was that I had been to the edge before. Only by taking yourself to the absolute limit will you know where that limit is. I've collapsed twice in races before and have come close numerous times in training. I knew the warning signs – wooziness, confusion, sudden lack of strength – and I wasn't getting any of the signs. The other inescapable truth was that I was simply unwilling to let my team down. I have let down everybody in my life over the years. Those closest to me have been wounded by my stupidity, laziness, fear, drunkenness and so many more character flaws that I could not even list here. I wasn't going to let down a new group of people.

I completed my sixth and seventh legs on the Sunday morning. My pace never dropped and I ran well to the end. We won by 20 kilometres.

24

Incentives

July 2011

I rang Ben halfway through his endurance feat, by accident, and I was surprised to hear him sound so tired on the day before the big run. But, of course, I had got the day wrong. The race was from Saturday 12 noon to Sunday 12 noon. It didn't start on the Sunday as I had thought. I rang him at about 8 p.m. on the hottest day of the year so far. He sounded tired.

'I'm OK,' he said. 'I've had a bowl of pasta.' He had already run three 10Ks on a hilly trail course in between 37 and 38 minutes. His team were in the lead at that point on the Saturday. He still had four 10Ks to go and the next one was due to start at 1 a.m. I apologised about getting the date wrong.

'It's OK,' he said. I felt like the bad father again, not even able to retain this simple information. He had to run 43 miles; I just had to remember the day and I couldn't even do that. It reminded me of my own childhood and all of the disappointments of my early life.

'I got 86 per cent in Latin,' I would tell my mother.

'Oh, very nice, son. When was the exam? Did you revise for it?'

'But you heard me, over and over again: "Dominus, domine, dominum; dominus, domine, dominum; dominus, domine, dominum." What did you think I was doing?'

'I don't know,' she said. 'It all sounds the same to me. It's all foreign, but is it any use? I heard that doctors have to write in Latin, but you're not going to be a doctor anyway, are you? You don't really like blood. You want to be a vet; you love animals but I don't think that you'd be any good at that either. If you're a vet you have to put animals down, you're too kind-hearted for that. You can be too kind-hearted you know, if you want to be a vet. A vet that is too kind-hearted would be unemployed like a lot around here and unemployable. And you don't need to write Latin if you're a vet. Animals can't read anyway. You could write in English and the animals would be none the wiser.'

I had run a 5K that morning in 21 something and then did an hour's yoga, and I felt like I had really pushed the boat out that day. I knew that it was going to be a night of shame ahead for me, waiting for him to finish. It was just going to be a night of shame but, of course, I was used to it.

I woke up the next morning anxious to learn how Ben had got on in his 24-hour race. I was pleased that he sounded much happier and fresher than the night before. His team had won the race. He said that all of the other competitors were talking about this team of professionals who had come down from Sheffield to compete, and it also turned out that all of his 10Ks were within a few minutes of each other.

'I was the most consistent of the lot,' he said. 'My average 10K was between 37 and 38 minutes and there was only about a 2-minute variation. Some of the other lads in the team had about 15 minutes between them. I now know that the marathon is my ideal distance.'

He had run 7 10Ks, 43 miles within a 24-hour period.

'How's the legs?' I asked.

'Fine,' he said 'but my running shoes are knackered.'

I felt very proud that Ben was turning out this way. 'Fine,' he said. I loved the brevity and the matter-of-factness of it all. It reminded me a bit of my brother.

'How was it?' I would ask excitedly about his climbing adventures in Afghanistan or the Alps.

'Fine,' he would say. 'It was not as hard as I thought it would be.'

Ben was named after my brother, Bill, but he was called Ben, which was Bill's nickname, after *Bill and Ben the Flowerpot Men*, a children's television programme from the black and white era. I drove back along the Pennines that afternoon and felt that I too needed to test myself with a longer run. Something that I could say 'fine' about in that sort of way which means that you don't really have to talk about it in order to make it important. I got back to Hollow Meadows quite late. Carol was sunbathing on the patio and Sam was out playing tennis. There was the usual mild discomfort as I said that I needed something to eat. Carol had been running that morning. 'I'm not waiting for you to turn up,' she had said. We talked about Ben's accomplishment the day before, but it seemed to be all about who knew most about what he had achieved and whom he was closest to, as if it was some sort of competition in parenthood.

When Ben and I had talked about writing this running book, Ben had said that it would be interesting to explore how my running and my life had shaped how he ran and how he might live his life, but Carol was rarely mentioned in these early discussions. I had said at the time that she must have been an incredible inspiration to him, a woman of her age, with one arm, running those sorts of times, first in her category week in and week out. But through his short and non-committal sentences he gave the clear impression that it was our connection that he wanted to explore. I sometimes feel that Carol is not that happy with the fact that Ben and I are possibly making up after all these years and my multiple misdemeanours. And who can blame her? Sam is very much more open and gregarious than Ben and he ambled into this frosty atmosphere.

'Have you had your run?' he said, implying that if I hadn't I would soon be disappearing again. Sam likes to greet me after a week's absence by insulting me and criticising my work. He was currently working as an intern for a local publisher that produces books on sustainability.

'Have you mentioned my book to your new boss?' I asked, referring to my latest book, *Why Aren't We Saving the Planet?*

'No,' he said, 'they wouldn't be interested, mate. They're only interested in quality. They're committed to environmental issues. You're only a dabbler, you dip it in here and you dip it in there.'

And his mother scowled across the room. But I had an inspirational plan for that day: I had decided to run from Hollow Meadows to Hathersage via Fulwood. It takes me about 1 hour 30 minutes, more or less a half marathon time. It's very hilly so it's less than 13 miles but feels like a proper run, like an adventure, a journey, an achievement. I asked Sam if he fancied doing it with me; it would be like a step back in time. It was a case of the errant father returning home and begging and cajoling his son to join him on his run so that they could spend some time together, after the uncomfortable absence.

'How much?' asked Sam.

'What? You want to be paid?'

'I sure do. You want me to run all that way with you. I've only done five miles before and I've just played two hours' tennis. How much would you give me to run to Hathersage with you?'

I laughed and glanced at Carol.

'Well, they take after you in one respect,' she said. 'It's all about money with them.'

'Fifty quid,' I said. 'Cash up front.'

He insisted that I go and get my wallet before he would even put on his running vest. I only had £45 but he let me off with the difference. I told him that I would dictate the pace because it was important not to set off too fast on a stifling hot afternoon, and the two of us, father and son, strode down the Snake Pass and then started climbing up Wyming Brook. He carried a small water bottle with him, and he would pass it to me every few miles or so. The scenery is quite breathtaking. The hills are very long and steep, but then you drift down into Hathersage and you can see this great view, and your spirits lift, and you can feel your stride lengthening.

I have told Sam many times that he could be a very good runner; he's got a powerful build, with broad shoulders and strong legs. I've even told him that he could perhaps be nearly as good as his brother, but he has expressed no real interest in running. He has always been a very good footballer and very good at lacrosse, in which he was captain at university and a county player (as was Ben), as well as playing for the British university team. As he strode into Hathersage he suddenly said that he would like to do the Sheffield Half Marathon next year.

'Just the Sheffield Half Marathon, though. I need you to run the first eight miles with me to show me the pace and then we'll see what happens.' He beat me to the garage in the centre of Hathersage where his mother was waiting with the car. The eyes of this father welled up as we reached our destination.

25

Endless Roundabouts

August 2011

The advice from Ben throughout this time was reasonably simple: 'Do not race on two consecutive days.' But the following week, I ignored his advice again. I was looking to do one of the parkruns in Manchester on the Saturday because I could have beaten the winning time the week before, or so I thought. I was nervous and slightly agitated the night before – expectant. I like this feeling but it is necessarily a private emotion, since you would never want to admit to it. To admit to it, you would have to confess your aspirations. I was very early for the race. I wanted to see exactly who would be turning up; I wanted to observe each new runner and work out my chances. There were only two runners when I got there, and both were old-timers. One was a very familiar face from my club: Don George, in his 70s, always cheery, with the same joke every time he sees me. He pretends to hit my right shoulder, the one that I dislocated in a race a year ago now. I still wince and he still smiles.

'Wouldn't it be awful if I forgot one day, and really hit you. Imagine the pain,' he said. It was a joke that I didn't really like; it reminded me of my own frailty, my own weakness.

But what would happen if that was the sum total of the opposition, how embarrassing would that be? Imagine ringing Ben or Carol to tell them that I had won a race. 'Who was in it?' they would ask, as they were bound to. It was just Don George and a few of the old codgers who have been around for years. It was just Don running along, and pretending to whack my arm every mile or so, to remind me of my own weakness. But then a few girls arrived in pink tops and running shoes with a matching pink flash; this didn't necessarily help. Carol would scrutinise all the times; some girls running a 5K in 26 minutes would not help my cause. And anyway, I wouldn't want things to be too easy after this long, long wait for a victory. Then there was a gap in the arrivals during which I daydreamed, seeing the finish with nobody in front of me, and my heart raced a little. But then my greatest fears were realised. Runners started to arrive in club vests, a few runners from Sale, solid runners, fast runners, certainly faster than me. There were a lot of cheery greetings, but nobody mentioned the fact that the previous winning time for this race was so slow. It was like a guilty little secret shared by all but never mentioned. There was lots of small talk but none about the past form for this race. It almost made me smile, all that private expectancy around that field.

Within three seconds of the start of the race, I could tell that I wasn't going to win it. At best it was going to be top ten, but winning was totally out of the question. The start was too quick, even for me, who likes fast starts. This 5K was run entirely on grass which was quite long and therefore very slow, which helped explain the poor winning time of the week before. The race was hard all the way round, and given my time – which I refuse even to mention because it was my worst time ever for a 5K (but a lot of runners did a PW that day, running on long grass, which is not easy) – absolutely pointless because I had a race the next morning and my legs were now tired. All my expectancy had evaporated and I was in a more depressive mood.

Carol picked me up from my house in Manchester on the Sunday and she laughed when I told her how hard the 5K had been the day before, and laughed again when I told her how much I had to drink on the Saturday night after the race. I often think that Carol's one driving ambition in her running is to beat me in a race. And sometimes, because I know her so well, I can literally see her visualising this and visualising my facial response and my humiliation when it finally happens. This, however, could just be my imagination.

We got to Birchwood near Warrington very early that morning and had plenty of time to find the toilets in the Birchwood shopping centre, a centre full of discount shops and a Home Bargains. I did my perfunctory warm-up outside Home Bargains while waiting for Carol to use the loo. When we changed in the car, I noticed that Carol's arm was covered in cuts and bruises. She'd had a fall in a fell race in Burbage on the Thursday night. She hadn't mentioned it to me, but her good arm now was in such a state. She saw me looking at it.

'Just scratches,' she said.

I felt that nauseous feeling of guilt in the pit of my stomach. Apparently, my son Sam had had to bathe the arm to pick the dirt out of it.

'He wasn't very happy about it,' said Carol, 'but he got over it.'

Given that my legs were already tired, I felt that I had to push myself at the start of this race to make sure that I got a really good start in order to pull away from Carol. And sure enough, I got the start that I was hoping for, and I felt safe that Carol would be a good distance behind.

Birchwood is, famously, a race full of endless roundabouts and on about the third or fourth roundabout I heard someone shout, 'Come on, Carol!'

I glanced back, and there she was, about 30 yards behind me. I needed to push. A mile later I heard someone else shout her name, in exactly the same way. I tried to push a bit harder but I felt like I was floundering. When I glanced around for the second time, I could make out her distinctive running movement, leaning forward and pushing with her one arm, determined, never smiling and fully focused on what she was trying to do.

I said, 'Fucking hell,' quietly to myself, but clearly not too quietly because the runner next to me in the Wilmslow vest asked me if everything was all right. I grunted and bit my tongue. At the final roundabout I glanced back one last time and couldn't see her any more, and I thought to myself, 'All I have to do is to beat her best time for a 10K which is 45 minutes and 8 seconds and I will be ahead of her. There is no way that she will do a PB today.' That was my one and only goal in this race and that is what I did.

As I approached the final 400 yards I felt happy. But then I noticed a runner in front of me in some trouble. He and his running partner were wearing matching light-blue vests. He was an older runner, he was leaning forward precariously, almost stumbling, and the man beside him wasn't helping. You could see that he was about to hit the pavement, and selfishly I just prayed that it wouldn't happen until after I had passed him because I didn't want the embarrassment of running past without trying to pick him up. And sure enough, a few seconds after I had passed, I heard the distinctive clatter as he landed face down on the road. It was a very hot day.

I was relieved that I had finished before Carol and I waited for her to finish, feeling nothing but guilt for the past and how I had behaved towards her.

I have images in my head of Carol that come to me from time to time. I can picture her tracking after me, as I stomped into university in my platform soles with my curly hair in ringlets falling over my tight, blue, fitted jacket in my Marc Bolan era. I was always slightly ahead, impatient to get to lectures but always running late, in black patent-leather clogs with four-inch heels and two-inch soles. I kept going over on my ankle, swearing. My flared jeans had red stars all over them, and were so tight they would give me a pain in my bladder; they had to be zipped up by lying on my back on the bed and pulling until my thumb bled with the pressure. Or beside a road just outside St-Tropez in July, both of us young, tanned and thin, optimistic and cosmopolitan, pretty, with a large suitcase full of vintage clothes and antique rings from the markets in Paris, and handmade jackets bought out of a student grant, waiting for a lift back towards Paris and Calais. I would be reassuring her that a driver would stop sooner or later, but that she would still have to do the talking because French sounded ridiculous in my working-class Belfast accent. Or her on a bed in a hospital in Sheffield with her left arm crushed by a train, about to be amputated, looking up at me and apologising for being so stupid as to try to board a moving train, with everything I had been through, my father, my brother, my mother's grief. She was always thinking of me first. I was wearing a brand-new white puffa jacket; my mother had bought it for me to cheer me up after Bill's death.

'You're a great one for the style,' she said the day she bought it for me – it was the most expensive gift I ever had from her – 'a great one for the style, just like your mother.'

The jacket was covered in Carol's blood as I tried to hold on to her left hand before they cut it off. The blood stains never came off the white puffa jacket, and this memory never faded. I would have been screaming on that bed if that had been me; they would have needed all the morphine in the world to shut me up and to stop me feeling the pain. But Carol just lay there and apologised. And when she got out of hospital after a month on morphine, she did her cold turkey without complaining once. I would have let every neighbour know what I was going through. Cold turkey would have had me on the run all right, and I would have screamed it out.

She seemed to be cursing slightly as she passed the finishing line. She came up to me without smiling.

'You saw me, didn't you?' she asked. 'You were starting to slow down but then you saw me, it was so bloody obvious, and then you started to speed up again to get away from me. It was like someone had bitten your arse!'

At first I just denied it and laughed, as it seemed quite funny. I nodded in the end, slightly embarrassed.

'You're right, I did speed up, but it wasn't just because I saw you. I like that bit of the course, it's a little bit faster.'

'You're such a bullshit merchant,' she said back. 'You know, the worst bit about the whole thing was that it wasn't even me they were shouting at, it was some other runner beside me called Carol. If they hadn't have shouted, you wouldn't even have spotted me. You looked as if you couldn't really be bothered today, to be honest. You looked tired and a bit fed up. Today could have been the day.'

'Shit!' she added after a slight pause.

We walked slowly back towards the car. I wanted her to be even more direct. Perhaps I was trying to provoke her, to glimpse her darker side.

'So how good would it be to actually beat me in a race, to actually get to the finish before me and to have to wait for me to come through, all knackered and miserable?'

'It would be amazing,' she said immediately, 'but do you know what one of my greatest fears in life is? That after all this time, it might turn out to be a bit of an anticlimax, and honestly, that thought really terrifies me.'

And we both laughed very loudly but maybe for complicated reasons.

26

Done In

Ben

Knackered. Again. This year I have averaged 76 miles per week. The longest break I've had from running is two days. I've raced about every two weeks. I've worn out 11 different pairs of running shoes so far this year and I've covered 2,500 miles. I'll have done 4,000 miles by the end of the year.

Every three months or so, my girlfriend Joanne and I go through a now familiar routine. The catalyst is always a bad performance, usually in a race but occasionally after a tough track session. It always starts the same way: 'I don't know why I bother,' I will say. It's an open sort of statement, addressed to no one in particular with no real context, and yet she understands. She stays silent but she knows what's coming next. 'Who else puts themselves through this much pain and sacrifice for a fucking hobby?' Again, there's just silence. Then the *coup de grâce*, delivered with an air of finality: 'I'm done with running. I'm going to have fun on my weekends like everyone else.'

It sounds like a threat. I sit there and imagine the new exciting ways I will spend all of my free time, my time now. It's a lovely dream. I train for about 12 hours a week. This is a major part of my life that I could utilise. But this frame of mind generally lasts less than a day. My record is announcing my retirement in Glossop on one side of the Pennines after a poor race in Manchester and changing my mind when I got to the other side, indeed changing my mind so dramatically that I actually got out of the car at the Ladybower Reservoir on the

Sheffield side to run the eight miles home, still in my race kit.

The hardest part is that the training never ends. It's a wonderful relief to write the week's mileage total in your diary on a Sunday night. The relief, however, lasts only seconds. The realisation soon hits you that a new week starts on a Monday. There is no break, no chance to enjoy the fruits of your labour, no chance to relax. Yet I choose to train every day, usually twice a day.

My week usually follows the same pattern. For the sake of the running diary it runs from Monday through to Sunday. I run easy twice on Monday. I do a session with the club on a Tuesday. I run twice on a Wednesday. I go to another club session on a Thursday as well as an easy run. On Friday I run twice and then train at the gym with my brother Sam. If I'm racing on a Sunday, I will run once easy on Saturday. If there's no race, I will run once easy and once either at tempo pace or do another session. If I'm not racing, Sunday will be a long run of up to 20 miles. The structure of my week will be familiar to all decent-standard club runners. The only variation comes in the routes and the type of sessions. I prefer it this way. I think the problem most people have is that there are too many distractions in their life, too many things competing for their time. That and the fact, of course, that they aren't mentally strong. They consider going for a run but then they begin to think about all of the other things that they could be doing. They will eventually find reasons why they shouldn't go and then justify the decision to themselves: 'It's raining', 'I have a niggle', 'I'm too tired.' I don't allow these thoughts to enter my head. I do not have that internal dialogue. Running is something that I must do, like going to work. I don't give myself a choice about either of these things. I find it a lot easier this way.

This determination and single-mindedness manifests itself in other ways as well. I am not yet an elite athlete. I have improved massively over the last four or five years and I continue to do so. But, however hard I work, I know that there will come a time when I reach some sort of plateau. I will stop achieving PBs due to my age and the state my body was in when I came back into running. I am acutely aware that because of these factors there is a limit to the level that I can reach. I am a lot better than most people, though, and because of this I am ridiculously competitive. I know the importance of easy runs; I have read all there is to read on active recovery. I know that there is no point in flying past a jogger just to prove a point, yet I can't help myself. I have a compulsive need to make people aware of my level of fitness and my speed, whether that means overtaking them when I'm meant to be running easy or casually dropping my UK ranking into conversation.

Recently I was in the gym putting on my kit, getting ready for an easy run just to turn the legs over on a Friday afternoon in preparation for a fast 10K on the Sunday. I vaguely recognised a guy in the changing room also putting on his running kit. I set off at the desired easy pace when suddenly out of the corner of my eye I saw the guy from the changing room coming up behind me. I had a split-second decision to make: should I be mature and wise, and let him go and carry on with my easy run; or should I be a bit of a twat and speed up to show him who the boss is at my gym? I went for the second option and speeded up, not massively (just under six minutes per mile), but it was clear to this other runner what my intention was. I went past him, he turned off our joint path and I immediately slowed back down to my easy pace. I carried on my looping run and on the way back I came across him again. I couldn't believe it, the competition was back. We were running towards each other this time and as we drew closer I speeded up again, I couldn't help myself. As we passed I gave him the nod of recognition that is customary with runners of a certain ability. Only then did I realise, to my absolute horror, that he wasn't just some bloke from down the gym but Jon Ridgeon, the world championship silver medal sprint hurdler. He was in Sheffield to cover a big athletics event for the television. God only knows what he thought of me, some lunatic with a point to prove, trying to run a stranger into the ground that was out for his relaxing lunchtime run.

27

California Dreamin'

September 2011

I was sitting on a beach in Santa Barbara, in Southern California, just round past the yachts of the rich and famous, including David Crosby's gleaming white yacht, the Mayan, and the fishing boats. Wild grey gulls were keeping a safe distance from me but watching me carefully. I was writing in a flesh-coloured notebook, in which they seemed to be inordinately interested – perhaps because of the colour; it looked like raw skin. Every time I went to paddle at the water's edge they would scurry towards my bag and tear at it looking for food. There was none. One bold, lone gull, which for some reason I concluded was female, with grey, speckled feathers and a slightly pink, indented beak, turned her head this way and that, trying to work out what I was doing and whether any of it involved something that was edible.

Two lone dog walkers approached each other on the sand, down towards the surf. One was a lady in her early 60s wearing grey linen trousers and a linen top of a slightly different hue of grey, and a straw hat with a grey ribbon around it. The other was a man of about the same age in a crimson Hawaiian shirt and grey shorts. He had a grey beard and was much less elegant than the lady. I started flicking through a magazine. I noticed that John Malkovich was performing in the West Coast premiere of *The Infernal Comedy: Confessions of a Serial Killer* for one night only at the Granada Theater at the University of California at Santa Barbara. He was probably dropping into his local. This place is full of Hollywood celebrities. The two walkers had similar types of dogs, similar but not identical, with large, feathery whiskers. They stood there at the water's edge admiring each other's canine specimen and walked for maybe a hundred yards together before the elegant lady burst into a flight of running; she appeared to be singing as she ran, her arms were all over the place. I think that the expression is 'in rapture'. That morning, two cyclists, one after the other, had passed me on the way to the beach. Both were singing very loudly. This surely is the home of happiness, no matter how forced, well-being and good vibes.

The previous night I had run from my hotel, along the coast road and up into the suburbs. It was about fifty minutes of running, maybe six and a half miles, passing every minute or so another very fit female runner. Most of them were very pretty and most of them impossibly blonde and fit looking. They were all very sexy in that wholesome, Californian sort of way. The run felt comfortable, but I couldn't take my eyes off the hills just outside the town. I was going to do the Pier to Peak Half Marathon in nine days' time, from the harbour in Santa Barbara to the La Cumbre Peak, a climb of about 4,000 feet. The gradient didn't seem that bad to me at first, but Ben had slowly and carefully explained to me that I would find this run extremely difficult. He put the emphasis on the 'extremely'.

'You live in Manchester,' he said. 'When was the last time you saw a hill, let alone tried to run up one? You don't do any hill training. That's what baffles me about you. For a seemingly intelligent guy, you do a lot of very stupid things.'

Funnily enough, my mother used to say something very similar, but then it wasn't necessarily about running, it was more general than that.

I had already walked past the start point of the race – the statue of the dolphins at Stearns Wharf in Santa Barbara – and I had tried to imagine the route. My imagination faded with the mist now enveloping the peaks. I was trying to prepare myself by using mental focus, by focusing on one single idea – it can't be that hard, it is California after all. And the lady in the grey linen top and the grey linen trousers of a slightly different hue, with the straw hat perched jauntily on her head, ran past me still singing. This encouraged me.

But then the sun disappeared and the beach got a little greyer. The sea turned a very funny grey colour indeed, and this seemed to be a signal to everybody on the beach because the beach started to empty almost immediately. A very odd-looking tanned man, of an indeterminate age and ethnicity with blond dreadlocks, sat quite close to me, staring into space. He took his phone out of his shorts and started to shout into it. We were now alone on the beach.

'Tell her I'm desperate, tell her I'm sad; tell her I'm at my wits' end.'

He jumped up and started pacing up and down the beach and then walked down into the water. 'I'm not well!' he shouted into his phone. 'I'm just not very well at the moment.'

I was too embarrassed to move away so I sat there and he came back and lay with his face down in the sand without a towel. And when he sat back up his wet face was now covered completely in sand, as if he were taking part in some religious ritual from some far-off country, the kind of country where there were still natives to engage in this kind of ritual in the first place, somewhere eerily primitive.

The beach had changed in perhaps 20 minutes from something sunny and Californian and gay and slightly crazy, to something very different, something that was dark and ominous and scary. My brain was saying, 'Charles Manson. Remember that was California, too.' The hills now looked much more menacing. They were just dark shapes that I could hardly make out. I couldn't see any paths and I started to think about the last time I had actually run up a hill. I couldn't really remember when that was. I was going to text Ben for a little reassurance, but then I thought that he would not be terribly sympathetic.

'You've made your bed,' he might have said. 'Now you fucking well lie in it.'

I woke the next morning to some shouting from outside my hotel window. It took me a few moments to begin to come to. I started to make out some individual words. 'You're killing it.'

'Killing' was the first word that I could make out in its entirety. I couldn't remember where I was. Perhaps I was back in Belfast. I was half asleep, still trying to dream. The shouting was very loud. Then again for a second time, louder this time, 'You're killing it.' The 'wow' came later and it took me a while to comprehend it. 'Wow!' That was the word, and then again and louder: 'Wow!'

What was going on? Was I back in Legmore Street, with the grey rain bouncing off the slate roofs with some guy in a balaclava, vague and ill defined, standing there in front of me, saying something about killing and death? I think I was dreaming. Then the shape took off his hood.

'It's only me, Beats. I had you going there for a while. It's only me. You didn't recognise me, did you? You can't forget your mates, you know. But even me ma wouldn't recognise me like this. I've got a parka jacket, the lot. I look good though, don't I? I look the fucking part. I'm big in the Organisation, you know. I'm Mr Big now.'

Wow! Again that shout. Was this me talking, from the American comics, Joe Palooka? Then more words, separate lines:

'Only a mile to go.'

'High five.'

'You're looking strong.'

'You're killing it.'

I heard it again this time at full volume. I got out of bed wearily. I glanced out onto the beach. I could just make out in the bright sunshine a long, thin line of runners in triathlon tops, all super fit, tanned and well muscled. Some broad-shouldered blonde was standing beside the cycle path shouting, 'High five!' at the triathletes, who all whooped and yelled as they high fived back.

When I used to do the Sheffield Marathon in the 1980s when Ben was a very young boy, if I decided on the day to do the half marathon instead, I would stand there with my children encouraging those who had done the full marathon, feeling ashamed that I wasn't there among them. My children for years afterwards would imitate what I said to the runners as they passed and they would also imitate how I said it: 'Well run,' I would say. 'Well run.' It was always the same with gentle applause, polite and quiet. They hated standing there for an extra two hours to encourage the runners back, but I tried to impress upon them what an accomplishment a full marathon was.

That afternoon I went to a running shop at the end of State Street to pick up my number and bib for the Pier to Peak Half Marathon; or rather, I tried to. I knew that I was a week early. But instead of getting my number, I bought several pairs of racing shoes, all with 50 per cent off in the sale, which I intended to wear in my 5K in Ventura the following day (I was always looking for the magic bullet at a clearance price). I had that 5K the following day, then one the following Wednesday, and then I was going to focus on the hardest half marathon in the world in the remaining four days. Ben would have been appalled.

The air was very clear that day and I could see exactly how high the peaks were. The young sales assistant in the shop explained that the gradient went up to 16 per cent for the last 5 miles. 'You'll be very, very sore the next day,' he said.

'If I finish it,' I added. I bought four gels and a fuel belt. Although, as I left the shop I thought to myself that I would never wear it. I couldn't bear the looks of derision from spectators at the race at the man in the brand-new shoes and the brand-new bottle belt who hadn't prepared for this race of all races. Instead I tried to think positive. I tried to visualise Ben's strength, his running gait, his demeanour. But a small blond boy came to mind for some reason; I couldn't understand why. It was Ben as a child – he was always the most beautiful of children, beautiful and vulnerable – and suddenly I felt very sad indeed on such a beautiful day with this one clear image from my past that I couldn't get out of my mind.

The next day, I found myself in the dark, unable to find the race. I had stumbled out of bed at 4.30 a.m. and my first and only goal was to find a 7-Eleven for a can of Red Bull. The night before, I had eaten a late dinner with wine, a lot more wine than I had intended, and I needed a pick-me-up. I had packed my new pair of Brooks racing shoes that I had bought the day before because I thought that the novelty might help. I didn't trust my Asics Hyperspeeds any more to protect the soles of my feet even though I thought that the race would be both flat and smooth on the roads around the harbour. The race was to be held at Ventura Harbour but although I drove up and down the sides of the harbour, there was no sign of any runners or any tents or any organisers. It still wasn't dawn and I was starting to panic. It was 6.22 a.m. and the race was due to start at 7.10 a.m. but I was quite lost and I needed the toilet. But at least I had a brand-new pair of running shoes. Then suddenly I saw an Asian girl standing by a car with all the paraphernalia of the modern American runner. Her easy-going Californian manner reassured me.

I had intended to run the half marathon but it was full so I had entered the 5K instead. At the starting line, the guy next to me looked serene, something I rarely feel. He told me that he would do the 5K in around 15.30 or thereabouts, and that he was running in the world triathlon championship in a month's time. He didn't ask about my time, but out of the blue I suddenly brought Ben into the conversation. I told the triathlete all about Ben's 5K, 10K and half marathon times and I even managed to introduce his 24-hour race, all as we stood at the start line waiting expectantly.

'That's impressive!' he said.

So this is what it feels like to be a proud parent? I had always worried that if I ever played the proud dad, it would become a sort of surrogate life, with surrogate achievements and goals. But I was proud of Ben, immensely so. I have always believed that Ben is the kind of person who really did need to excel at something in order to be happy and I was pleased that he had found this thing.

I looked down the course to the first turn. 'Best of luck!' I said to the tall Californian.

'Tell your son best of luck from me. That is impressive, man.'

The start was fast and the tall blond triathlete led the field. I started quickly but at two miles or so (vague because there were no mile markers) a small pack of three runners went past me. I finished 10th overall with a very modest 21.31. My only relief was that I hadn't worn the Asics because part of the course was on sharp gravel. I went and stood towards the end of the half marathon course to applaud the athletes as they passed. The first runner came through, then a large fat woman with a strawberry tattoo on her leg ambled past dragging a poodle behind her.

'Is that the finish line?' she asked.

'Yeah,' I replied, 'and the first runner has just come through,' I added.

She looked at me quizzically. 'I'm not doing the race, you know,' she said, as if I had just implied that some athlete, the winner, had just beaten her to the finish. 'I'm not taking part today,' she added, somewhat unnecessarily.

'Oh, OK,' I said.

But I couldn't understand how her mind was working. Did she really think that I believed that she could do a half marathon in anything like that time, or indeed in any time?

She stood opposite me, watching the runners. 'I wish I was running today,' she shouted over to me. 'Running is awesome!'

Then she unpacked a cheeseburger and started eating it. The poodle sat expectantly, looking up at her, waiting for great dollops of cheese and fat to land in its mouth. The dog was seriously overweight, too.

The half marathon runners came back in a long thin line accompanied by 5K runners who were still finishing. One hour twenty minutes for a 5K (and not even the slowest 5K of the day) did not seem impressive.

'Good job!' shouted the lady with the tattoo. This was directed at both sets of runners simultaneously. It seemed strange to me. 'They're just awesome!' she shouted at me between great messy bites of her mega burger. 'Just awesome!'

After the race I headed with my category prize – an eco bag full of nuts and dried bananas and pineapple, the kind of stuff that I would never eat – down to Malibu and Zuma Beach to bathe my tired muscles in the surf. I drove down past the canyons with rocks crumbling off, the cliffs overhanging the road dressed in huge hair nets to stop the rockfall. Two hundred or so Hell's Angels rode past on their Harley-Davidsons accompanied by five or six highway patrol cars.

I lay on my back in the sand, slightly contented and very fatigued, and fell asleep within seconds. Dreams came to me almost immediately, dreams about running. I woke up 40 minutes later with a real tiredness in my legs. I could feel some dry saliva at the sides of my mouth. I needed a drink of water; the run had been very hot. The hire car, a sleek black Avenger, was parked on the main road, that stretch of the Pacific Coast Highway that streams through Malibu itself. I had been very lucky; I had found a car parking space almost immediately. Very lucky, given that it was a busy Sunday and the beach was jam-packed with family groups of whites and Mexicans. Some of the Mexican children were seriously overweight and they sat in the sand eating almost incessantly.

I ambled towards the car, happy to be alive on this bright summer's day. And then I saw it, or rather, I didn't see it. There was just a gap instead of my car. I looked quickly around to get my bearings, but that was the spot, the exact spot where I had left it. Everything that I had for this whole trip – my wallet, my passport, my driving licence, my brand-new running shoes, not yet worn in – were all in the boot of the car. I just thought to myself that I was going to be left here, in Malibu, unable to get anywhere, unable to buy anything, unable to have a drink. My eyes, for some inexplicable reason, moved upwards, away from the sand patch where I had parked the car and away from the tyre marks that I could clearly make out in the sand where it had been, to a white sign with some red lettering which read 'No Parking, Tow Away'. I was feeling helpless.

Then I saw a runner and his dog about to cross the road, and I asked him where they might have towed an illegally parked car to. Fortunately he knew exactly. It was some high-school car park up in the canyons; not only did he know where this car park was but he returned a few minutes later, without request or prompting, and offered me a lift up to it. It was the camaraderie of runners and I felt like part of some great, invisible club. We chatted the whole way up the canyon road, and again I talked about Ben's times. When we got to the car park, there sat the gleaming black Avenger in a baking-hot car lot. I got out and thanked the runner, then walked towards a short, stocky woman in a wire-mesh kiosk, who seemed to beckon me over.

I stood there, without a top ('You need to put your top on!' the woman kept shouting at me. 'You're in California now!'), and without any shelter, as I and a few other unfortunates, all Europeans I noticed, waited for the sheriff, who eventually came after an hour or two and nonchalantly filled in the paperwork. It was a lucrative business: $186 for the towing and $58 for the fine.

'The recession,' explained the small, rotund lady in the cowboy hat, who seemed to be in charge of the whole thing and stood in her little kiosk with the wire grating, processing us all slowly, one by one. A tall, thin man in a Croatian football shirt gave her abuse at regular intervals.

'You're a bad lady,' he said several times, but she quietly ignored him, for the most part that is, and then dealt with me before him, even though he had been there first.

'You punish me even more,' he said. 'I never leave this hole.

My wife and family are on the beach; they will be dead from the sun. You are a wicked lady.'

And then he turned on me for allowing myself to be processed ahead of him. 'Give me your name!' he shouted. 'Yes, you queue jumper, you, the man in the shorts! What the hell are you wearing? Put your top on, I will complain, I will never return to California. Never ever, do you hear me?'

But by now nobody did.

I got my car back and drove to Pointe Dume and walked to the top of the cliff where the Chumash Indians worshipped in the days before the white man, but where the film stars now live. I read the 'notification of filming' sign pinned to one of the houses. A major Hollywood film was to be made here, the stars leaving their 25-million-dollar homes to walk to the bottom of the street for their day's work.

I decided that I would drive around the Pier to Peak course, just to make sure that I hadn't got carried away with my own dreams in this land of sweet dreams and bitter disappointments.

28

The Start of a Great Adventure

September 2011

It probably was the limits of my imagination. The Pier to Peak Half Marathon is billed as the toughest half marathon in the world. It climbs 4,000 feet from the harbour in Santa Barbara to La Cumbre Peak. Ben had patiently explained that this climb would be too tough for me and that, in fact, it would be tougher than the mountain stage of the Tour de France. Plus, he explained, 'You don't like hills. You don't train on hills and if there's a hill in a race you complain for days afterwards, and now you're intending to run up a freaking mountain in the heat without any preparation. How many times have you passed out in a race? This one could kill you.'

I suspect that Ben did not have much faith in me, but he had himself successfully completed the 24-hour race several weeks before and I needed a personal challenge. Not just another 5K that I could do at my own preferred pace. The one positive thought that I kept inside, which I kept reassuring myself with, was that the race was being held in California. California, the Big Easy, 'California Dreamin'', the Beach Boys, this great golden dream as seen from 1960s Belfast.

The Avenger pulled along State Street and then into Haley Street and up Santa Barbara Street to Mission Street. I noted the incline as I made my race preparations. Then the Avenger turned into Mountain Drive and the limits of my imagination were exposed. I can map gradients out with my hands as they signal geometric angles, but I can't imagine these angles in my legs and in my body the way that cyclists in the Tour de France presumably can, or maybe even Ben. The gradients were 1 in 10, 1 in 8, 1 in 7, 1 in 6 and climbing. It made me feel woozy. There were steep drops on the side of the road and barren dry scrub with nothing moving. I parked the car by the side of the road and tried running up the course for perhaps 800 metres. I felt out of breath and I started to sweat. I glanced down from my current vista to Santa Barbara. I could feel my ears popping. If on a good day I can run a half marathon in 1.38 or 1.39, how long might this one take? How long does it take me to run up any hill, never mind hills like this? Ten minutes for a mile, eleven minutes for a mile. This race could take me two and a half hours, maybe quite a bit more, and that was without any walking or leg spasms or cramps. That is to say, without any problems. The publicity emails which were becoming more and more frequent as the race day approached described the race as 'an endurance event'. But it suddenly occurred to me that I am not an endurance athlete. I never have been. I don't like enduring anything. I am more of a spontaneous pleasure-seeking athlete with slight narcissistic tendencies. So why did I enter the race? Because in one mad, spontaneous moment, I thought that I would impress Ben in a single act, something I feel that I failed to do with a lifetime of academic accomplishments. It's something I share with my brother Bill, the great romantic gesture, the spur-of-the-moment, devil-may-care attitude. 'Let's do it!' as Gary Gilmore had said to his executioners in Utah State Prison. And look where that attitude had taken Bill, and Gary Gilmore; but I suppose that Gilmore only wasted a few seconds with his last directive.

I had sent Ben a jokey email about the half marathon, telling him about the course and my reaction to it, and how ill prepared I was for the whole thing. 'Wish me luck,' I had written at the end. He didn't reply. I never say or write things like 'wish me luck', it's just not an expression I use. They were, however, the last words ever written by my brother in his diary on his fateful expedition to Nanda Devi. After his death, all I got was his diary and then only for a short time because my mother said that it would upset me too much to spend time reading it. The diary was a tale of sickness and diarrhoea and what seemed like poor preparation, both individual and collective.

Bill had got married a few months before the expedition, and I just felt that he really didn't want to be there, about to climb this mountain. The diary was really a love letter to his new wife; I felt that I shouldn't really be reading it. It finished with 'wish me luck' and that was the end.

Now we live in a different era. I checked my emails again to make sure I had sent the email I had intended to send to Ben. I checked the wording, I checked my in-box, but Ben had definitely not replied. The picture in my head was of a slightly disapproving look. Ben has never lacked confidence in his opinions; he can be very forthright. Did he start an email and think better of it? Was he waiting to see the outcome of the half marathon before he replied, and was he therefore hedging his bets? Was he storing his admonishments for when I would tell him that I had dropped out just after the Santa Barbara Mission because of lack of preparation?

Ben is big on preparation, both physical and psychological. I am big on neither. I sometimes find it hard to keep a focus. It was now Thursday with three days to go before the big race. I had run a 5K race the night before in 21.41 but it had been surprisingly hard, first, because the first half of the race was all uphill and second, because I had gone for a run the night before on the sandy beach of Santa Barbara itself, and my legs were tired and sore; but I enjoyed the race and the family atmosphere afterwards. The live band, the beer, the children racing in the sand and hundreds of Californians all congratulating each other on a 'good job'. I had met a Geordie at the start of the race with a curious Californian twang. He worked in advertising and looked as if he did. Again I bragged about Ben's performance; it was becoming a bit of a habit, but he was impressed, as was everyone. On the run as we passed on the out and back course he shouted at me, 'Great work, Geoff!' far too loudly and energetically to be in the middle of a run. It was all a bit over the top.

That afternoon I walked back into town and watched a stick-thin black man perform backflips for a dollar on State Street, and further up I spotted three rather overweight youths holding up a sign asking for food, but they were clearly on their way back from school or college. One very short and very thin Vietnamese man with a moustache, dressed from head to toe in a single sheet, stopped and unpacked a loaf of bread carefully and broke it into three parts of exactly equal size. The youths tried to smile but couldn't hide their puzzlement. The Vietnamese man tried to engage them in conversation, but he was distracting them from their core business of panhandling from the rich citizens of Santa Barbara.

I walked slowly down State Street trying to get myself into a positive frame of mind for the race on Sunday, but sometimes I am too easily distracted by the world out there. Another large lady sat with her own sign. It read:

I NEED MONEY FOR:
DOG FOOD
SOUP (CHEAPEST AVAILABLE)
BREAD
(DEFINITELY NO CIGARETTES OR ALCOHOL)
A LITTLE SHAMPOO
BECAUSE IT'S IMPORTANT TO SMELL NICE AT ALL
TIMES.

One emaciated old lady, perhaps in her late 70s or early 80s, dripping with gold jewellery and with a white peaked cap to shield her from the sun, was asking the beggar to go through the list one more time with her to make sure that she had got it right. It was all very Californian.

'It's very important to present yourself well,' said the beggar. 'First impressions count.'

'They sure do,' said the old lady.

'You only get one chance to make a good first impression,' said the large beggar.

'You are sure right on that,' said the old lady back.

'You have to make it count,' said the beggar. 'I could have brought my lovely doggy with me today to help me out in this enterprise but I wouldn't want to take her away from her lovely bed. She's tucked up back at home now in her lovely doggy basket.'

The old lady smiled.

'She's counting on me to bring back some money to pay for her lovely doggy food,' said the woman who was begging. 'She knows I only eat soup and dry bread; she gets all that lovely doggy food to herself.'

The old lady looked back at her, without smiling this time, and said absolutely nothing. She rotated slightly to the side and then shuffled off without putting her hand anywhere near her pocket or her purse. The woman who was begging made a huffing sound, and then made it a second time, but louder this time, as if she was trying to call the old woman back. It still got no response.

It was all a little depressing, but I couldn't look away. Mental preparation, I feel that's the hardest thing. I get distracted too easily by life's little events, and then my mood changes.

The next day it was just two days to go before the Pier to Peak and my rational brain was urging me to rest, but the irrational side wanted me to get going, to try the beginning of the course at least. Ben had still not replied. I had asked for his advice, explicitly and politely, by email. He had offered none. Perhaps he thought that I was beyond advice, beyond persuasion, beyond hope.

Everywhere you go in Santa Barbara you can't help seeing the peaks of the mountains that I was going to run up. This range runs parallel to the shore, dry, barren and cruel.

'Testing', is how endurance athletes might put it. Just sitting there, waiting to test the body and the will. I like to think of myself as courageous, but perhaps this is just a myth that I perpetuate to myself.

My brother Bill could be reckless; I had to learn from his recklessness. I had seen close up what recklessness could do to a family, in producing a grieving mother, inconsolable, turning her anger outwards.

'I wish it had been you,' she would say, when the grief got too much for her. 'Why was it him? Why did it have to be Bill?'

I never knew what she expected me to say or do on the back of these outbursts. They always occurred late into the night and after she had had a drink or two, maybe more. Perhaps she wanted an argument to make her feel better. But I was already a psychologist in my 20s, a psychologist who had to listen; a frustrated listener, one who tried to understand and had to keep it all inside. I would say nothing back and she would just sit there staring into her glass, a shiny abyss with no handholds, her falling headlong into this abyss not of her own making.

To be truly courageous you need to have some recklessness, but I had had to abandon this trait, if I ever had it. I couldn't afford to be reckless. To be honest I wasn't even that reckless with my friends back on the streets of Belfast. I could be cautious when I had to be. One friend asked me to look after a gun for him, to hide it in my bedroom. I refused, against all the rules of our street, to help him out. I lied to him, I said that my mother tidied my bedroom almost daily, when she clearly hadn't been anywhere near it for years. The friend subsequently got three years for possession of a gun. I was then safe across the water in university and well out of it. My mother liked to remind me of this.

'All of your friends are defending Ulster, but what are you doing? You're looking after number one, as usual, that's all you ever do, and chasing women. Looking after number one and chasing women is basically your life.'

I was never really reckless; I couldn't ever afford to be. But I've always had something inside – I don't know what to call it – this desire just to get there, to say, 'Fuck it, the talking's over, let's just do it.'

I used to get angry after some marathons. I would bump into friends or colleagues and tell them what I had done that day and what I had achieved, and sometimes they would say something like, 'Yes, I could do that, if I had the time to train,' simultaneously belittling the accomplishment and taking the moral high ground. Once in a pub on the evening of the Sheffield Marathon one ex-student asked me what time I had done that day. It was probably around 3.14 or 3.15. Sheffield was always a hard marathon, hilly and held at the height of summer.

'3.15!' he exclaimed. 'I'd have done it in about 2.30. I did 2 miles the other night and I did them in about 15 or 16 minutes and the marathon is about 22 miles or 26 miles, whatever. Yeah, about 2.30, that's about the kind of time I'd do. Fucking hell, man, you're not even trying.'

I hate bullshit merchants and so does Ben. That's why I knew in my heart that I would get up that mountain with the 16 per cent gradient without walking. I'd be doing it for my brother. He would understand. Once in a half marathon in flat, windy Lincoln, I felt him beside me. He ran for maybe two or three miles with me as I hit the wall. He was encouraging me like the wind.

'I can't believe you're giving it a go today,' he was saying. 'I didn't know you could put your books down that long. The truth is that you're not that bad. Not as good as me, of course, but not bad either. Not that bad looking either, but not as good looking as me. You've a way to go.'

The Lincoln wind whispered to me all the way through the wall for the final few miles and I finished effortlessly and without even feeling tired. Carol and the kids were there to watch me.

'Were you talking to someone?' Carol asked afterwards. 'You looked like you were talking to somebody.'

So that morning, I set out on State Street, then on to Santa Barbara Street, then on to Mission Street, then Mountain Drive, all the places on the course etched out in my mind. I found a pace that might work. I wore the bright-orange New Balance 828s. This race was going to draw upon my character, forged in the streets of Belfast, the fucking ghetto, that's what they called it in the media (even journalists did to my face) and in my school: 'You're from the fucking ghetto, Beattie; Ligoniel, what a shit hole.' That character that told all the boys around him what would work and what wouldn't work in those streets in our little gang; that young boy who brought some logic and forward planning to a strange, unpredictable world of instant, searing violence, which meant that we often got away. That young boy who tramped with a half-wild Alsatian– collie crossbreed over Divis and Cavehill on Sundays in the pouring rain before sitting down to do five or six straight hours of Russian homework on a card table in the front room before an uncomprehending mother, sitting there chatting to her friends in the same room, all blowing smoke my way, presumably hoping that I would leave so that they could chat in peace about what was on their minds.

'Our Geoffrey never goes out on a Sunday, except with that bloody wild dog from down the street,' she would say. 'All his friends are out there enjoying themselves, out with the wee girls, and he's sitting there talking to himself all bloody day. I don't know if it's Russian or Latin or just shite he's talking; I just know that I don't understand a bloody word of it.'

What's a fucking half marathon up a fucking baking-hot mountain to a man like me? I'll tell you what, it's fuck all, mate; it's just fuck all.

29

Heaven and Hell

September 2011

The Pier to Peak Half Marathon started at Stearns Wharf, just five minutes from my hotel. I wandered down just after 5 a.m. to pick up my number. I was disappointed that there were only five or six runners milling about in the dark. It would not be dawn for another few hours yet. I had slept well, which was a good sign, but the sleep was full of vivid dreams that did not seem to connect to running. Most, nevertheless, were anxiety dreams of one sort or another, such as being caught out of doors without clothes, exposed in public. The latent meaning was obvious: this could be my greatest exposure as a weak fraud without any defence.

After I picked up my number I went back to my hotel and, curiously, did 100 bench presses, then some sit-ups and finally some stretches. When I looked at my watch again it was 6.15 a.m. The race started at 6.30 a.m. so, despite the best of intentions, there was a last-minute rush down to the start line. I declined to wear my fuel pack, but I carried a GU gel. Ben hadn't written back to me with any advice, but I suspected that carrying the gel would have been the only advice that he would have given me.

A term I hate from my ten years working on *Big Brother* is 'game plan', but here it was more appropriate than in most situations. My game plan was to run the half marathon, as simple and as basic as that, without walking and without stopping, just run it. Not race it, or despair when some runner passed me, or compete, just run it.

The race started promptly, almost suddenly, after a few basic words of encouragement. We made our way up State Street in the dark. I could see that the runners were strong and confident, peak-capped with good strong strides, but for once this didn't worry me. We hit the Mission at about three miles; the Mission marked the end of the 'flat' part of the race. To my mind, we had already been climbing from the start but I knew that things would feel different as soon as we hit Mountain Drive, and it did feel different more or less instantly. My strides got shorter; the sides of my shoes seemed to be scraping the road in almost a shuffle. The runners didn't talk as they passed; there was nothing to say. I thought that I would break the ice.

'Hell, isn't it?' I said to one, but he ignored me, so I kept my thoughts to myself from then on.

During my drive up Mountain Drive I had thought that the one redeeming feature of this race was that I would be able to see the summit at all times and that this would give me a tangible goal to aim for; but the summit was shrouded in mist and invisible on the race day. It was like ascending a long tunnel that was jacked up on one side, giving it an odd slant.

Then something miraculous happened: the sun came out, the mist evaporated, and I found myself in a bright, visually intense place, with all the colours accentuated; it was like being on acid. We used to drop tabs back then in the Belfast of the Troubles, and it makes me laugh now to think about surviving long, sleepless nights out on the streets with bombs thundering in the background, sometimes streets away, with the colours of the explosions reverberating in my brain, because there were always colours. I remember the maniacal laughter as we tried to reassure each other, the after-images from the arcing hand moving through space to tell us that the trip was starting, and Cream singing 'Born Under a Bad Sign' when we nipped into the house for some brief respite, but having to move again before our oddness was detected. We often dropped the tabs up at a house in the

Glencairn estate, the estate where the Shankill Butchers would dump their mutilated Catholic victims in their depraved attempts to 'terrorise the terrorist', in their own words; some of the victims almost decapitated by hatchets, their heads hanging on by just a flap of skin. But the colours of the trip took us away from all of this to another world that was sometimes hard to just imagine, and the colours that day on the run suddenly felt exactly that vivid and that intense. It felt spiritual, and I prayed for the soul of my brother, a long prayer asking for him to be forgiven for anything wrong he might have done.

We climbed and climbed up a dry, winding mountain path where nothing grew. My field of vision became limited to the metre or so in front of my leading foot. There was no point in looking up; it would have just killed the spirit. One very fit blonde woman with muscular shoulders and well-defined legs wearing a yellow top ran beside me and then past me. Two hundred yards ahead of me, she stopped and did some power-walking. I had vowed not to walk but I could hardly close the gap on her even while she was walking. Her running and power-walking kept her level with me as we climbed up and up. She had back-up, a four-by-four stacked with drinks, driven by another woman with blonde hair and a yellow top who handed her a drink every mile or so.

I was now judging the passing of distance and time by the stops made by this four-by-four, and my progress was frustrating in the extreme. My rational mind suggested to me that it might make sense to walk the odd stretch, but my unconscious will rejected this; that would not work for me, that was not why I was here. I could see Ben's scornful face, I could hear my brother calling out to me, 'The Alps, the Hindu Kush, the Himalayas, I've been up them all; it's only fucking Ben Nevis, for God's sake, get a fucking grip.'

I kept to my task. I tried to swallow my gel at about seven miles but instantly felt like vomiting. It dried my mouth. I couldn't see any mile markers, so I wasn't timing my run –

which was probably just as well in the circumstances. At 11 miles I thought that my right knee had gone but I kept on running with the mental image of Ben and the voice of my brother in my head. It was a weird but compelling combination. I only wish that they had met. I am sure that Bill would have been a better role model for Ben than I ever was.

I was surprised to realise I had run 12 miles when I saw the 12-mile feeding station. It seemed to come up suddenly. Despite running more slowly than I had ever run, the miles were now passing quickly. The last mile of the race held the greatest climb. One regular of this run tells me that at times the gradient in this stretch is 16 per cent in places; I could easily believe it. The final few yards were again very steep, almost like climbing, and then it was all over, in 2 hours 35 minutes. But how do you gauge a time like that on a race with that kind of gradient?

I stood on the mountain looking back down to the sea. I thought that what I had just done was impossible, for me at least. And then I felt very alone because everyone else seemed to be in pairs or in groups. I picked up two beers and sat on a tree stump, reflecting on what Bill would think of the climb; after all, he would have seen it.

I started to chastise myself for not pushing harder. Weirdly, I was hardly out of breath. I got a quick massage on a shaky table that nearly tipped over, and then went to look at the results pinned on the back of a truck. There was only one person older than me in front of me in the whole race and he was the same age as my brother Bill, or rather the same age as my brother would have been. It was like a message from somewhere. I felt positive for the first time in weeks and smiled to myself that I had done it, without complaining and without any problems, with his help.

The following Monday, my legs were still stiff. Instead of doing a second recovery run, I decided to do a bit of sightseeing on foot by running out of Santa Barbara down to Montecito. Santa Barbara is an exclusive town, with its marinas and its hippy shops and its upmarket boutiques – I didn't once see a piece of litter or a daub of graffiti – but Montecito is where the real celebrities live, behind gated estates that slope down to the sea. Oprah had apparently just bought a $50-million property in Montecito; the day before, a girl on the pier at Santa Barbara informed her friend and, by chance, me, that Justin Bieber was just moving in.

I jogged slowly along the cycle path with a seemingly endless line of fit, blonde girls and well-muscled, bare-chested men coming towards me. My miles of running in California must have been starting to pay off because many of the more serious runners were starting to smile back at me. Young, blonde mums with tight butts pushed their children along in pushchairs with a husky or an Irish wolfhound or some cute chihuahua trotting behind.

I first came to Santa Barbara in the mid-1980s and thought that I had found my spiritual home. There were just so many runners and for once I felt that I fitted in, that I belonged. But I had done nothing about it, although there might have been opportunities at the time, if I had pursued them.

I followed the path along the beach and then briefly went onto the road, turned right at Santa Barbara Cemetery and headed up the hill. Then I saw the grand houses, in all their magnificent glory: colonial mansions, French chateaux, English Tudor houses, Spanish villas – every shape and design, every decade and century blended and mixed together, architecture from all over the world built afresh here and right next to each other. Each property proclaimed one simple message: 'We are very rich and we are very proud of this. Forget taste, forget decency, forget culture, we have made it.'

I ran down past the Four Seasons Hotel, then past a gated community with large ornamental gates and immaculate security on duty at the entrance, who eyed me suspiciously, and finally I hit the beach. I watched some cormorants sit so still on top of a building right on the beach that I thought that they were black marble statues, until one of them finally moved. A sandpiper eyed the tide impatiently, and I could hear a sea lion maybe 50 yards offshore.

I jogged further along past some Mexican gardeners tending some beautiful red flowers by another large, open, ornamental gate. I ran through it and they all smiled and said hello. I kept running. What better way to see the world than by running slowly past it, taking it all in? There were houses worth maybe $12–16 million. I would have loved to have moved here earlier on in my career, if I could have afforded it, but of course, when you have children, you have fewer options, less freedom; any freedom that you get you have to work for.

I ran as far as I could until I realised that I had come to another large, ornamental fence, just like the ones I had seen earlier, with more security. I had somehow managed to jog my way into this community of the stars without anyone noticing. I ran back the way I had come and then realised that the gate I had come through earlier was now locked. I was effectively locked inside this exclusive estate. The gardeners had clearly thought that the runner, bronzed, fit and healthy, somehow belonged here. This misinterpretation felt good for a short while, until I realised my predicament.

I traced my way back around the perimeter fence and found a bit where I could climb over, though it was a long drop on tired legs. But I had to do it; I was just relieved to get out. I ran back to Santa Barbara realising that I had somehow found the American dream, and it reminded me of long ago, back with my family on our Sunday drive, down to Holywood and those big houses with their lights on in the middle of the day, my mother gazing up at them and saying to my father and Bill and me, 'Imagine living in one of those, imagine having the kind of money to live there, with no work to do and just able to sit on your arse all day.'

I suddenly realised that I had found part of the dream out there in California, the good part that keeps your arse in more or less perpetual motion.

30

Happiness Is a Choice

September 2011

I flew to Chicago from Santa Barbara to talk at the university about my new research on implicit racism, which seemed to show that most people do have a significant unconscious bias against others from different racial or ethnic groups to themselves; and to run the half marathon. The Chicago Half Marathon was on the coming Sunday and the Great North Run was the following Sunday. I had three half marathons in a row, hardly worth mentioning in the grand scheme of achievements, but tough enough for me. Ben and I had obtained 'celebrity' entry into the famous north-east race, and Ben was torn between his natural reticence and the thought of starting beside world-class runners. He hated masquerading as a celebrity or even the son of a 'celebrity'. He hated people recognising me on the street because he felt embarrassed by this kind of attention. He doesn't like to be in the spotlight unless he is in control of the process (like through his running where he maintains personal control).

One example of this from earlier in his life that springs vividly to mind was when he was bullied at secondary school. He was probably about 14 at the time. His elder sister, Zoe, told me about it. They were boys from her form, around sixteen, two years older than Ben, taller and stronger, and very middle class, which made the whole thing worse in a way. She explained that Ben wouldn't come to me with this issue but she had witnessed it at first hand. He didn't want any attention to be drawn to it. I remember her saying that because I was a psychologist I could probably get to the root of the problem, whatever it was. It seemed awfully mature for a 16-year-old girl. I had a colleague at the university who was internationally known for his research on bullying. He was thin with red hair and glasses; his chosen research career was perhaps easy to fathom. I told him all about Ben, and how he was now reluctant to go to school. My colleague told me that I had to set up an immediate dialogue with his teacher.

'Cooperation is the name of the game,' he earnestly explained. 'Bullies try to isolate their victims, to intimidate them, to keep them from talking. We need to build alliances, to shift the power balance.'

I listened for what seemed like hours and I realised that none of this would work. Ben, with all his reticence and natural discomfort, did not want to build alliances; he just wanted the bullying to stop. I tried a different approach. I put on a leather jacket and some Wranglers, and slapped my dog Louis about the head so much that he thought we were going to play a game of 'escaped prisoners', where one of the children's friends would run off, watched by Louis and me, and then Louis would be released to stop him (with me whispering 'escaped prisoners' in his ear). We eventually had to call a halt to this game because Louis was 'stopping' the escaped prisoners by biting them. Louis and I stood by the school gates waiting; Zoe had pointed the two boys out in photographs so that I would recognise them.

All I remember thinking was how big they were and how angry I felt. Louis could sense my anger and when I walked in front of them, I had to pull his choker lead because I swear he would have bitten both of them. Words came tumbling out in my strong Belfast accent. I was no longer the doctor and lecturer from the university, I was back at the turn-of-the-road, back to where I probably belong. There was just a confidence in how I spoke.

'If you ever fucking touch my son again, I'll fucking well

knock the fuck out of the pair of you, do you understand me?'

The dog was pulling itself closer to the pair of them and they were right up against the well-manicured hedge. Both of the boys were ashen-faced but the dog was enjoying himself; he thought that I had invented a new game.

For days afterwards, I enquired of Zoe as to whether she had witnessed any further bullying, but she told me that she had not; it had stopped as quickly as it had started. She asked me whether I had talked to them, whether I had set up a dialogue. I said that I had.

'They're intelligent boys,' I said. 'I simply sketched out some broader context for each of them. We discussed the underlying issues like intelligent adults.'

'Thank God, the psychology is of some use then,' said Zoe.

Ben asked me what I had done, but I said nothing, even when I got a letter from the boys in question in which they said that they had decided to become friends with Ben, not 'because I had threatened to beat the shit out of them' but because they now recognised Ben's good points. Their P.S. was the funniest bit of their letter. They wrote that they were shocked that some people would stoop to 'the intimidation tactics of the IRA when simple dialogue would have worked'. I nearly wrote back to tell them that I was a proud Protestant and that they needed to learn to discriminate more (but because I had been brought up as a Protestant in Ulster I was already good at discrimination), but they might not have understood the joke.

I never mentioned to Ben what I had done, he would have been far too embarrassed, but it was my life in Belfast that had made the difference here and not my university life. I had been pulled back to my past, whether I liked it or not.

Chicago felt cold after California. I went for a run that night along Lake Shore Drive. The waters of Lake Michigan looked grey and angry, noisy, crashing onto the cycle path and the route all the runners take so I had to run nearer the road, congested at rush hour, at a strange, unfamiliar angle that caused a pain in my left hip. A dwarf on a bicycle nearly ran me over; the waves were so loud that I couldn't hear him coming. He wore glasses and swore at me so violently that his glasses shifted on his face. All I could think of was that my running career could have ended there and then, at the hands of a person of diminutive stature.

There was a constant line of runners coming towards me, a long string of individuals with thick knots of club runners, all getting ready for the half marathon that weekend. None of them smiled; I had been spoiled by Southern California. Last year I had done a disappointing 1.41 but this year I was hoping for something better. Last year, I had run a 5K race the day before, coming first in my category, but this year I vowed to be more sensible. The only problem was that my legs were still tired from the weekend, more than tired, genuinely fatigued. I have perhaps always been over-optimistic about my powers of recovery. I seem to think that a good night's sleep is all that I require to recover. I don't plan in weeks or months when it comes to recovery, just days – usually one day. Perhaps it's because when I was a child, I didn't sleep that well. I had my reasons. I would stay awake at nights, watchful and observant, and fall asleep towards dawn on many, many occasions. There was always something magical in my mind about a good night's sleep, with all of its restorative powers. Perhaps that's why I race on consecutive days, against all sensible advice. My insomnia got so great that my mother took me to the chemist's for something to knock me out. But I never took any of the drugs for it. I stayed awake and longed for days when I could feel more secure, like now.

I had a number of good nights' sleep ahead of me. What more could I ask for?

A few days later, it was time for some serious reflection on the nature of happiness. They say that happiness is a choice, or rather some say that. They say that all we have to do to feel happy is to make certain critical decisions in our everyday life, like what to do in the day. Generally speaking, it is better to do something rather than nothing. When we do something, we become immersed in the 'flow' of life and we forget ourselves temporarily, and forgetting ourselves seems to be a good thing, it seems to make us happy. When we do nothing, on the other hand, we get the chance to reflect on all of the bad things that have happened to us that day, or before, and we end up just feeling sad and sometimes downright miserable.

Many people look forward to the weekend and their long lie-in on a Sunday morning. They lie there with the papers on their lap and reflect and reflect on everything that has happened in the past week, usually the bad things, with the result that by the time they have decided to get up they have got all of these painful and difficult memories right at the forefront of their consciousness, and their Sunday is now ruined. So choosing what to do in the day can be rather important to how we feel.

We can also consciously choose what to reflect on to make us feel happy. So, some psychologists say, we should focus on the five best things that have happened to us that day when we are brushing our teeth last thing at night rather than the two or three bad things that have happened to us. Psychologists say that if we do this, we can prime our positive memories and make them more accessible. The argument goes that these accessible memories then influence our mood state. These ideas derive from the pioneering research of Aaron Beck (who had just written an extraordinarily good endorsement of my latest book *Get the Edge*), who reversed the traditional thinking from Freud's time and before, which was that our mood influences our thoughts and that this is the essence of the relationship between thinking and emotion. Beck argued that this may be true, on occasion, but it is more often the reverse: that our thoughts, our cognitions, our memories shape our moods and that if we can just redirect our thoughts and our cognitions, then we can reshape our moods and our more enduring emotional states.

I know all of this, and yet I was sitting outside a Starbucks on the day after the Chicago Half Marathon, in a deep, black, sombre mood that would not lift. I was depressed, worse than depressed, down in the dumps, down and out, unable to communicate, barely able to talk, even to myself. I'd had several bits of good news that morning. The last review of the manuscript of my new book on implicit racism had just arrived from the publishers. It was from David McNeill of the University of Chicago and it was extremely positive, they told me ('a rave review, in fact'). I had also just heard from my other publishers that my book *Get the Edge* had gone into the business chart at number nine in the WHSmith listings. Normally these things would produce a burst of good feeling, a burst of spontaneous joy, but that day – nothing. I felt that nothing would have done the trick on that particular day; nothing would have lifted my mood. I couldn't even think offhand of any positive events to focus on; that was how bad it was.

The half marathon had not gone well and I was sitting there, unable to bend down to go to the toilet and when I tried to walk down a flight of steps it felt as if wooden splints had been attached to my legs. People were staring at me as I walked, like a man with false legs. The expo the day before the half marathon, which had been held on Navy Pier, had been great. Motivational speakers had explained to us all how to stay 'truly motivated' in our lifelong pursuit of running, and what to avoid before big races, including the obvious: any change in diet, any change in running shoes, any change in schedule. Yet I had changed both my diet and my running shoes in the days before the race, and throughout that long 13.1 miles I badly needed the toilet and I could feel that my feet were getting terribly blistered. At eleven miles the fatigue from the Pier to Peak Half Marathon set in, and the last two miles were extremely slow; it was like running through deep water. Runners streamed past me but I was beyond caring. It just didn't feel like me, and that's the truth. It was also very hot, maybe touching 90 degrees, and I stopped at every feeding station, clocking up the minutes all the way through the race to my obvious emotional discomfort. Despite arriving in very good time on a shuttle bus that morning, I had nearly missed the beginning of the race and I had to run to the start, I forgot my gel that I had planned to take at the 10-mile mark, and I couldn't get my watch started on the starting line. It was one of those days.

And then there was something there on the course itself that made the whole thing that much worse. At four miles or thereabouts, and also (because it was an out and back course) at eleven miles, there stood a tall man in a green outfit. I think he was dressed as a leprechaun, but I'm not entirely sure – this might have been my mind playing tricks on me. I didn't really want to look up at him, but all I remember seeing was the green outfit and his weird tall hat, and all I remember hearing was his message, over and over again. He kept shouting at all of the runners as they passed:

'Happiness is a choice.

'You can choose to be happy or not.

'You all still have to run the same distance.

'But how do you want to run it?

'Happy or sad?

'It's your choice.'

And the message kept repeating over and over again:

'Happiness is a choice . . .'

I hated this leprechaun, as much as I hated myself at that point in time.

The Chicago Half Marathon was being held on the tenth anniversary of 9/11 and patriotism, not surprisingly, was the theme of the day. The run started to someone singing the 'Star-Spangled Banner' and there was a Marine guard of honour on the start line. The endurance runner Dane Rauschenberg ran the whole course with a large, flapping American flag, although he still managed to do it in a reasonable time. I expected to be highly moved by all of this – I can be extremely emotional in this kind of situation – but when the singer started I was queuing for the toilet because of my new diet (steak and potatoes for three consecutive nights because it was on special offer at T.G.I. Friday's), unable to go. My mind was on other things and I didn't have the time or the opportunity to focus on my sentimentality.

There was nothing good about the run and I sat with the sweat dripping off me on the grass for maybe three hours afterwards, without moving much, if at all. I drank two bottles of Gatorade, two bottles of water and maybe five more cups of water. It's unlike me to drink anything after a race. Indeed, I sat there for so long that I just caught the last shuttle bus back to the hotel.

The driver was a very large, fat, black woman who said, 'You sure are late, honey. You like to cut things real fine. This bus is leavin' now. Do you hear me, sugar? We're not waiting for no one.' She was directing this very loudly at me. I could see the fat on her stomach wobbling as she emphasised every word and syllable. It was one of those days where I hated most people.

I didn't want to talk on the bus. I didn't want anyone to ask me what time I did. It wasn't quite a PW but it was very close, 1.46. I was disappointed with my 1.41 the previous year and I had been hoping to do 1.36 this year, so this time of mine was a huge disappointment. I was too embarrassed to tell Carol or Ben or anyone else the time. To be honest, I didn't really feel like running again. I emailed my daughter Zoe that night and she said, 'Why not just pack it in?' And, for a split second, maybe for the first time ever, I contemplated it, for that short period at least.

I had the Great North Run the following Sunday and I realised, through a simple computation, that I was going to have to run three half marathons in two weeks. Given that I hadn't recovered from the Pier to Peak, I was getting extremely concerned about how tired I was going to be feeling the following Sunday. I was not in a happy mood and I wasn't sure how to change it. I would have liked a choice, but it did not seem to be forthcoming.

I couldn't stop thinking about the leprechaun on the course and his mantra, 'Happiness is a choice.' It was an emotionally charged image, imbued with negative emotion, mainly loathing, with a great deal of self-loathing mixed in. But all I could think of was my response to his insistent barrage, which was now fully articulated, if not necessarily profound. It was, 'Well, maybe, maybe not.' I do know something for absolute certainty, Mr Leprechaun: running isn't a choice. I have no choice here, and if you don't see that, then you shouldn't have been there that day, advising or trying to advise those who do know this in that heat in Chicago.

31

What Really Spurs You On?

Ben

When people find out that I'm a runner they will often ask me two questions: 'Why do you do it?' and 'What are you trying to achieve?' Hopefully, I've been able to articulate some of the reasons why I run (although, to be absolutely honest, I don't fully understand a lot of them myself). The question of what I'm trying to achieve is, if anything, even more difficult to answer.

When I first got back into running, as I've said, my immediate motivation was to beat my dad. Looking back now, I can't believe that this was because of some Hamlet-esque need to depose him but rather because it made sense, it was right. It was wrong for a man 30 years my senior to beat me in a physical challenge. So now I think my primary goal was to beat him; nothing more, nothing less. It's all a bit too tidy though, a bit too simple, and I'm not sure that this is the full truth. The real reasons are a bit deeper and I've been frank about these towards the start. As Dad highlighted earlier, for years I didn't want to see him or speak to him; I didn't even like to hear his name mentioned. I would fantasise about a time when I would be stronger and I could hurt him, he made me so angry. My mother didn't deserve the treatment and disrespect she got. So I would imagine a time when I would be able to beat him – literally. In hindsight, maybe becoming a better runner than him was my way to prove my manhood and at the same time take something away from him. Certain of his achievements I could never take away from him, but I could take away his achievements in running; achievements that he was incredibly proud of. After beating him in a head-to-head race, the next obvious target to focus on was my dad's personal bests, and that's what I've been doing in the past few years.

A lot of the running he did as a young man was over cross-country. Cross-country by its nature is not quantifiable. The courses are so varied in length, terrain and weather conditions that you cannot compare one race against another. It is completely subjective. The only way to judge yourself against another runner in cross-country is to compete directly against them. So cross-country was out. The next option was 10K but when my dad was younger, 10K as a distance wasn't widely run. Races tended to be measured in imperial distances, hence the proliferation of 5- and 10-mile races that have now sadly dropped from the race calendar. So 10K was out.

The two distances that Dad raced over the most were the marathon and half marathon. He raced these while he was at the peak of his powers and running his fastest times. At this stage I certainly wasn't ready for a full marathon (I may not be ready still!). I had 'raced' a half before, though, and knew I could cover the distance. So my target became 1.26. I made it clear to him that this was my goal: to break the Beattie record. It did, however, seem like an incredible time. It was about 20 minutes faster than I had ever covered the distance in, and I must admit, I feared that it was completely unattainable. I had a couple of near misses in 2008 and my dad could hardly conceal the delight that he took in still being faster than me. I remember walking with him from Don Valley Stadium after running 1.28 in the Sheffield Half and he couldn't stop smiling; he was so smug. Now, as a psychologist he should have known that this would only spur me on. I'm sure that he will claim that that was his aim all along, although I'm not convinced.

The time of 1.26 was my aim for a long while but when I finally achieved it I took almost no satisfaction in the result.

The problem I have with goals and targets in running is that I can never concentrate on the one in hand but am always thinking about the next one. By the time that I achieved a sub-1.26, clocking my expectations had already moved far beyond that; 1.26 was a logical step on my way to achieving my next target. It was never in doubt and was purely a stepping stone on my way to achieving a sub-1.20 half marathon, which I achieved in 2010.

So that's where I find myself now. My latest aim is to run sub-70. My current PB is 72.54. Most people would focus on the next logical step, sub-72 maybe, but that's not the way my brain works. I look at sub-70 and know how difficult it is; I also know that sub-70 is around the standard that you can start to get 'elite' entry for races. If you had offered me a sub-73-minute half marathon 5 years ago I would have taken it in an instant. In fact, if you'd offered me a sub-85-minute half marathon 5 years ago I would have taken it. But expectations and hopes move on. I look at the elite and know what I want to be. It is only recently that I've gained any insight into the world of the elite athlete. Up to now I was restricted solely to reading the blogs of people like Andi Jones, Ryan McLeod and Jonny Mellor. I read their training diary entries meticulously in the hope, I suppose, that I will discover some great secret, some missing ingredient that will turn me from an average club runner into an elite. Unfortunately, there is no magic formula. It's a mixture of hard work and natural talent. I don't have the talent part but I do seem to have the capacity to train myself to exhaustion. So I'm willing to keep trying, to work harder than I've ever done for no reward whatsoever. People ask why. I honestly don't know but I'm not going to stop. I may never achieve anything of note but I'm willing to do whatever it takes to try.

Recently, thanks to the incredible hospitality of Nova International, I have had a chance to see what it is like to be an elite athlete. As a 'celebrity' entrant to the Bupa Great North and South runs, I was able to see at first hand the treatment they get. I think the biggest surprise for me was that they are treated better than the celebrities, but this is just the way it should be, in my opinion. They are chaperoned everywhere and all their requirements taken care of. I felt an incredible pang of jealousy when on the morning of the race at the Great South Run I had to stand and watch as the elites were led out of the hotel and my dad and I were left with just the celebrities for company. Well, just the celebrities and a middle-aged Italian talking to a young Kenyan. The Italian was Renato Canova and he was giving the Kenyan Leonard Komon his final instructions before he tried – and ultimately, spectacularly failed – to break the world record for 10 miles at the Great South Run. All the other elites had already left the hotel reception and were boarding the bus on the way to the start. Only the favourite and his mentor remained. Canova made it abundantly clear that Komon must go after the record from the gun. His tone was insistent, bordering on irate. When they finally left, there could have been no doubt in Komon's mind what he had to do in order to appease his coach. When watching the footage of the race later, it was clear that the message had got through as he went off from the start and ran a suicidal 4.15 first mile. He could never have sustained that sort of pace and blew up around the sixth mile. He finished two minutes off Haile Gebrselassie's world record.

Maybe, like me, he should have aimed at a more realistic target and been satisfied rather than constantly striving for the next goal. But it's easy to be philosophical about other people; it's a bit harder when you have to be philosophical about yourself.

32

D.N.F.

December 2011

Somehow, I always envisaged this book as having a neat, logical structure. The book started just after the Great North Run and it was to finish there. I didn't leave Ben at Newcastle station like I said in Chapter 1, just sitting on his own reading his book, I couldn't. I went back to him and, even though it was slightly out of my way, I travelled back towards Sheffield with him and then on to Manchester from York. I think that he was secretly pleased. The deed itself wasn't that great, but the gesture felt magnificent. I just couldn't leave him. The train from Newcastle was full of runners, some of whom recognised me from the television, so that started the conversations, but I kept telling them all how well Ben had done in the race. When I left him he was still chatting away. He was the star of that particular train carriage; they were all talking about his time and I could see that he was very, very happy.

I also imagined the book having a neat linear structure as Ben and I worked hard to put the past behind us, and sat down, deliberately and seriously, to examine what had occurred and write about how we felt about each other and our chosen sport. The narrative was meant to be driven by Ben's thrust towards elite status, which in my view he is fast approaching (I seem more optimistic about this than Ben himself), and my continuation in this loneliest and most reflective of sports. The underlying psychology was meant to be clear and positive, cathartic in every sense, in the words of Freud and Breuer, who in their classic book *Studies in Hysteria* spent some time extolling the principles of catharsis and the role of emotion in the whole process: 'The patient only gets free from the . . . symptom by reproducing the pathogenic impressions that caused it and by giving utterance to them with an expression of affect.' Or, as the famous American psychologist Jamie Pennebaker wrote in *Advances in Experimental Social Psychology*:

> *Confronting a trauma helps individuals to understand and ultimately assimilate the event. By talking or writing about . . . experiences, individuals translate the event into language. Once encoded linguistically, individuals can more readily understand, find meaning in, or attain closure of the experience.*

This, of course, is all about trauma; but just ask Ben: he would say that much of his childhood was genuinely traumatic for a sensitive boy like him.

So I knew from the start that the whole thing was going to be emotional and fraught, but I thought that it might just work, and it nearly did. Can you put the past behind you in this sort of way? Can you come to terms with things like that by writing and talking about them? Can you articulate emotional hurt and pain and feel better as a consequence? Can you attain closure by writing about highly charged emotional experiences? Well, maybe.

In October 2011 Ben and I went off to do the Great South Run, as guests, as Ben has already said, of Nova International. It was odd because there was a lot of uncertainty about whether we should do this particular race or not, which is really not like either of us; we usually make up our minds pretty quickly about most things. But eventually we decided to go, and Carol decided to run the Worksop Half Marathon instead that same day. Ben and I had a great weekend in

Portsmouth. We got there in good time, I was able to drink some wine without complaint, and lots of people recognised me in the restaurant but Ben seemed happy enough with this for a change.

'They obviously watch a lot of TV down here,' he said, although he may possibly have said 'shit TV', I'm not sure which.

It was a 10-mile race and on the day I felt great and cruised around effortlessly in 74 minutes 50 seconds. I was 1,122nd out of nearly 30,000 runners; Ben ran 55 minutes 52 seconds and was 54th overall. It was the kind of course which backtracks on itself, so Ben could see me running. Afterwards, he even complimented me – and that is so rare.

'You were running effortlessly and surrounded by good, fit young runners.'

I told him that he looked superb; he had passed a number of the elite athletes. He was on the verge himself of elite status.

Of course, I had this book in mind as we got onto the train back to London, and how to finish it. I knew that we hadn't yet achieved complete reconciliation but things were much better than they had ever been. We stopped at St Pancras for some supper and I have never felt so close to him, not since he was a child, and I suspect that he had never felt so close to me. Carol was to pick us up at Sheffield station so I rang her to confirm the time. As soon as she answered I knew that something was the matter. Her speech was faint, barely audible; I could just about make out what she was saying. She had had an accident, another fall in a race. She had passed out at the finish of the half marathon; she couldn't stop herself from going down with her one good arm, and she had landed on her face and been unconscious for a little while. Ben could see my face and hear what I was saying. There was no point in trying to disguise it. I started to explain what had happened in my own words, and he just got angrier and angrier.

'Why doesn't she eat more? She starves herself. Why does she have to push it, the way she does? You just bloody well cruise around, smiling all around you. Why does she have to hurt herself like this?'

By the time we got to Sheffield station Ben was hardly talking to me; he was that worried about his mother. My running in Portsmouth wasn't just forgotten; it had been completely reinterpreted and buried. It was no longer an effortless good run, attributable to years of training, but a shoddy day out where I hadn't troubled myself yet again. We saw Carol standing in the shadows as we came down the station steps, as if she was trying to hide. Ben just said, 'Bloody hell,' when he saw her. She looked as if she'd been in a car accident, with cuts and deep-blue bruises all over her face, and a black eye. Ben didn't speak to me in the car on the way back home, and the next piece he wrote for the book was all about how much he had hated me in the not so distant past. Any chance of complete reconciliation had now gone. It was as simple as that.

The next race we all did together was the Leeds Abbey Dash in November 2011. I had a sore Achilles tendon all week but got conflicting advice about whether to risk it or not by racing. I took some painkillers on the day of the race and went off well. The pain, however, just got worse and worse until just past 9K when it became unbearable, and I had to stop and walk, agonisingly slowly, with 800 or so metres to go, with the crowd shouting at me so that that I would know, in case I didn't already, that I was nearly there. After a few minutes Carol passed me but didn't stop. She apologised on the way past, with a half-look back. I immediately stepped off the course and limped very, very slowly towards the finishing area, embarrassed, in despair and inconsolable. It was the first race that I had dropped out of (while still conscious) in forty-odd years and, two weeks later, I still couldn't run or even walk properly with my ruptured Achilles. When I later told Ben about Carol not stopping in the race but apologising, he just said, 'What has she got to apologise about?' And he left it at that.

A fortnight after that race Carol and Ben did the Percy Pud 10K in Sheffield in the freezing, driving sleet of a Yorkshire December. I was confined to gym work. They ran in their vests and shorts, the two hardiest souls in the whole race, standing out a mile, and it would have been obvious to anyone who looked that they were mother and son. I didn't go to watch. Ben wasn't happy with his time (34 minutes 7 seconds) and he ran all the way out to Hollow Meadows as a 'warm-down' then was immediately sick in the front garden. He looked pale and gaunt. I felt as if I had blown my chances of any real reconciliation but I instinctively knew that we had some deep and never-ending connection between us, this fundamental and shared inability to feel genuinely content, ever, and this great desire to keep going and going and going, both driven by unknowable forces, maybe the same, maybe different.

I waited a few weeks before I looked up the results of the Leeds Abbey Dash. I wanted to see exactly how Ben and Carol had performed in the race. Ben had done the 10K in 33.36; Carol had run it in 45.29. My results for that race simply read 'D.N.F.', 'did not finish', and I thought to myself: the book and this whole deliberate and self-conscious attempt at reconciliation has to stop here. The running, of course, will continue for both of us – or in my case, as soon as I can walk again.